AFRICAN GAME TRAILS

The "white" rhino.

Drawn by Philip R. Goodwin from photographs and from descriptions furnished by Mr. Roosevelt.

AFRICAN GAME TRAILS

AN ACCOUNT OF THE

AFRICAN WANDERINGS

OF AN

AMERICAN HUNTER–NATURALIST

BY

THEODORE ROOSEVELT

VOLUME II

NEW YORK
CHARLES SCRIBNER'S SONS
1926

CONTENTS

Contents

vi

ILLUSTRATIONS

AFRICAN GAME TRAILS

CHAPTER XI

THE GUASO NYERO; A RIVER OF THE EQUATORIAL DESERT

WHEN I reached Neri, after coming down from killing my first elephant on Kenia, I was kept waiting two or three days before I could gather enough Kikuyu porters. As I could not speak a word of their language I got a couple of young Scotch settlers, very good fellows, to take charge of the safari out to where I intended to hunt. There was a party of the King's African Rifles camped at Neri; the powerful-looking enlisted men were from the south, chiefly from one of the northernmost tribes of Zulu blood, and their two officers were of the best Kipling-soldier type. Then there was another safari, that of Messrs. Kearton and Clark who were taking some really extraordinary photographs of birds and game. Finally, Governor and Mrs. Jackson arrived from a trip they had been making round Kenia; and I was much pleased to be able to tell the Governor, who had helped me in every way, about my bull elephant, and to discuss with him some of the birds we had seen and the mammals we

329

had trapped. A great ingowa, a war-dance of the natives, was held in his honor, and the sight was, as always, one of interest and of a certain fascination. There was an Indian trader at Neri from whom we had obtained donkeys to carry to our elephant camp "posho," or food for the porters. He announced that they were all in readiness in a letter to Cuninghame, which was meant to be entirely respectful, but which sounded odd, as it was couched in characteristic Baboo English. The opening lines ran: " Dear K-ham, the donkeys are altogether deadly."

At last fifty Kikuyus assembled—they are not able to carry the loads of regular Swahili porters—and I started that moment, though it was too late in the afternoon to travel more than three or four miles. The Kikuyus were real savages, naked save for a dingy blanket, usually carried round the neck. They formed a picturesque safari; but it was difficult to make the grasshopper-like creatures take even as much thought for the future as the ordinary happy-go-lucky porters take. At night if it rained they cowered under the bushes in drenched and shivering discomfort; and yet they had to be driven to make bough shelters for themselves. Once these shelters were up, and a little fire kindled at the entrance of each, the moping, spiritless wretches would speedily become transformed into beings who had lost all remembrance of ever having been wet or cold. After their posho had been distributed and eaten they would sit, huddled and cheerful, in their shelters, and sing steadily for a couple of hours. Their songs were much wilder than those of the regular porters, and were often warlike. Occasionally, some " shanty man," as he would be called on shipboard, improvised or repeated a kind of story in short sentences or strophes; but the main feature of each song was the endless repetition of some refrain, musically chanted in chorus by the whole party. This repetition of a short sentence or refrain is a characteristic of many kinds of savage music; I have seen the Pawnees grow almost maddened by their triumph song, or victory song, which consisted of nothing whatever but the fierce, barking, wolf-like repetition of the words, " In the morning the wolves feasted."

Our first afternoon's march was uneventful; but I was amused at one of our porters and the " safari " ants. These safari ants are so called by the natives because they go on foraging expeditions in immense numbers. The big-headed warriors are able to inflict a really painful bite. In open spaces, as where crossing a path, the column makes a little sunken way through which it streams uninterruptedly. Whenever we came to such a safari ant column, in its sunken way, crossing our path, the porter in question laid two twigs on the ground as a peace-offering to the ants. He said that they were on safari, just as we were, and that it was wise to propitiate them.

That evening we camped in a glade in the forest.

At nightfall dozens of the big black-and-white horn-bill, croaking harshly, flew overhead, their bills giving them a curiously top-heavy look. They roosted in the trees near by.

Next day we came out on the plains, where there was no cultivation, and instead of the straggling thatch and wattle, unfenced villages of the soil-tilling Kikuyus, we found ourselves again among the purely pastoral Masai, whose temporary villages are arranged in a ring or oval, the cattle being each night herded in the middle, and the mud-daubed, cow-dung-plastered houses so placed that their backs form a nearly continuous circular wall, the spaces between being choked with thorn-bushes. I killed a steinbuck, missed a tommy, and at three hundred yards hit a Jackson's hartebeest too far back, and failed in an effort to ride it down.

The day after we were out on plains untenanted by human beings, and early in the afternoon struck water by which to pitch our tents. There was not much game, and it was shy; but I thought that I could kill enough to keep the camp in meat so I sent back the two Scotchmen and their Kikuyus, after having them build a thorn boma, or fence, round the camp. One of the reasons why the Masai had driven their herds and flocks off this plain was because a couple of lions had turned man-eaters, and had killed a number of men and women. We saw no sign of lions, and believed they had followed the

From a photograph by Theodore Roosevelt.

My boma when
I was camped
afoot
T. R.

Masai; but there was no use in taking needless chances.

The camp was beside a cold, rapid stream, one of the head-waters of the Guaso Nyero. It was heavily fringed with thorn timber. To the east the crags and snow-fields of Kenia rose from the slow swell of the mountain's base. It should have been the dry season, but there were continual heavy rains, which often turned into torrential downpours. In the overcast mornings as I rode away from camp, it was as cool as if I were riding through the fall weather at home; at noon, if the sun came out, straight overhead, the heat was blazing; and we generally returned to camp at nightfall, drenched with the cold rain. The first heavy storm, the evening we pitched camp, much excited all my followers. Ali came rushing into the tent to tell me that there was "a big snake up high." This certainly seemed worth investigating, and I followed him outside where everybody was looking at the " snake," which proved to be a huge, funnel-shaped, whirling cloud, careering across the darkened sky. It was a kind of waterspout or cyclone; fortunately it passed to one side of camp.

The first day I hunted I shot only a steinbuck for the table. The country alternated between bare plains and great stretches of sparse, stunted thorns. We saw zebra, and two or three bands of oryx; big, handsome antelope strongly built and boldly colored,

with long, black, rapier-like horns. They were very
wary, much more so than the zebra with which they
associated, and we could not get anywhere near them.

Next day I hunted along the edges of a big swamp.
We saw waterbuck, but were unable to get within
shot. However, near the farther end of the swamp,
in an open swale, we found four eland feeding. The
eland is the king of antelope; and not only did I
desire meat for camp, but I wished the head of a
good bull as a trophy for myself, the eland I had
hitherto shot being for the National Museum. The
little band included a big bull, a small bull, and two
cows; at a distance the big bull looked slaty blue.
The great, sleek, handsome creatures were feeding
in the long grass just like cattle, switching their long
tails at the flies. The country looked like a park,
with clumps of thorn-trees scattered over the grassy
sward. Carefully I crept on all-fours from tree
clump to tree clump, trying always to move when the
elands' heads were down grazing. At last I was
within three hundred yards, when one of the cows
caught a glimpse of me and alarmed the others.
They were startled, but puzzled, and after trotting
a few rods turned to stare at the half-seen object of
their alarm. Rising to my knee I shot the big bull
in the throat as with head erect he gazed in my direction. Off he went with a rush, the others bounding and leaping as they accompanied him, and we
followed on the blood spoor. Bakhari and Gouvi-

mali trotted fast on the trail, and in order to be fresh
for the shot I mounted Tranquillity. Suddenly out
bounced the wounded bull from some bushes close
by, and the horse nearly had a fit; I could hardly
get off in time to empty my magazine at long range
—fortunately with effect. It was a magnificent bull
of the variety called Patterson's eland, with a fine
head. Few prize oxen would be as heavy, and
in spite of its great size, its finely moulded limbs
and beautiful coat gave it a thoroughly game
look.

Oryx were now what I especially wished, and we
devoted all of the following day to their pursuit. We
saw three bands, two of them accompanying herds
of zebra, after the manner of kongoni. Both species
were found indifferently on the bare, short-grass
flats and among the thin, stunted thorn-trees which
covered much of the plains. After a careful stalk,
the latter part on all-fours, I got to within about
three hundred yards of a mixed herd, and put a
bullet into one oryx as it faced me, and hit another
as it ran. The first, from its position, I thought I
would surely kill if I hit it at all, and both of the
wounded beasts were well behind the herd when it
halted a mile away on the other side of the plain.
But as we approached they all went off together,
and I can only hope the two I hit recovered; at any
rate, after we had followed them for miles, the tough
beasts were still running as strongly as ever.

All the morning I manœuvred and tramped hard, in vain. At noon, I tried a stalk on a little band of six, who were standing still, idly switching their tails, out in a big flat. They saw me, and at four hundred yards I missed the shot. By this time I felt rather desperate, and decided for once to abandon legitimate proceedings and act on the Ciceronian theory, that he who throws the javelin all day must hit the mark some time. Accordingly I emptied the magazines of both my rifles at the oryx, as they ran across my front, and broke the neck of a fine cow, at four hundred and fifty yards. Six or seven hundred yards off the survivors stopped, and the biggest bull, evidently much put out, uttered loud bawling grunts and drove the others round with his horns. Meanwhile I was admiring the handsome dun gray coat of my prize, its long tail and long, sharp, slender horns, and the bold black and white markings on its face. Hardly had we skinned the carcass before the vultures lit on it; with them were two marabou storks, one of which I shot with a hard bullet from the Springfield.

The oryx, like the roan and sable, and in striking contrast to the eland, is a bold and hard fighter, and when cornered will charge a man or endeavor to stab a lion. If wounded it must be approached with a certain amount of caution. The eland, on the other hand, in spite of its huge size, is singularly mild and inoffensive, an old bull being as inferior

to an oryx in the will and power to fight as it is in
speed and endurance. "Antelope," as I have said,
is a very loose term, meaning simply any hollow-
horned ruminant that isn't an ox, a sheep, or a goat.
The eland is one of the group of tragelaphs, which
are as different from the true antelopes, such as the
gazelles, as they are from the oxen. One of its kinsfolk is the handsome little bushbuck, about as big
as a white-tail deer; a buck of which Kermit had
killed two specimens. The bushbuck is a wicked
fighter, no other buck of its size being as dangerous;
which makes the helplessness and timidity of its huge
relative all the more striking.

I had kept four Kikuyu with me to accompany me
on my hunts and carry in the skins and meat. They
were with me on this occasion; and it was amusing
to see how my four regular attendants, Bakhari and
Gouvimali the gun-bearers, Simba the sais, and Kiboko the skinner, looked down on their wild and
totally uncivilized brethren. They would not associate with the "shenzis," as they called them; that
is, savages or bush people. But the "shenzis" always amused and interested me; and this was especially true on the afternoon in question. Soon after
we had started campwards with the skin and meat
of the oryx, we encountered a succession of thunder-storms. The rain came down in a deluge, so that
the water stood ankle deep on the flats, the lightning
flashed continuously on every side, and the terrific

peals of thunder made one continuous roll. At first it maddened my horse; but the uninterrupted blaze and roar, just because uninterrupted, ended by making him feel that there was nothing to be done, and he plodded stolidly forward through the driving storm. My regular attendants accepted it with an entire philosophy, which was finally copied by the Kikuyus, who at first felt frightened. One of them had an old umbrella which he shared with a crony. He himself was carrying the marabou stork; his crony had long strips of raw oryx meat wound in a swollen girdle about his waist; neither had a stitch on save the blankets which were wrapped round their throats; and they clasped each other in a tight embrace as they walked along under the battered old umbrella.

In this desolate and lonely land the majesty of the storms impressed on the beholder a sense of awe and solemn exaltation. Tossing their crests, and riven by lightning, they gathered in their wrath from every quarter of the heavens, and darkness was before and under them; then, in the lull of a moment, they might break apart, while the sun turned the rain to silver and the rainbows were set in the sky; but always they gathered again, menacing and mighty,— for the promise of the bow was never kept, and ever the clouds returned after the rain. Once as I rode facing Kenia the clouds tore asunder, to right and left, and the mountain towered between, while across

its base was flung a radiant arch. But almost at once
the many-colored glory was dimmed; for in splendor
and terror the storm strode in front, and shrouded
all things from sight in thunder-shattered sheets of
rain.

These days alone in the wilderness went by very
pleasantly, and, as it was for not too long, I
thoroughly enjoyed being entirely by myself, so far
as white men were concerned. By this time I had
become really attached to my native followers, who
looked after my interest and comfort in every way;
and in return I kept them supplied with plenty of
food, saw that they were well clothed, and forced
them to gather enough firewood to keep their tents
dry and warm at night—for cold, rainy weather is
always hard upon them.

Ali, my faithful head tent boy, and Shemlani his
assistant—poor Bill the Kikuyu had left because of
an intricate row with his fellows—were both, as they
proudly informed me, Arabs. On the East African
coast the so-called Arabs almost all have native blood
in them and speak Swahili; the curious, newly
created language of the descendants of the natives
whom the Arabs originally enslaved, and who themselves may have in their veins a little Arab blood; in
fact, the dividing line between Swahili and Arab
becomes impracticable for an outsider to draw
where, as is generally the case, it is patent that the
blood of both races is mixed to a degree at which it

is only possible to guess. Ali spoke some English; and he and Shemlani were devoted and efficient servitors. Bakhari the gun-bearer was a Swahili, quite fearless with dangerous game, rather sullen, and unmoved by any emotion that I could ever discover. He spoke a little English, but it could not be called idiomatic. One day we saw two ostriches, a cock and a hen, with their chicks, and Bakhari with some excitement said, " Look, sah! ostrich! bull, cow, and pups! " The other gun-bearer, Gouvimali, in some ways an even better hunter, and always good-tempered, knew but one English phrase; regularly every afternoon or evening, after cleaning the rifle he had carried, he would say, as he left the tent, his face wreathed in smiles, " G-o-o-d-e-bye! " Gouvimali was a Wakamba, as were Simba and my other sais, M'nyassa, who had taken the place of Hamisi (Hamisi had broken down in health, his legs, as he assured me, becoming " very sick "). The cook, Roberti, was a mission boy, a Christian; we had several Christians with the safari, one being a headman, and all did excellently. I mention this because one so often hears it said that mission boys turn out worthless. Most of our men were heathens; and of course many, both of the Christians and the Mohammedans, were rather thinly veneered with the religions they respectively professed.

When in the morning we started on our hunt my

gun-bearers and sais, and the skinners, if any were along, walked silently behind me, on the lookout for game. Returning, they were apt to get in front, to pilot me back to camp. If, as at this time was generally the case, we returned with our heads bent to the rushing rain, they trudged sturdily ahead in dripping silence. If the weather was clear the spirits of the stalwart fellows were sure to rise until they found some expression. The Wakamba might break into song; or they might all talk together in Swahili, recounting the adventures of the day, and chaffing one another with uproarious laughter about any small misadventure; a difference of opinion as to the direction of camp being always a subject, first for earnest discussion, and then for much mirth at the expense of whom ever the event proved mistaken.

My two horses, when I did not use them, grazed contentedly throughout the day near the little thorn boma which surrounded our tents; and at nightfall the friendly things came within it of their own accord to be given their feed of corn and be put in their own tent. When the sun was hot they were tormented by biting flies; but their work was easy, and they were well treated and throve. In the daytime vultures, kites, and white-necked ravens came round camp, and after nightfall jackals wailed and hyenas uttered their weird cries as they prowled outside the thorn walls. Twice, at midnight, we heard the ominous sighing or moaning of a hungry lion, and I looked to my rifle, which always stood, loaded, at the head of my bed. But on neither occasion did he come near us. Every night a fire was kept burning in the entrance to the boma, and the three askaris watched in turn, with instructions to call me if there was any need.

I easily kept the camp in meat, as I had guessed that I could do. My men feasted on oryx and eland, while I reserved the tongues and tenderloins for myself. Each day I hunted for eight or ten hours, something of interest always happening. I would not shoot at the gazelles; and the game I did want was so shy that almost all my shots were at long range, and consequently a number of them did not hit. However, I came on my best oryx in rather thick bush, and killed it at a hundred and twenty-five yards, as it turned with a kind of sneeze of alarm or curiosity, and stood broadside to me, the sun glinting on its handsome coat and polished black horns. One of my Kikuyu followers packed the skin entire to camp. I had more trouble with another oryx, wounding it one evening at three hundred and fifty yards, and next morning following the trail and after much hard work and a couple of misses killing it with a shot at three hundred yards. On September 2 I found two newly born oryx calves. The color of the oryx made them less visible than hartebeest when a long way off on the dry plains. I noticed that whenever we saw them mixed in a herd with zebra, it was the zebra that first struck our eyes. But in bright sunlight, in bush, I also noticed that the zebra themselves were hard to see.

One afternoon, while skirting the edge of a marsh teeming with waders and water-fowl, I came across four stately Kavirondo cranes, specimens of which bird the naturalists had been particularly anxious to secure. They were not very shy for cranes, but they would not keep still, and I missed a shot with the Springfield as they walked along about a hundred and fifty yards ahead of me. However, they were unwise enough to circle round me when they rose, still keeping the same distance, and all the time uttering their musical call, while their great wings flapped in measured beats. Wing shooting with the rifle, even at such large birds of such slow and regular flight, is never easy, and they were rather far off; but with the last cartridge in my magazine —the fifth—I brought one whirling down through the air, the bullet having pierced its body. It was a most beautiful bird, black, white, and chestnut, with an erect golden crest, and long, lanceolate gray feathers on the throat and breast.

There were waterbuck and impalla in this swamp. I tried to get a bull of the former but failed. Several times I was within fifty yards of doe impalla and cow waterbuck, with their young, and watched them as they fed and rested, quite unconscious of my presence. Twice I saw steinbuck, on catching sight of me, lie down, hoping to escape observation. The red coat of the steinbuck is rather conspicuous, much more so than the coat of the duiker; yet it often tries to hide from possible foes.

Late in the afternoon of September 3, Cuninghame and Heller, with the main safari, joined me, and I greeted them joyfully; while my men were equally pleased to see their fellows, each shaking hands with his especial friends. Next morning we started toward Meru, heading north-east, toward the foot-hills of Kenia. The vegetation changed its character as we rose. By the stream where we had camped grew the great thorn-trees with yellow-green trunks which we had become accustomed to associate with the presence of herds of game. Out on the dry flats were other thorns, weazened little trees, or mere scrawny bushes, with swellings like bulbs on the branches and twigs, and the long thorns far more conspicuous than the scanty foliage; though what there was of this foliage, now brilliant green, was exquisite in hue and form, the sprays of delicate little leaves being as fine as the daintiest lace. On the foot-hills all these thorn-trees vanished. We did not go as high as the forest belt proper (here narrow, while above it the bamboos covered the mountain side), but tongues of juniper forest stretched down along the valleys which we

crossed, and there were large patches of coarse deer
fern, while among many unknown flowers we saw
blue lupins, ox-eyed daisies, and clover. That night
we camped so high that it was really cold, and we
welcomed the roaring fires of juniper logs.

We rose at sunrise. It was a glorious morning,
clear and cool, and as we sat at breakfast, the table
spread in the open on the dew-drenched grass, we
saw in the southeast the peak of Kenia, and through
the high, transparent air the snow-fields seemed so
close as almost to dazzle our eyes. To the north
and west we looked far out over the wide, rolling
plains to a wilderness of mountain ranges, barren
and jagged. All that day and the next we journeyed eastward, almost on the equator. At noon the
overhead sun burned with torrid heat; but with the
twilight—short compared to the long northern twilights, but not nearly as short as tropical twilights
are often depicted—came the cold, and each night
the frost was heavy. The country was untenanted
by man. In the afternoon of the third day we began to go downhill, and hour by hour the flora
changed. At last we came to a broad belt of woodland, where the strange trees of many kinds grew
tall and thick. Among them were camphor-trees,
and trees with gouty branch tips, bearing leaves like
those of the black walnut, and panicles of lilac flowers, changing into brown seed vessels; and other
trees, with clusters of purple flowers, and the seeds

or nuts enclosed in hard pods or seed vessels like huge sausages.

On the other side of the forest we came suddenly out on the cultivated fields of the Wa-Meru, who, like the Kikuyu, till the soil; and among them, farther down, was Meru boma, its neat, picturesque buildings beautifully placed among green groves and irrigated fields, and looking out from its cool elevation over the hot valleys beneath. It is one of the prettiest spots in East Africa. We were more than hospitably received by the Commissioner, Mr. Horne, who had been a cow-puncher in Wyoming for seven years—so that naturally we had much in common. He had built the station himself, and had tamed the wild tribes around by mingled firmness and good treatment; and he was a mighty hunter, and helped us in every way.

Here we met Kermit and Tarlton, and heard all about their hunt. They had been away from us for three weeks and a half, along the Guaso Nyero, and had enjoyed first-rate luck. Kermit had been particularly interested in a caravan they had met, consisting of wild spear-bearing Borani, people like Somalis, who were bringing down scores of camels and hundreds of small horses to sell at Nairobi. They had come from the north, near the outlying Abyssinian lands, and the caravan was commanded by an Arab of stately and courteous manners. Such an extensive caravan journey was rare in the old

days before English rule; but one of the results of
the " Pax Europaica," wherever it obtains in German, French, or English Africa, is a great increase
of intercourse, commercial and social, among the
different tribes, even where widely separated. This
caravan had been followed by lions; and a day or
two afterward Kermit and Tarlton ran into what
were probably these very lions. There were eleven
of them: a male with a heavy mane, three lionesses,
and seven cubs, some of them about half grown.
As Kermit and Tarlton galloped after them, the lion
took the lead, the cubs coming in the middle, while
three lionesses loped along in the rear, guarding
their young. The lion cared little for his wives
and offspring, and gradually drew ahead of them,
while the two horsemen, riding at full speed, made
a wide détour round the others in order to reach
him; so that at last they got between him and the
ten lionesses and cubs, the big lion coming first, the
horsemen next, and then the lesser lions, all headed
the same way. As the horsehooves thundered
closer the lion turned to bay. Kermit—whose horse
had once fallen with him in the chase—and Tarlton
leaped off their horses, and Kermit hit the lion with
his first shot, and, as it started to charge, mortally
wounded it with a second bullet. It turned and
tried to reach cover, and Tarlton stopped it with a
third shot; for there was no time to lose, as they
wished to tackle the other lions. After a sharp gal-

lop they rounded up the lionesses and cubs. Kermit killed one large cub, which they mistook for a lioness; wounded a lioness which for the time being escaped; killed another with a single bullet from his 30-40 Winchester—for the others he used his .405 Winchester—and hit the third as she crouched facing him at two hundred yards. She at once came in at full speed, making a most determined charge. Kermit and Tarlton were standing near their horses. The lioness came on with great bounds so that Kermit missed her twice, but broke her shoulder high up when she was but thirty yards off. She fell on her head and, on rising, galloped, not at the men, but at the horses, who, curiously enough, paid no heed to her. Tarlton stopped her with a bullet in the nick of time, just before she reached them, and with another bullet Kermit killed her. Two days later they came on the remaining cubs and the wounded lioness, and Kermit killed the latter; but they let the cubs go, feeling it unsportsmanlike to kill them —a feeling which I am by no means certain I share, for lions are scourges not only to both wild and tame animals but to man himself.

Kermit also rode down and killed two cheetahs and a serval, and got a bad tumble while chasing a jackal, his horse turning a complete somersault through a thorny bush. This made seven cheetahs that he had killed, a record unequalled for any other East African trip of the same length; and the finding and galloping down of these cheetahs—going at breakneck speed over any and every kind of ground, and then shooting them either from foot or horseback—made one of the noteworthy features of our trip. One of these two cheetahs had just killed a steinbuck. The serval was with its mate, and Kermit watched them for some time through his glasses before following them. There was one curious feature of their conduct. One of them was playing about, now near the other, now leaving it; and near by was a bustard, which it several times pretended to stalk, crawling toward it a few yards, and then standing up and walking away. The bustard paid no heed to it; and, more singular still, two white-necked ravens lit close to it, within a few yards on either side; the serval sitting erect between them, seemingly quite unconcerned for a couple of minutes, and then strolling off without making any effort to molest them. I can give no explanation of the incident; it illustrates afresh the need of ample and well-recorded observations by trustworthy field naturalists, who shall go into the wilderness before the big game, the big birds, and the beasts of prey vanish. Those pages of the book of nature which are best worth reading can best be read far from the dwellings of civilized man; and for their full interpretation we need the services, not of one man, but of many men, who in addition to the gift of accurate observation shall if possible possess the power

fully, accurately, and with vividness to write about
what they have observed.

Kermit shot many other animals, among them
three fine oryx, one of which he rode down on horseback, manœuvring so that at last it galloped fairly
closely across his front, whereupon he leaped off his
horse for the shot; an ardwolf (a miniature hyena
with very weak teeth) which bolted from its hole
at his approach; gerenuk, small antelope with necks
relatively as long as giraffes', which are exceedingly
shy and difficult to obtain; and the Grevy's zebra,
as big as a small horse. Most of his hunting was
done alone, either on foot or on horseback; on a
long run or all-day tramp no other member of our
outfit, black or white, could quite keep up with him.
He and Tarlton found where a leopard had killed
and partly eaten a nearly full-grown individual of
this big zebra.   He also shot a twelve-foot crocodile.
The ugly, formidable brute had in its belly sticks,
stones, the claws of a cheetah, the hoofs of an impalla, and the big bones of an eland, together with
the shell plates of one of the large river-turtles; evidently it took toll indifferently from among its fel-
low-denizens of the river, and from among the
creatures that came to drink, whether beasts of
pasture or the flesh eaters that preyed upon them.

He also shot three buffalo bulls, Tarlton helping
him to finish them off, for they are tough animals,
tenacious of life and among the most dangerous of

African game. One turned to charge, but was disabled by the bullets of both of them before he could come on. Tarlton, whose experience in the hunting field against dangerous game had been large, always maintained that, although lion hunting was the most dangerous sport, because a hunted lion was far more apt to charge than any other animal, yet when a buffalo bull did charge he was more dangerous than a lion, because harder to kill or turn. Where zebra and other game are abundant, as on the Athi Plains, lion do not meddle with such formidable quarry as buffalo; on Heatley's farm lions sometimes made their lairs in the same papyrus swamp with the buffalo, but hardly ever molested them. In many places, however, the lion preys largely, and in some places chiefly, on the buffalo. The hunters of wide experience with whom I conversed, men like Tarlton, Cuninghame, and Horne, were a unit in stating that where a single lion killed a buffalo they had always found that the buffalo was a cow or immature bull, and that whenever they had found a full-grown bull thus killed, several lions had been engaged in the job. Horne had once found the carcass of a big bull which had been killed and eaten by lions, and near by lay a dead lioness with a great rip in her side, made by the buffalo's horn in the fight in which he succumbed. Even a buffalo cow, if fairly pitted against a single lion, would probably stand an even chance; but of course the fight never is fair, the lion's aim being to take his prey unawares and get a death grip at the outset; and then, unless his hold is broken, he cannot be seriously injured.

Twenty years ago the African buffalo were smitten with one of those overwhelming disasters which are ever occurring and recurring in the animal world. Africa is not only the land, beyond all others, subject to odious and terrible insect plagues of every conceivable kind, but is also peculiarly liable to cattle murrains. About the year 1889, or shortly before, a virulent form of rinderpest started among the domestic cattle and wild buffalo almost at the northern border of the buffalo's range, and within the next few years worked gradually southward to beyond the Zambesi. It wrought dreadful havoc among the cattle, and in consequence decimated by starvation many of the cattle-owning tribes; it killed many of the large bovine antelopes, and it wellnigh exterminated the buffalo. In many places the buffalo herds were absolutely wiped out, the species being utterly destroyed throughout great tracts of territory, notably in East Africa; in other places the few survivors did not represent the hundredth part of those that had died. For years the East African buffalo ceased to exist as a beast of the chase. But all the time it was slowly regaining the lost ground, and during the last decade its increase has been rapid. Unlike the slow-breeding elephant and rhinoceros, buffalo multiply apace, like domestic cattle, and in many places the herds have now become too numerous. Their rapid recovery from a calamity so terrific is interesting and instructive.* Doubtless for many years after man, in recognizably human form, appeared on this planet, he played but a small part in the destruction of big animals, compared to plague, to insect pests and microbes, to drought, flood, earth upheaval, and change of temperature. But during the geological moment covering the few thousand years of recorded history man has been not merely the chief, but practically the sole factor in the extermination of big mammals and birds.

At and near Meru boma we spent a fortnight hunting elephant and rhinoceros, as described in the preceding chapter. While camped by the boma white-necked vulturine ravens and black and white crows came familiarly around the tents. A young eland bull, quite as tame as a domestic cow, was picketed, now here, now there, about us. Horne was breaking it to drive in a cart.

During our stay another District Commissioner, Mr. Piggott, came over on a short visit; it was he who the preceding year, while at Neri, had been obliged to undertake the crusade against the rhinos, because, quite unprovoked, they had killed various natives. He told us that at the same time a man-

* On our trip along the Guaso Nyero we heard that there had been a fresh outbreak of rinderpest among the buffalo; I hope it will not prove such a hideous disaster.

eating leopard made its appearance, and killed seven children. It did not attack at night, but in the daytime, its victims being the little boys who were watching the flocks of goats; sometimes it took a boy and sometimes a goat. Two old men killed it with spears on the occasion of its taking the last victim. It was a big male, very old, much emaciated, and the teeth worn to stumps. Horne told us that a month or two before our arrival at Meru a leopard had begun a career of woman-killing. It killed one woman by a bite in the throat, and ate the body. It sprang on and badly wounded another, but was driven off in time to save her life. This was probably the leopard Heller trapped and shot, in the very locality where it had committed its ravages; it was an old male, but very thin, with worn teeth. In these cases the reason for the beast's action was plain: in each instance, a big savage male had found his powers failing, and had been driven to prey on the females and young of the most helpless of animals, man. But another attack, of which Piggott told us, was apparently due to the queer individual freakishness always to be taken into account in dealing with wild beasts. A Masai chief, with two or three followers, was sitting eating under a bush, when, absolutely without warning, a leopard sprang on him, clawed him on the head and hand, without biting him, and as instantly disappeared. Piggott attended to the wounded man.

In riding in the neighborhood, through the tall dry grass, which would often rattle in the wind, I was amused to find that if I suddenly heard the sound I was apt to stand alertly on guard, quite unconsciously and instinctively, because it suggested the presence of a rattlesnake. During the years I lived on a ranch in the West I was always hearing and killing rattlesnakes, and although I knew well that no African snake carries a rattle, my subconscious senses always threw me to attention if there was a sound resembling that made by a rattler. Tarlton, by the way, told me an interesting anecdote of a white-tailed mongoose and a snake. The mongoose was an inmate of the house where he dwelt with his brother and was quite tame. One day they brought in a rather small puff adder, less than two feet long, put it on the floor, and showed it to the mongoose. Instantly the latter sprang toward the snake, every hair in its body and tail on end, and halted five feet away, while the snake lay in curves like the thong of a whip, its head turned toward the mongoose. Both were motionless for a moment. Then suddenly the mongoose seemed to lose all its excitement; its hair smoothed down; and it trotted quietly up to the snake, seized it by the middle of the back—it always devoured its food with savage voracity—and settled comfortably down to its meal. Like lightning the snake's head whipped round. It drove its fangs deep into the snout or lip of the mongoose, hung on for a moment, and then repeated the blow. The mongoose paid not the least attention, but went on munching the snake's body, severed its backbone at once, and then ate it all up, head, fangs, poison, and everything; and it never showed a sign of having received any damage in the encounter. I had always understood that the mongoose owed its safety to its agility in avoiding the snake's stroke, and I can offer no explanation of this particular incident.

There were eland on the high downs not far from Meru, apparently as much at home in the wet, cold climate as on the hot plains. Their favorite gait is the trot. An elephant moves at a walk or rather rack; a giraffe has a very peculiar leisurely looking gallop, both hind legs coming forward nearly at the same time, outside the forelegs; rhino and buffalo trot and run. Eland when alarmed bound with astonishing agility for such large beasts—a trait not shown by other large antelope, like oryx—and then gallop for a short distance; but the big bulls speedily begin to trot, and the cows and younger bulls gradually also drop back into the trot. In fact, their gaits are in essence those of the wapiti, which also prefer the trot, although wapiti never make the bounds that eland do at the start. The moose, however, is more essentially a trotter than either eland or wapiti; a very old and heavy moose never, when at speed, goes at any other gait than a trot, except that under the pressure of great and sudden danger it may perhaps make a few bounds.*

While at Meru boma I received a cable, forwarded by native runners, telling me of Peary's wonderful feat in reaching the North Pole. Of course we were all overjoyed, and in particular we Americans could not but feel a special pride in the fact that it was a fellow-countryman who had performed the great and noteworthy achievement. A little more than a year had passed since I said good-by to Peary as he started on his Arctic quest; after leaving New York in the *Roosevelt*, he had put into Oyster Bay to see us, and we had gone aboard the *Roosevelt*, had examined with keen interest how she was fitted for the boreal seas and the boreal winter, and had then waved farewell to the tall, gaunt explorer, as he stood looking toward us over the side of the stout little ship.†

On September 21, Kermit and Tarlton started southwest, toward Lake Hannington, and Cuning-

* A perfectly trustworthy Maine hunter informed me that in the spring he had once seen in the snow where a bear had sprung at two big moose, and they had bounded for several rods before settling into the tremendous trot which is their normal gait when startled. I have myself seen signs that showed where a young moose had galloped for some rods under similar circumstances; and I have seen big moose calves, or half-grown moose, in captivity gallop a few yards in play, although rarely. But the normal, and under ordinary circumstances the only, gait of the moose is the trot.

† When I reached Neri I received from Peary the following cable: "Your farewell was a royal mascot. The Pole is ours. —PEARY."

hame and I north toward the Guaso Nyero. Heller
was under the weather, and we left him to spend a
few days at Meru boma, and then to take in the elephant skins and other museum specimens to Nairobi.

As Cuninghame and I were to be nearly four
weeks in a country with no food supplies, we took
a small donkey safari to carry the extra food for our
porters—for in these remote places the difficulty of
taking in many hundred pounds of salt, as well as
skin tents, and the difficulty of bringing out the
skeletons and skins of the big animals collected,
make such an expedition as ours, undertaken for
scientific purposes, far more cumbersome and un-
wieldy than a mere hunting trip, or even than a
voyage of exploration, and trebles the labor.

A long day's march brought us down to the hot
country. That evening we pitched our tents by a
rapid brook, bordered by palms, whose long, stiff
fronds rustled ceaselessly in the wind. Monkeys
swung in the tree tops. On the march I shot a
Kavirondo crane on the wing with the little Springfield, almost exactly repeating my experience with
the other crane which I had shot three weeks before,
except that on this occasion I brought down the bird
with my third bullet, and then wasted the last two
cartridges in the magazine at his companions. At
dusk the donkeys were driven to a fire within the
camp, and they stood patiently round it in a circle
throughout the night, safe from lions and hyenas.

Next day's march brought us to another small
tributary of the Guaso Nyero, a little stream twisting rapidly through the plain, between sheer banks.
Here and there it was edged with palms and beds
of bulrushes. We pitched the tents close to half a
dozen flat-topped thorn-trees. We spent several
days at this camp. Many kites came around the
tents, but neither vultures nor ravens. The country
was a vast plain bounded on almost every hand by
chains of far-off mountains. In the south-west,
just beyond the equator, the snows of Kenia lifted
toward the sky. To the north the barren ranges
were grim with the grimness of the desert. The
flats were covered with pale, bleached grass which
waved all day long in the wind; for though there
were sometimes calms, or changes in the wind, on
most of the days we were out it never ceased blowing from some point in the south. In places the
parched soil was crumbling and rotten; in other
places it was thickly strewn with volcanic stones;
there were but few tracts over which a horse could
gallop at speed, although neither the rocks nor the
rotten soil seemed to hamper the movements of the
game. Here and there were treeless stretches.
Elsewhere there were occasional palms; and trees
thirty or forty feet high, seemingly cactus or aloes,
which looked even more like candelabra than the
euphorbia which is thus named; and a scattered
growth of thorn-trees and bushes. The thorn-trees

were of many kinds. One bore only a few leathery leaves, the place of foliage being taken by the mass of poisonous-looking, fleshy spines which, together with the end of the branches, were bright green. The camel-thorn was completely armed with little, sharply hooked thorns which tore whatever they touched, whether flesh or clothes. Then there were the mimosas, with long, straight thorn spikes; they are so plentiful in certain places along the Guaso Nyero that almost all the lions have festering sores in their paws because of the spikes that have broken off in them. In these thorn-trees the weaver birds had built multitudes of their straw nests, each with its bottle-shaped mouth toward the north, away from the direction of the prevailing wind.

Each morning we were up at dawn, and saw the heavens redden and the sun flame over the rim of the world. All day long we rode and walked across the endless flats, save that at noon, when the sky was like molten brass, we might rest under the thin half shade of some thorn-tree. As the shadows lengthened and the harsh, pitiless glare softened, we might turn campward; or we might hunt until the sun went down, and the mountains in the far-off west, and the sky above them, grew faint and dim with the hues of fairyland. Then we would ride back through the soft, warm beauty of the tropic night, the stars blazing overhead and the silver moonlight flooding the reaches of dry grass; it was so bright that our shadows were almost as black and clear-cut as in the day. On reaching camp I would take a cup of tea with crackers or gingersnaps, and after a hot bath and a shave I was always eager for dinner.

Scattered over these flats were herds of zebra, oryx, and gazelle. The gazelle, the most plentiful and much the tamest of the game, were the northern form of the Grant's gazelle, with straighter horns which represented the opposite extreme when compared with the horns of the Roberts' type which we got on the Sotik. They seemed to me somewhat less in size than the big gazelle of the Kapiti Plains. One of the bucks I shot, an adult of average size (I was not able to weigh my biggest one), weighed one hundred and fifteen pounds; a very big true Grant's buck which I shot on the Kapiti Plains weighed one hundred and seventy-one pounds; doubtless there is complete intergradation, but the Guaso Nyero form seemed slimmer and lighter, and in some respects seemed to tend toward the Somaliland gazelles. I marked no difference in the habits, except that these northern gazelle switched their tails more jerkily, more like tommies, than was customary with the true Grant's gazelles. But the difference may have been in my observation. At any rate, the gazelles in this neighborhood, like those elsewhere, went in small parties, or herds of thirty or forty individuals, on the open plains or where there were a few scat-

tered bushes, and behaved like those in the Sotik or
on the Athi Plains. A near kinsman of the gazelle,
the gerenuk, a curious creature with a very long
neck, which the Swahilis call " little giraffe," was
scattered singly or in small parties through the
brush, and was as wild and wary as the common
gazelle was tame. It seemed to prefer browsing,
while the common gazelle grazes.

The handsome oryx, with their long horns carried by both sexes, and their coloring of black,
white, and dun gray, came next to the gazelle in
point of numbers. They were generally found in
herds of from half a dozen to fifty individuals, often
mixed with zebra herds. There were also solitary
bulls, probably turned out of the herds by more vigorous rivals, and often one of these would be found
with a herd of zebras, more merciful to it than its
own kinsfolk. All this game of the plains is highly
gregarious in habit, and the species associate freely
with one another. The oryx cows were now generally accompanied by very young calves, for, unlike
what we found to be the case with the hartebeest on
the Athi, the oryx on the Guaso Nyero seem to have
a definite calving time—September.* I shot only

* Of course this represents only one man's experience. I
wish there were many such observations. On the Athi in
May I found new-born wildebeest and hartebeest calves, and
others several months old. In June in the Sotik I saw new-
born eland calves, and topi calves several months old. In
September on the Guaso Nyero all the oryx calves were new-
born. The zebra foals were also very young.

bulls (there was no meat, either for the porters or ourselves, except what I got with the rifle), and they were so wary that almost all those I killed were shot at ranges between three hundred and five hundred yards; and at such ranges I need hardly say that I did a good deal of missing. One wounded bull which, the ground being favorable, I galloped down, turned to bay and threatened to charge the horse. We weighed one bull; it tipped the scales at four hundred pounds. The lion kills we found in this neighborhood were all oryx and zebra; and evidently the attack was made in such fashion that the oryx had no more chance to fight than the zebra.

The zebra were of both species, the smaller or Burchell's, and the Grevy's, which the porters called kangani. Each animal went in herds by itself, and almost as frequently we found them in mixed herds containing both species. But they never interbreed, and associate merely as each does with the oryx. The kangani is a fine beast, much bigger than its kinsman; it is as large as a polo pony. It is less noisy than the common zebra, the " bonte quagga " of the Boers, and its cry is totally different. Its gaits are a free, slashing trot and gallop. When it stands facing one the huge fringed ears make it instantly recognizable. The stripes are much narrower and more numerous than those on the small zebra, and in consequence cease to be distinguishable at a shorter distance; the animal then looks gray,

like a wild ass. When the two zebras are together
the coloring of the smaller kind is more conspicuous.
In scanning a herd with the glasses we often failed
to make out the species until we could catch the
broad black and white stripes on the rump of the
common "bonte quagga." There were many
young foals with the kangani; I happened not to
see any with the Burchell's. I found the kangani
even more wary and more difficult to shoot than the
oryx. The first one I killed was shot at a range of
four hundred yards; the next I wounded at that distance, and had to ride it down, at the cost of a hard
gallop over very bad country and getting torn by the
" wait a bit " thorns.

There were a number of rhinos on the plains, dull
of wit and senses, as usual. Three times we saw
cows with calves trotting at their heels. Once,
while my men were skinning an oryx, I spied a
rhino less than half a mile off. Mounting my horse
I cantered down, and examined it within a hundred
yards. It was an old bull with worn horns, and
never saw me. On another occasion, while we were
skinning a big zebra, there were three rhinoceros,
all in different places, in sight at the same time.

There were also ostriches. I saw a party of
cocks, with wings spread and necks curved backward, strutting and dancing. Their mincing,
springy run is far faster than, when the bird is near
by, it seems. The neck is held back in running, and

when at speed the stride is twenty-one feet. No game is more wary or more difficult to approach. I killed both a cock and a hen—which I found the naturalists valued even more than a cock. We got them by stumbling on the nest, which contained eleven huge eggs, and was merely a bare spot in the sand, surrounded by grass two feet high; the bird lay crouched, with the neck flat on the ground. When we accidentally came across the nest the cock was on it, and I failed to get him as he ran. The next day we returned, and dismounted before we reached the near neighborhood of the nest. Then I advanced, cautiously, my rifle at the ready. It seemed impossible that so huge a bird could lie hidden in such scanty cover, but not a sign did we see until, when we were sixty yards off, the hen, which this time was on the nest, rose, and I killed her at sixty yards. Even this did not make the cock desert the nest; and on a subsequent day I returned, and after missing him badly, I killed him at eighty-five yards; and glad I was to see the huge black-and-white bird tumble in the dust. He weighed two hundred and sixty-three pounds and was in fine plumage. The hen weighed two hundred and forty pounds. Her stomach and gizzard, in addition to small, white quartz pebbles, contained a mass of vegetable substance; the bright-green leaves and twig tips of a shrub, a kind of rush with jointed stem and tuberous root, bean pods from different

kinds of thorn-trees, and the leaves and especially
the seed vessels of a bush, the seed vessels being enclosed in cases or pods so thorny that they pinched
our fingers, and made us wonder at the bird's palate.
Cock and hen brood the eggs alternately. We
found the heart and liver of the ostrich excellent eating; the eggs were very good also. As the cock
died it uttered a kind of loud, long-drawn grunting
boom that was almost a roar. Its beautiful white
wing plumes were almost unworn. A full-grown
wild ostrich is too wary to fall into the clutches of a
lion or leopard, save by accident, and it will master
any of the lesser carnivora; but the chicks are preyed
on by jackals and wild cats, and of course by the
larger beasts of prey also; and the eggs are eagerly
sought by furred and feathered foes alike. Seemingly trustworthy settlers have assured me that vultures break the tough shells with stones. The cock
and hen will try to draw their more formidable foes
away from the nest or the chicks by lingering so
near as to lure them into pursuit; and anything up
to the size of a hyena they will attack and drive
away, or even kill. The terrific downward stroke
of an ostrich's leg is as dangerous as the kick of a
horse; the thump will break a rib or backbone of any
ordinary animal, and in addition to the force of the
blow itself the big nails may make a ghastly rip.
Both cock and hen lead about the young brood and
care for it. The two ostriches I shot were swarm-

ing with active parasitic flies, a little like those that were on the lions I shot in the Sotik. Later the porters brought us in several ostrich chicks. They also brought two genet kittens, which I tried to raise, but failed. They were much like ordinary kittens, with larger ears, sharper noses, and longer tails, and loved to perch on my shoulder or sit on my lap while I stroked them. They made dear little pets, and I was very sorry when they died.

On the day that I shot the cock ostrich I also shot a giraffe. The country in which we were hunting marks the southern limit of the " reticulated " giraffe, a form or species entirely distinct from the giraffe we had already obtained in the country south of Kenia. The southern giraffe is blotched with dark on a light ground, whereas this northern or north-eastern form is of a uniform dark color on the back and sides, with a net-work or reticulation of white lines placed in a large pattern on this dark background. The naturalists were very anxious to obtain a specimen of this form from its southern limit of distribution, to see if there was any intergradation with the southern form, of which we had already shot specimens near its northern, or at least north-eastern, limit. The distinction proved sharp.

On the day in question we breakfasted at six in the morning, and were off immediately afterward; and we did not eat anything again until supper at quarter to ten in the evening. In a hot climate a hunter does not need lunch; and though in a cold climate a simple lunch is permissible, anything like an elaborate or luxurious lunch is utterly out of place if the man is more than a parlor or drawing-room sportsman. We saw no sign of giraffe until late in the afternoon. Hour after hour we plodded across the plain, now walking, now riding, in the burning heat. The withered grass was as dry as a bone, for the country had been many months without rain; yet the oryx, zebra, and gazelle evidently throve on the harsh pasturage. There were innumerable game trails leading hither and thither, and, after the fashion of game trails, usually fading out after a few hundred yards. But there were certain trails which did not fade out. These were the ones which led to water. One such we followed. It led across stretches of grassland, through thin bush, thorny and almost leafless, over tracts of rotten soil, cracked and crumbling, and over other tracts where the unshod horses picked their way gingerly among the masses of sharp-edged volcanic stones. Other trails joined in, and it grew more deeply marked. At last it led to a bend in a little river, where flat shelves of limestone bordered a kind of pool in the current where there were beds of green rushes and a fringe of trees and thorn thickets. This was evidently a favorite drinking-place. Many trails converged toward it, and for a long distance round the ground was worn completely bare by the hoofs of

the countless herds of thirsty game that had travelled thither from time immemorial. Sleek, handsome, long-horned oryx, with switching tails, were
loitering in the vicinity, and at the water hole itself
we surprised a band of gazelles not fifty yards off;
they fled panic-struck in every direction. Men and
horses drank their fill; and we returned to the sunny
plains and the endless reaches of withered, rustling
grass.

At last, an hour or two before sunset, when the
heat had begun a little to abate, we spied half a
dozen giraffes scattered a mile and a half ahead of
us, feeding on the tops of the few widely separated
thorn-trees. Cuninghame and I started toward
them on foot, but they saw us when we were a mile
away, and after gazing a short while, turned and
went off at their usual rocking-horse canter, twisting and screwing their tails. We mounted and rode
after them. I was on my zebra-shaped brown
horse, which was hardy and with a fair turn of
speed, and which by this time I had trained to be a
good hunting horse. On the right were two giraffe which eventually turned out to be a big cow
followed by a nearly full-grown young one; but
Cuninghame, scanning them through his glasses,
and misled by the dark coloration, pronounced them
a bull and cow; and after the big one I went. By
good luck we were on one of the rare pieces of the
country which was fitted for galloping. I rode at

an angle to the giraffe's line of flight, thus gaining
considerably; and when it finally turned and went
straight away I followed it at a fast run, and before
it was fully awake to the danger I was but a hundred yards behind. We were now getting into bad
country, and jumping off I opened fire and crippled
the great beast. Mounting, I overtook it again in a
quarter of a mile and killed it.

In half an hour the skinners and porters came up
—one of the troubles of hunting as a naturalist is
that it necessitates the presence of a long tail of men
to take off and carry in the big skins, in order that
they may ultimately appear in museums. In an
hour and a half the giraffe's skin, with the head and
the leg bones, was slung on two poles; eight porters
bore it, while the others took for their own use all
the meat they could carry. They were in high
good-humor, for an abundant supply of fresh meat
always means a season of rejoicing, and they started
campwards singing loudly under their heavy bur-
dens. While the giraffe was being skinned we had
seen a rhinoceros feeding near our line of march
campwards, and had watched it until the light grew
dim. By the time the skin was ready night had
fallen, and we started under the brilliant moon. It
lit up the entire landscape; but moonlight is not sunlight, and there was the chance of our stumbling on
the rhino unawares, and of its charging; so I rode
at the head of the column with full-jacketed bullets

in my rifle.   However, we never saw the rhino, nor
had we any other adventure; and the ride through
the moonlight, which softened all the harshness, and
gave a touch of magic and mystery to the landscape,
was so pleasant that I was sorry when we caught the
gleam of the camp-fires.

Next day we sent our porters to bring in the rest
of the giraffe meat and the ostrich eggs.   The giraffe's heart was good eating.   There were many
ticks on the giraffe, as on all the game hereabouts,
and they annoyed us a little also, although very far
from being the plague they were on the Athi Plain.
Among the flies which at times tormented the
horses and hung around the game, were big gad-
flies with long wings folded longitudinally down the
back, not in the ordinary fly fashion; they were
akin to the tsetse flies, one species of which is fatal
to domestic animals, and another, the sleeping-sickness fly, to man himself.   They produce death by
means of the fatal microbes introduced into the
blood by their bite; whereas another African fly, the
seroot, found more to the north, in the Nile countries, is a scourge to man and beast merely because
of its vicious bite, and where it swarms may drive
the tribes that own herds entirely out of certain districts.

One afternoon, while leading my horse because
the ground was a litter of sharp-edged stones, I
came out on a plain which was crawling with zebra.

In every direction there were herds of scores or of
hundreds.   They were all of the common or small
kind, except three individuals of the big kangani,
and were tame, letting me walk by within easy shot.
Other game was mixed in with them.   Soon, walking over a little ridge of rocks, we saw a rhino sixty
yards off.   To walk forward would give it our
wind; I did not wish to kill it; and I was beginning
to feel about rhino the way Alice did in Looking
Glass country, when the elephants " did bother so."
Having spied us the beast at once cocked its ears
and tail, and assumed its usual absurd resemblance
to a huge and exceedingly alert and interested pig.
But with a rhino tragedy sometimes treads on the
heels of comedy, and I watched it sharply, my rifle
cocked, while I had all the men shout in unison to
scare it away.   The noise puzzled it much; with
tail erect and head tossing and twisting, it made
little rushes hither and thither, but finally drew off.
Next day, in shifting camp, Cuninghame and I were
twice obliged to dismount and keep guard over the
safari while it marched by within a hundred yards
of a highly puzzled rhino, which trotted to and fro
in the bush, evidently uncertain whether or not to
let its bewilderment turn into indignation.

The camp to which we thus shifted was on the
banks of the Guaso Nyero, on the edge of an open
glade in a shady grove of giant mimosas.   It was a
beautiful camp, and in the soft tropic nights I sat

outside my tent and watched the full moon rising
through and above the tree tops. There was absolutely no dew at night, by the way. The Guaso
Nyero runs across and along the equator, through a
desert country, eastward into the dismal Lorian
swamp, where it disappears, save in very wet sea-
sons, when it continues to the Tana. At our camp
it was a broad, rapid, muddy stream infested with
crocodiles. Along its banks grew groves of ivory-
nut palms, their fronds fan-shaped, their tall trunks
forked twenty or thirty feet from the ground, each
stem again forking—something like the antlers of
a black-tail buck. In the frond of a small palm of
this kind we found a pale-colored, very long-tailed
tree mouse, in its nest, which was a ball of chopped
straw. Spurfowl and francolin abounded, their
grating cries being heard everywhere; I shot a few
as well as one or two sandgrouse; and with the rifle
I knocked off the heads of two guinea fowls. The
last feat sounds better in the narration than it was
in the performance; for I wasted nearly a beltful of
cartridges in achieving it, as the guineas were shy
and ran rapidly through the tall grass. I also ex-
pended a large number of cartridges before securing
a couple of gerenuk; the queer, long-legged, long-
necked antelope were wary, and as soon as they
caught a glimpse of me off they would go at a
stealthy trot or canter through the bushes, with neck
outstretched. They had a curious habit of rising

on their hind legs to browse among the bushes; I do not remember seeing any other antelope act in this manner. There were waterbuck along the river banks, and I shot a couple of good bulls; they belonged to the southern and eastern species, which has a light-colored ring around the rump; whereas the western form, which I saw at Naivasha, has the whole rump light-colored. They like the neighborhood of lakes and rivers. I have seen parties of them resting in the open plains during the day, under trees which yielded little more shade than telegraph poles. The handsome, shaggy-coated waterbuck has not the high withers which mark the oryx, wildebeest, and hartebeest, and he carries his head and neck more like a stag or a wapiti bull.

One day we went back from the river after giraffe. It must have been a year since any rain had fallen. The surface of the baked soil was bare and cracked, the sparse tussocks of grass were brittle straw, and the trees and bushes were leafless; but instead of leaves they almost all carried thorns, the worst being those of the wait-a-bit, which tore our clothes, hands, and faces. We found the giraffe three or four miles away from the river, in an absolutely waterless region, densely covered with these leafless wait-a-bit thorn-bushes. Hanging among the bare bushes, by the way, we roused two or three of the queer, diurnal, golden-winged, slate-colored bats; they flew freely in the glare of the sunlight,

minding it as little as they did the furnace-like heat.
We found the really dense wait-a-bit thorn thickets
quite impenetrable, whereas the giraffe moved
through them with utter unconcern. But the giraffe's indifference to thorns is commonplace compared to its indifference to water. These particular
giraffe were not drinking either at the river or at
the one or two streams which were running into it;
and in certain places giraffe will subsist for months
without drinking at all. How the waste and evap-
oration of moisture from their huge bodies is supplied is one of the riddles of biology.

We could not get a bull giraffe, and it was only a
bull that I wanted. I was much interested, however,
in coming up to a cow asleep. She stood with her
neck drooping slightly forward, occasionally stamp-
ing or twitching an ear, like a horse when asleep
standing. I saw her legs first, through the bushes,
and finally walked directly up to her in the open,
until I stood facing her at thirty yards. When she
at last suddenly saw me, she came nearer to the exe-
cution of a gambol than any other giraffe I have
ever seen.

Another day we went after buffalo. We left
camp before sunrise, riding along parallel to the
river to find the spoor of a herd which had drunk
and was returning to the haunts, away from the
river, in which they here habitually spent the day.
Two or three hours passed before we found what

we sought; and we at once began to follow the trail.
It was in open thorn-bush, and the animals were
evidently feeding. Before we had followed the
spoor half an hour we ran across a rhinoceros. As
the spoor led above wind, and as we did not wish to
leave it for fear of losing it, Cuninghame stayed
where he was, and I moved round to within fifty
yards of the rhino, and, with my rifle ready, began
shouting, trying to keep the just mean as regards
noise, so as to scare him, and yet not yell so loudly
as to reach the buffalo if they happened to be near
by. At last I succeeded, and he trotted sullenly off,
tacking and veering, and not going far. On we
went, and in another half-hour came on our quarry.
I was the first to catch a glimpse of the line of bulky
black forms, picked out with white where the sun
glinted on the horn bosses. It was ten o'clock, a
hot, windless morning on the equator, with the sun
shining from a cloudless sky; yet these buffalo were
feeding in the open, miles from water or dense
cover. They were greedily cropping the few tufts
of coarse herbage that grew among the sparse thorn-
bushes, which here were not more than two feet
high. In many places buffalo are purely nocturnal
feeders, and do not come into the hot, bare plains in
the scorching glare of daylight; and our experience
with this herd illustrates afresh the need of caution
in generalizing about the habits of game.

We crept toward them on all-fours, having left

the porters hidden from sight. At last we were within rather long range—a buffalo's eyesight is good, and cannot be trifled with as if he were a rhino or elephant—and cautiously scrutinized the herd through our glasses. There were only cows and perhaps one or two young bulls with horns no bigger than those of cows. I would have liked another good bull's head for myself; but I also wished another cow for the museum. Before I could shoot, however, a loud yelling was heard from among the porters in our rear; and away went the buffalo. Full of wrath, we walked back to inquire. We found that one porter had lost his knife, and had started back to look for it, accompanied by two of his fellows, which was absolutely against orders. They had come across a rhino, probably the one I had frightened from our path, and had endeavored to avoid him; but he had charged them, whereupon they scattered. He overtook one and tossed him, goring him in the thigh; whereupon they came back, the two unwounded ones supporting the other, and all howling like lost souls. I had some crystals of permanganate, an antiseptic, and some cotton in my saddle pocket; Cuninghame tore some of the lining out of his sleeve for a bandage; and we fixed the man up and left him with one companion, while we sent another in to camp to fetch out a dozen men with a ground-sheet and some poles, to make a litter in which the wounded man could be carried. While

we were engaged in this field surgery another rhino
was in sight half a mile off.

Then on we went on the trail of the herd. It led
straight across the open, under the blazing sun; and
the heat was now terrific. At last, almost exactly
at noon, Cuninghame, who was leading, stopped
short. He had seen the buffalo, which had halted,
made a half-bend backward on their tracks, and
stood for their noonday rest among some scattered,
stunted thorn-trees, leafless and yielding practically
no shade whatever. A cautious stalk brought me
to within a hundred and fifty yards. I merely
wounded the one I first shot at, but killed another as
the herd started to run. Leaving the skinners to
take care of the dead animal, a fine cow, Cuninghame and I started after the herd, to see if the
wounded one had fallen out. After a mile the trail
led into some scant cover. Here the first thing we
did was to run into another rhinoceros. It was
about seventy yards away, behind a thorn-tree, and
began to move jerkily and abruptly to and fro, gazing toward us. "Oh, you malevolent old idiot!"
I muttered, facing it with rifle cocked; then, as it
did not charge, I added to Cuninghame, "Well, I
guess it will let us by, all right." And let us by it
did. We were anxious not to shoot it, both because
in a country with no settlers a rhino rarely does
harm, and I object to anything like needless
butchery, and furthermore because we desired to

avoid alarming the buffalo. Half a mile farther on
we came on the latter, apparently past their fright.
We looked them carefully over with our glasses; the
wounded one was evidently not much hurt, and
therefore I did not wish to kill her, for I did not
need another cow; and there was no adult bull. So
we did not molest them; and after a while they got
our wind and went off at a lumbering gallop. Returning to the dead cow, we found the skin ready
and marched back to camp, reaching it just as the
moon rose, at seven; we had been away thirteen
hours, with nothing to eat and only the tepid water
in our canteens to drink.

We were in the country of the Samburu, and several of their old men and warriors visited us at this
camp. They are cattle-owning nomads like the
Masai; but in addition to cattle, sheep and goats
they own herds of camels, which they milk but do
not use as beasts of burden. In features they are
more like Somalis than negroes.

Near this camp was the remains of the boma or
home camp of Arthur Neuman, once the most famous elephant hunter between Tana and Lake Ru-
dolf. Neuman, whose native name was Nyama
Yango, was a strange moody man who died by his
own hand. He was a mighty hunter, of bold and
adventure-loving temper. With whites he was un-
social, living in this far-off region exactly like a
native, and all alone among the natives; living in

some respects too much like a native. But, from the native standpoint, and without making any effort to turn the natives into anything except what they were, he did them good, and left a deep impression on their minds. They talked to us often about him, in many different places; they would not believe that he was dead; and when assured it was so they showed real grief. At Meru boma, when we saw the Meru tribesmen dance, one of the songs they sung was: " Since Nyama Yango came, our sheep graze untouched by the Samburu," and, rather curiously, the Samburu sing a similar song reciting how he saved them from the fear of having their herds raided by the nomads farther north.

After leaving this camp we journeyed up the Guaso Nyero for several days. The current was rapid and muddy, and there were beds of reeds and of the tall, graceful papyrus. The country round about was a mass of stony, broken hills, and the river wound down among these, occasionally cutting its way through deep gorges, and its course being continually broken by rapids. Whenever on our hunts we had to cross it, we shouted and splashed and even fired shots, to scare the crocodiles. I shot one on a sandbar in the river. The man the rhino had wounded was carried along on a litter with the safari.

Sometimes I left camp with my sais and gunbearer before dawn, starting in the light of the waning moon, and riding four or five hours before halting to wait for the safari; on the way I had usually shot something for the table—a waterbuck, impalla, or gazelle. On other occasions Cuninghame and I would spend the day hunting in the waterless country back of the river, where the heat at mid-day was terrific. We might not reach camp until after nightfall. Once as we came to it in the dark it seemed as if ghostly arms stretched above it; for on this evening the tents had been pitched under trees up which huge rubber vines had climbed, and their massive dead-white trunks and branches glimmered pale and ghostly in the darkness.

Twice my gun-bearers tried to show me a cheetah; but my eyes were too slow to catch the animal before it bounded off in safety among the bushes. Another time after an excellent bit of tracking, the gun-bearers brought me up to a buffalo bull, standing for his noonday rest in the leafless thorns a mile from the river. I thought I held the heavy Holland straight for his shoulder, but I must have fired high; for though he fell to the shot he recovered at once. We followed the blood spoor for an hour, the last part of the time when the trail wandered among and through the heavy thickets under the trees on the river banks; here I walked beside the tracker with my rifle at full cock, for we could not tell what instant we might be charged. But his trail finally crossed the river, and as he was

going stronger and stronger we had to abandon the
chase. In the waterless country, away from the
river, we found little except herds of zebra, of both
kinds, occasionally oryx and eland, and a few
giraffe. A stallion of the big kangani zebra which I
shot stood fourteen hands high at the withers and
weighed about eight hundred and thirty pounds,*
according to the Seton beam. I shot another kangani just at nightfall, a mile or so from camp, as it
drank in a wild, tree-clad gorge of the river. I was
alone, strolling quietly through the dusk, along the
margin of the high banks by the stream, and saw
a mixed herd of zebras coming down to a well-worn
drinking-place, evidently much used by game, on
the opposite side of the river. They were alert and
nervous, evidently on the lookout for both lions and
crocodiles. I singled out the largest, the leader of
the troop, and shot it across the stream; I have
rarely taken a shot among more picturesque surroundings.

At our final camp on the river, before leaving it
on our week's steady trek southward to Neri, we

* The aggregate of the weights of the different pieces was
778 pounds; the loss of blood and the drying of the pieces
of flesh in the intense heat of the sun we thought certainly
accounted for 50 pounds more. The stallion was not fat.
At any rate it weighed between 800 and 850 pounds. Its
testicles, though fully developed, had not come down out of
the belly skin; one of those shot by Kermit showed the same
peculiarity; Cuninghame says it is a common occurrence with
this species. Moreover the stallions did not have their
canine teeth developed.

found a spot in which game abounded. It was about
ten miles back from the river, a stretch of plain
sparsely covered with thorn-trees, broken by koppies,
and bounded by chains of low, jagged mountains,
with an occasional bold, isolated peak. The crags
and cliff walls were fantastically carved and chan-
nelled by the weathering of ages in that dry climate. It was a harsh, unlovely spot in the glare of
the hot daylight; but at sunset it was very lovely,
with a wild and stern beauty.

Here the game abounded, and was not wary. Before starting out on our week's steady marching I
wished to give the safari a good feed; and one day
I shot them five zebra and an oryx bull, together
with a couple of gazelle for ourselves and our immediate attendants—enough of the game being
hallalled to provide for the Mohammedans in the
safari. I also shot an old bull giraffe of the northern
form, after an uneventful stalk which culminated in
a shot with the Winchester at a hundred and seventy
yards. In most places this particular stretch of
country was not suitable for galloping, the ground
being rotten, filled with holes, and covered with tall,
coarse grass. One evening we saw two lions half a
mile away; I tried to ride them, but my horse fell
twice in the first hundred and fifty yards and I could
not even keep them in sight. Another day we got
a glimpse of two lions, quarter of a mile off, gliding
away among the thorns. They went straight to the

river and swam across it.   More surprising was the
fact that a monkey, which lost its head when we
surprised it in a tree by the river, actually sprang
plump into the stream, and swam, easily and
strongly, across it.

One day we had a most interesting experience
with a cow giraffe. We saw her a long way off and
stalked to within a couple of hundred yards before
we could make out her sex. She was standing under
some thorn-trees, occasionally shifting her position
for a few yards, and then again standing motionless
with her head thrust in among the branches. She
was indulging in a series of noon naps. At last,
when she stood and went to sleep again, I walked up
to her, Cuninghame and our two gun-bearers, Bakhari and Kongoni, following a hundred yards behind.
When I was within forty yards, in plain sight,
away from cover, she opened her eyes and looked
drowsily at me; but I stood motionless and she dozed
off again. This time I walked up to within ten feet
of her. Nearer I did not care to venture, as giraffe
strike and kick very hard with their hooves, and,
moreover, occasionally strike with the head, the
blow seemingly not being delivered with the knobby,
skin-covered horns, but with the front teeth of the
lower jaw. She waked, looked at me, and then, rearing slightly, struck at me with her left foreleg, the
blow falling short. I laughed and leaped back, and
the other men ran up shouting. But the giraffe

would not run away. She stood within twenty feet
of us, looking at us peevishly, and occasionally pout-
ing her lips at us, as if she were making a face.
We kept close to the tree, so as to dodge round it,
under the branches, if she came at us; for we would
have been most reluctant to shoot her. I threw a
stick at her, hitting her in the side, but she paid no
attention; and when Bakhari came behind her with
a stick she turned sharply on him and he made a
prompt retreat. We were laughing and talking all
the time. Then we pelted her with sticks and clods
of earth, and, after having thus stood within twenty
feet of us for three or four minutes, she cantered
slowly off for fifty yards, and then walked away with
leisurely unconcern. She was apparently in the best
of health and in perfect condition. She did not get
our wind; but her utter indifference to the close
presence of four men is inexplicable.*

On each of the two days we hunted this little district we left camp at sunrise, and did not return
until eight or nine in the evening, fairly well tired,
and not a little torn by the thorns into which we
blundered during the final two hours' walk in the
darkness. It was hot, and we neither had nor
wished for food, and the tepid water in the canteens

---

* After writing the above account I read it over to Mr.
Cuninghame so as to be sure that it was accurate in all its
details. All the game was tame in this locality, even the
giraffe, but no other giraffe allowed us to get within two
hundred yards, and most of them ran long before that distance was reached, even when we were stalking carefully.

lasted us through. The day I shot the giraffe the porters carrying the skin fell behind, and never got in until next morning. Coming back in the late twilight a party of the big zebra, their forms shadowy and dim, trotted up to us, evidently attracted by the horses, and accompanied us for some rods; and a hedgehog, directly in our path, kept bleating loudly, like an antelope kid.

The day we spent in taking care of the giraffe skin we, of course, made no hunt. However, in the afternoon I sauntered upstream a couple of miles to look for crocodiles. I saw none, but I was much interested in some zebra and waterbuck. The zebra were on the opposite side of the river, standing among some thorns, and at three, mid-afternoon, they came down to drink; up to this time I had generally found zebra drinking in the evening or at night. Then I saw some waterbuck, also on the opposite bank, working their way toward the river, and seeing a well-marked drinking-place ahead I hastened toward it, and sat down in the middle of the broad game trail leading down to the water on my side. I sat perfectly still, and my clothes were just the color of the ground, and the waterbuck never noticed me, though I was in plain view when they drank, just opposite me, and only about fifty yards off. There were four cows and a bull. It was four o'clock in the afternoon. The cows came first, one by one, and were very alert and suspicious.

Each continually stopped and stood motionless, or looked in every direction, and gave little false starts of alarm. When they reached the green grass by the water's edge each cropped a few mouthfuls, between times nervously raising its head and looking in every direction, nostrils and ears twitching. They were not looking for crocodiles, but for land foes, lions or leopards. Each in turn drank, skipping up to the top of the bank after a few mouthfuls, and then returning to the water. The bull followed with rather less caution, and before he had finished drinking the cows scurried hurriedly back to the thorn-trees and the open country. We had plenty of meat in camp, and I had completed my series of this species of waterbuck for the museum; and I was glad there was no need to molest them.

The porters were enjoying the rest and the abundance of meat. They were lying about camp or were scattered up and down stream fishing. When, walking back, I came to the outskirts of camp, I was attracted by the buzzing and twanging of the harp; there was the harper and two friends, all three singing to his accompaniment. I called "Yambo" (greeting), and they grinned and stood up, shouting "Yambo" in return. In camp a dozen men were still at work at the giraffe skin, and they were all singing loudly, under the lead of my gun-bearer, Gouvimali, who always acted as shanty man, or improvisatore, on such occasions.

For a week we now trekked steadily south across the equator, heel and toe marching, to Neri. Our first day's journey took us to a gorge riven in the dry mountain. Half-way up it, in a side pocket, was a a deep pool, at the foot of a sloping sheet of rock, down which a broad, shallow dent showed where the torrent swept during the rains. In the trees around the pool black drongo shrikes called in bell-like tones, and pied hornbills flirted their long tails as they bleated and croaked. The water was foul; but in a dry country one grows gratefully to accept as water anything that is wet. Klipspringers and baboons were in the sheer hills around; and among the rocks were hyraxes (looking like our Rocky Mountain conies or Little Chief hares), queer diurnal rats, and bright blue-green lizards with orange heads. Rhinos drank at this pool; we frequently saw them on our journey, but always managed to avoid wounding their susceptibilities, and so escaped an encounter. Each day we endeavored to camp a couple of hours before sundown so as to give the men plenty of chance to get firewood, pitch the tents, and put everything in order. Sometimes we would make an early start; in which case we would breakfast in the open, while in the east the crescent of the dying moon hung over the glow that heralded the sunrise.

As we reached the high, rolling downs the weather grew cooler, and many flowers appeared;

those of the aloes were bright red, standing on
high stalks above the clump of fleshy, spined leaves,
which were handsomely mottled, like a snake's back.
As I rode at the head of the safari I usually, in the
course of the day, shot a buck of some kind for the
table. I had not time to stalk, but simply took the
shots as they came, generally at long range. One
day I shot an eland, an old blue bull. We needed
the skin for the museum, and as there was water
near by we camped where we were; I had already
shot a waterbuck that morning, and this and the
eland together gave the entire safari a feast of meat.

On another occasion an eland herd afforded me
fun, although no profit. I was mounted on
Brownie, the zebra-shaped pony. Brownie would
still occasionally run off when I dismounted to shoot
(a habit that had cost me an eland bull); but he
loved to gallop after game. We came on a herd of
eland in an open plain; they were directly in our
path. We were in the country where the ordinary
or Livingstone's eland grades into the Patterson's;
and I knew that the naturalists wished an additional
bull's head for the museum. So I galloped toward
the herd; and for the next fifteen or twenty minutes
I felt as if I had renewed my youth and was in the
cow camps of the West, a quarter of a century ago.
Eland are no faster than range cattle. Twice I
rounded up the herd—just as once in the Yellow-
stone Park I rounded up a herd of wapiti for John

Burroughs to look at—and three times I cut out of the herd a big animal, which, however, in each case, proved to be a cow. There were no big bulls, only cows and young stock; but I enjoyed the gallop.

From Neri we marched through mist and rain across the cold Aberdare table-lands, and in the forenoon of October 20 we saw from the top of the second Aberdare escarpment the blue waters of beautiful Lake Naivasha. On the next day we reached Nairobi.

CHAPTER XII

A T Nairobi Kermit joined me, having enjoyed a notably successful hunt during the month since we had parted, killing both Neuman's hartebeest and koodoo. The great koodoo, with its spiral horns and striped coat, is the stateliest and handsomest antelope in the world. It is a shy creature, fond of bush and of rocky hills, and is hard to get.

After leaving me at Meru Kermit and Tarlton had travelled hard to Rumeruti. They had intended to go to Lake Hannington, but finding that this was in the reserve they went three days toward the northwest, stopping a score of miles east of Barengo. The country, which showed many traces of volcanic action, was rough, rocky, and dry; the hunting was exhausting, and Kermit was out from morning to night. Tarlton had been very sick on the Guaso Nyero, and although he was better he was in no shape to accompany Kermit, who therefore hunted only with his gun-boys, taking them out alternately so as to spare them as much as possible. It took three days' steady work before he got his first koodoo. On the third day he hunted fruitlessly all the morning, came back to camp, picked up a fresh gun-bearer, Juma Yohari, and started out again. At four in the afternoon he came to the brink of a great hollow a mile across, perhaps an extinct crater, and looking from the rimrock, spied a koodoo bull in the bottom. The steep sides of the hollow were covered with a tangled growth of thorn scrub and cactus, traversed by rhinoceros paths. The bottom was more open, strewn with bushy mounds or hillocks, and on one of these stood a noble koodoo bull. He stood with his massive spiral horns thrown back, and they shifted slowly as he turned his head from side to side. Kermit stole down one of the rhino paths, save for which the scrub would have been practically impenetrable; it was alive with rhinos; Kermit heard several, and Juma who followed some distance behind saw three. The stalk took time; and the sun was on the horizon and the light fading when, at over two hundred yards, Kermit took his shot. The first bullet missed, but as for a moment the bull paused and wheeled Kermit fired again and the second bullet went home. The wounded beast ran, Kermit, with Juma, hard on the trail; and he overtook and killed it just as darkness fell. Then back to camp they stumbled and plunged through the darkness, Kermit tearing the sole completely off one shoe. They reached camp at ten and Juma, who had only been working half the day, took out some porters to the dead bull, which they skinned, and then slept by until morning. Later, on his birthday, he killed a cow, which completed the group; the two koodoo cost him ten days' steady labor. The koodoo were always found on steep, rocky hills; their stomachs contained only grass, for both beasts when shot were grazing (I do not know whether or not they also browse). The midday hours, when the heat was most intense, they usually spent resting; but once Kermit came on two which were drinking in a stream exactly at noon.

From the koodoo camp the two hunters went to Lake Hannington, a lovely lake, with the mountains rising sheer from three of its sides. The water was saline, abounding with crocodiles and hippos; and there were myriads of flamingoes. They were to be seen swimming by thousands on the lake, and wading and standing in the shallows; and when they rose they looked like an enormous pink cloud; it was a glorious sight. They were tame; and Kermit had no difficulty in killing the specimens needed for the Museum. Here Kermit also killed an impalla ram which had met with an extraordinary misadventure. It had been fighting with another ram, which had stabbed it in the chest with one horn. The violent strain and shock, as the two vigorous beasts bounded together, broke off the horn, leaving the broken part, ten inches long, imbedded in the other buck's chest; about three inches of the point being fixed firmly in the body of the buck, while the rest stuck out like a picket pin. Yet the buck seemed well and strong.

Two days after leaving Lake Hannington they camped near the ostrich-farm of Mr. London, an American from Baltimore. He had been waging war on the lions and leopards, because they attacked his ostriches. He had killed at least a score of each, some with the rifle, some with poison or steel traps. The day following their arrival London went out hunting with Kermit and Tarlton. They saw nothing until evening, when Kermit's gun-bearer, Kassitura, spied a leopard coming from the carcass of a zebra which London had shot to use as bait for his traps. The leopard saw them a long way off and ran; Kermit ran after it and wounded it badly, twice; then Tarlton got a shot and hit it; and then London came across the dying beast at close quarters and killed it just as it was gathering itself to spring at him.

Thence they went to Nakuru, where Kermit killed two Neuman's hartebeest. They were scarce and wild, and Kermit obtained his two animals by long shots after following them for hours; following them until, as he expressed it, they got used to him, became a little less quick to leave, and gave him his chance.

While on this trip Kermit passed his twentieth birthday. While still nineteen he had killed all the kinds of African dangerous game—lion, leopard, elephant, buffalo, and rhino.

Heller also rejoined us, entirely recovered. He

had visited Mearns and Loring at their camp high up on Mount Kenia, where they had made a thoroughly biological survey of the mountain. He had gone to the line of perpetual snow, where the rock peak rises abruptly from the swelling downs, and had camped near a little glacial lake, whose waters froze every night. The zones of plant and animal life were well marked; but there are some curious differences between the zones on these equatorial African snow mountains and those on similar mountains in the northern hemisphere, especially America. In the high mountains of North America the mammals are apt to be, at least in part, of totally different kinds from those found in the adjacent warm or hot plains, because they represent a fauna which was once spread over the land, but which has retreated northward, leaving faunal islands on the summits of the taller mountains. In this part of Africa, however, there has been no faunal retreat of this type, no survivals on the peaks of an ancient fauna which in the plains and valleys has been replaced by another fauna; here the mammals of the high mountains and table-lands are merely modified forms of the mammals of the adjacent lowlands, which have gradually crept up the slopes, changing in the process. High on Mount Kenia, for instance, are hyraxes, living among the snow fields, much bigger than their brethren of the forests and rocky hills below; and light-colored mole rats, also much bigger

than those of the lower country. Moreover, the
lack of seasonal change is probably accountable
for differences in the way that the tree zones are
delimited. The mountain conifers of America are
huge trees on the middle slopes, but higher up gradually dwindle into a thick, low scrub, composed of
sprawling, dwarfed individuals of the same species.
On Mount Kenia the tree zone ceases much more
abruptly and with much less individual change
among the different kinds of trees. Above this zone
are the wet, cold downs and moors, with a very peculiar vegetation, plants which we know only as
small flowering things having become trees. The
giant groundsell, for instance, reaches a height of
twenty feet, with very thick trunk and limbs which,
though hollow, make good firewood; and this is only
one example of the kind.

At Nairobi we learned, as usual, of incident after
incident, which had happened among our friends and
acquaintances, of exactly the type which would occur were it possible in North America or Europe
suddenly to mix among existing conditions the men
and animals that died out some hundreds of thousands of years ago. In a previous chapter I mentioned on one occasion meeting at dinner three men,
all of whom had been mauled by lions; one being our
host, Mr. F. A. Ward, who had served as a captain
in the South African War, and was now one of
the heads of the Boma Trading Company. Among

our fellow guests at this dinner was Captain Douglas Pennant of the British Army. When we went north to Kenia he went south to the Sotik. There he made a fine bag of lions; but having wounded a leopard and followed it into cover it suddenly sprang on him, apparently from a tree. His life was saved by his Somali gun-bearer who blew out the leopard's brains as it bore him to the ground, so that it had time to make only one bite; but this bite just missed crushing in the skull, broke the jaw, tore off one ear, and caused ghastly wreck. He spent some weeks in the hospital at Nairobi, and then went for further treatment to England; his place in the hospital being taken by another man who had been injured by a leopard.

There had been quite a plague of wild beasts in Nairobi itself. One family had been waked at midnight by a leopard springing on the roof of the house and thence to an adjacent shed; it finally spent a couple of hours on the veranda. A lion had repeatedly wandered at night through the outlying (the residential) portion of the town. Dr. Milne, the head of the Government Medical Department, had nearly run into it on his bicycle, and, as a measure of precaution, guests going out to dinner usually carried spears or rifles. One night I dined with the Provincial Commissioner, Mr. Hobley, and the next with the town clerk, Captain Sanderson. In each case the hostess, the host, and the house were

all delightful, and the evening just like a very pleasant evening spent anywhere in civilization; the
houses were only half a mile apart; and yet on the
road between them a fortnight previously a lady on
a bicycle, wheeling down to a rehearsal of " Trial
by Jury," had been run into and upset by a herd of
frightened zebras. One of my friends, Captain
Smith, Director of Surveys in the Protectorate, had
figured in another zebra incident to which only Mark
Twain could do justice. Captain Smith lived on the
outskirts of the town, and was much annoyed by the
zebras tearing through his ground and trampling
down his vegetables and flowers. So one night, by
his direction, his Masai servant sallied out and
speared a zebra which was tangled in a wire fence.
But the magistrate, a rigid upholder of the letter
of the law, fined the Masai for killing game without
a license! (A touch quite worthy of comparison with
Mark Twain's account of how, when he called for
assistance while drowning, he was arrested for disturbing the peace.) Captain Smith decided that
next time there should be no taint of illegality about
his behavior, so he got ropes ready, and when the
zebras returned he and his attendants again chased
them toward the wire fences, and tied up one which
got caught therein; and then with much difficulty
he led it down town, *put it in the pound,* and notified
Captain Sanderson, the town clerk, what he had
done. This proceeding was entirely regular; and so

was all that followed. For seven days the zebra was
kept in the pound, while the authorities solemnly ad-
vertised for a highly improbable owner; then it was
sold at auction, being brought to the sale, bucking,
rolling, and fighting, securely held by ropes in the
hands of various stalwart natives, and disposed of
to the only bidder for five rupees. The Court rec-
ords are complete. The District Court criminal reg-
ister, under date of February, 1 1909, contains the
entry of the prosecution by the Crown through
" Mutwa Wa. Najaka A.N." of the Masai for " killing zebra without a license (under section 4/35
Game Regulations of 15th April, 1906," and of the
infliction of a fine of twenty rupees. The sequel appears in the Nairobi Municipality Pound Book under date of August 6, 1909. In the column
headed " Description of Animal " is the entry " 1
zebra "; under the heading " By whom impounded "
is the entry " Major Smith, R.E."; under the heading " Remarks " is the entry " Sold by Public Auc-
tioneers Raphael & Coy on 24/8/09."

We had with us several recent books on East African big game; Chapman's " On Safari," dealing
alike with the hunting and the natural history of big
game; Powell Cotton's accounts of his noteworthy
experiences both in hunting and in bold exploration;
Stigand's capital studies of the spoor and habits of
big game (it is to be regretted that he was too modest to narrate some of his own really extraordinary

adventures in the chase of dangerous beasts) ; and Buxton's account of his two African trips. Edward North Buxton's books ought to be in the hands of every hunter everywhere, and especially of every young hunter, because they teach just the right way in which to look at the sport. With Buxton big-game hunting is not a business but a pastime, not allowed to become a mania or in any way to interfere with the serious occupations of life, whether public or private; and yet as he has carried it on it is much more than a mere pastime, it is a craft, a pursuit of value in exercising and developing hardihood of body and the virile courage and resolution which necessarily lie at the base of every strong and man-ly character. He has not a touch of the game butcher in him; nor has he a touch of that craving for ease and luxury the indulgence in which turns any sport into a sham and a laughing-stock. Big-game hunting, pursued as he has pursued it, stands at the opposite pole from those so-called sports car-ried on primarily either as money-making exhibi-tions, or, what is quite as bad—though the two evils are usually found in different social strata—in a spirit of such luxurious self-indulgence as to render them at best harmless extravagances, and at worst forces which positively tend to the weakening of moral and physical fibre.

On October 26, Tarlton, Kermit, Heller, and I started from the railroad station of Londiani, for the

Uasin Gishu plateau and the 'Nzoi River, which flows not far from the foot of Mount Elgon. This stretch of country has apparently received its fauna from the shores of Lake Victoria Nyanza, and contains several kinds of antelope, and a race or variety of giraffe, the five-horned, which are not found to the eastward, in the region where we had already hunted.

On the 27th we were marching hard, and I had no chance to hunt; I would have liked to take a hunt, because it was my birthday. The year before I had celebrated my fiftieth birthday by riding my jumping horse, Roswell, over all the jumps in Rock Creek Park, at Washington. Roswell is a safe and good jumper, and a very easy horse to sit at a jump; he took me, without hesitation or error, over everything, from the water jump to the stone wall, the rails, and the bank, including a brush hurdle just over five feet and a half high.

For the first four days our route led among rolling hills and along valleys and ravines, the country being so high that the nights were actually cold, although we crossed and recrossed the equator. The landscape in its general effect called to mind southern Oregon and northern California rather than any tropical country. Some of the hills were bald, others wooded to the top; there were wet meadows, and hill-sides covered with tussocks of rank, thick-growing grass, alternating with stretches of forest;

and the chief trees of the forest were stately cedars, yews, and tall laurel-leaved olives. All this was, at least in superficial aspect, northern enough; but now and then we came to patches of the thoroughly tropical bamboo, which in East Africa, however, one soon grows to associate with cold, rainy weather, for it only grows at high altitudes. In this country, high, cold, rainy, there were several kinds of buck, but none in any numbers. The most interesting were the roan antelope, which went in herds. Their trails led everywhere, across the high, rolling hill pastures of coarse grass, and through the tangled tree groves and the still, lifeless bamboo jungle. They were found in herds and lived in the open, feeding on the bare hill-sides and in the wet valleys at all hours; but they took cover freely, and when the merciless gales blew they sought shelter in woodland and jungle. Usually they grazed, but once I saw one browsing. Both on our way in and on our way back, through this hill country, we shot several roan, for, though their horns are poor, they form a distinct sub-species, peculiar to the region. The roan is a big antelope, nearly as tall, although by no means as bulky, as an eland, with curved scimitar-like horns, huge ears, and face markings as sharply defined as those of an oryx. It is found here and there, in isolated localities, throughout Africa south of the Sahara, and is of bold, fierce temper. One of those which Kermit shot was only crippled by the first bullet, and charged the gun-bearers, squealing savagely, in addition to using its horns; an angry roan, like a sable, is said sometimes to bite with its teeth. Kermit also killed a ratel or honey badger, in a bamboo thicket; an interesting beast; its back snow white and the rest of its body jet black.

As on the Aberdares and the slopes of Kenia, the nights among these mountains were cold; sometimes so cold that I was glad to wear a mackinaw, a lumberman's jacket, which had been given me by Jack Greenway, and which I certainly never expected to wear in Africa.

The porters always minded cold, especially if there was rain, and I was glad to get them to the Uasin Gishu, where the nights were merely cool enough to make one appreciate blankets, while the days were never oppressively hot. Although the Swahilis have furnished the model for all East African safari work, and supply the lingua franca for the country, they no longer compose the bulk of the porters. Of our porters at this time about two-fifths were stalwart M'nuwezi from German East Africa, two-fifths were Wakamba, and the remainder Swahilis with half a dozen Kavirondos and Kikuyus. The M'nuwezi are the strongest of all, and make excellent porters. They will often be as much as two or three years away from their homes; for safari work is very attractive to the best type of natives, as they live much better than if travelling on their own account, and as it offers almost the only way in which they can earn money. The most severe punishment that can be inflicted on a gun-bearer, tent boy, sais, or porter is to dismiss him on such terms as to make it impossible for him again to be employed on a safari. In camp the men of each tribe group themselves together in parties, each man sharing any unwonted delicacy with his cronies.

Very rarely did we have to take such long marches as to exhaust our strapping burden-bearers; usually they came into camp in high good humor, singing and blowing antelope horns; and in the evening, after the posho had been distributed, cooked, and eaten, the different groups would gather each around its camp fire, and the men would chant in unison while the flutes wailed and the buzzing harps twanged. Of course individuals were all the time meeting with accidents or falling sick, especially when they had the chance to gorge themselves on game that we had killed; and then Cuninghame or Tarlton—than whom two stancher and pleasanter friends, keener hunters, or better safari managers are not to be found in all Africa—would have to add the functions of a doctor to an already multifarious round of duties. Some of the men had to be watched lest they should malinger; others were always complaining of trifles; others never complained at all. Gosho, our excellent headman came in the last category. On this Uasin Gishu trip we noticed him limping one evening; and inquiry developed the fact that the previous night, while in his tent, he had been bitten by a small poisonous snake. The leg was much swollen, and looked angry and inflamed; but Gosho never so much as mentioned the incident until we questioned him, and in a few days was as well as ever. Heller's chief feeling, by the way, when informed what had happened, was one of indignation because the offending snake, after paying the death penalty, had been thrown away instead of being given to him as a specimen.

The roans were calving in early November; whereas, when we went thirty miles on, at an elevation a thousand feet less, we at first saw no very young fawns accompanying the hartebeests, and no very young foals with the zebras. These hartebeests, which are named after their discoverer, Governor Jackson, are totally different from the hartebeests of the Athi and the Sotik countries, and are larger and finer in every way. One bull I shot weighed, in pieces, four hundred and seventy pounds. No allowance was made for the spilt blood, and, inasmuch as he had been hallalled, I think his live weight would have been nearly four hundred and ninety pounds. He was a big, full-grown bull, but not of extraordinary size; later I killed much bigger ones, unusually fine specimens, which must have weighed well over five hundred pounds. The horns, which are sometimes two feet long, are set on great bony pedicels, so that the face seems long and homely even for a hartebeest. The first two or three of these hartebeests which I killed were shot at long range, for, like all game, they are sometimes exceedingly wary; but we soon found that normally they were as tame as they were plentiful. We frequently saw them close by the herds of the Boer settlers. They were the common game of the plains. At times of course they were difficult to approach; but again and again, usually when we were riding, we came upon not only individuals but herds, down wind and in plain view, which permitted us to approach to within a hundred yards before they definitely took flight. Their motions look ungainly until they get into their full speed stride. They utter no sound save the usual hartebeest sneeze.

There were bohor reedbuck also, pretty creatures, about the size of a white-tail deer, which lay close in the reed beds, or in hollows among the tall grass, and usually offered rather difficult running shots or very long standing shots. Still prettier were the little oribi. These are grass antelopes, frequenting much the same places as the duiker and steinbuck and not much larger. Where the grass was long they would lie close, with neck flat along the ground, and dart off when nearly stepped on, with a pig-like rush like that of a reedbuck or duiker in similar thick cover. But where the grass was short, and especially where it was burned, they did not trust to lying down and hiding; on the contrary, in such places they were conspicuous little creatures, and trusted to their speed and alert vigilance for their safety. They run very fast, with great bounds, and when they stand— usually at a hundred and fifty or two hundred yards —they face the hunter, the forward-thrown ears being the most noticeable thing about them. We found that each oribi bagged cost us an unpleasantly large number of cartridges.

One day we found where a large party of hyenas had established their day lairs in the wet seclusion of some reed beds. We beat through these reed beds, and, in the words once used by an old plains friend in describing the behavior of a family of black bears under similar circumstances, the hyenas " came bil- in' out." As they bolted Kermit shot one and I an- other; his bit savagely at a stick with which one of the gun-bearers poked it. It is difficult at first glance to tell the sex of a hyena, and our followers stoutly upheld the wide-spread African belief that they are bi-sexual, being male or female as they choose. A wounded or trapped hyena will of course bite if seized, but shows no sign of the ferocious courage which marks the leopard under such circumstances; for the hyena is as cowardly as it is savage, although its size and the tremendous power of its jaws ought to make it as formidable as the fierce spotted cat.

The day after this incident we came on a herd of giraffe. It was Kermit's turn for a giraffe; and just

as the herd got under way he wounded the big bull.
Away went the tall creatures, their tails twisting and
curling, as they cantered along over the rough veldt
and among the thorn bushes, at that gait of theirs
which looks so leisurely and which yet enables them
to cover so much ground.   After them we tore, Kermit and Tarlton in the lead; and a fine chase we had.
It was not until we had gone two or three miles that
the bull lagged behind the herd.   I was riding the
tranquil sorrel, not a speedy horse; and by this time
my weight was telling on him.   Kermit and his horse
had already turned a somersault, having gone into
an ant-bear hole, which the tall grass concealed; but
they were up and off in an instant.   All of Tranquillity's enthusiasm had vanished, and only by constant
thumping with heels and gun butt could I keep him
at a slow hand gallop, and in sight of the leaders.
We came to a slight rise, where the rank grass grew
high and thick; and Tranquillity put both his forelegs into an ant-bear hole, and with obvious relief
rolled gently over on his side.   It was not really a
tumble; he hailed the ant-bear burrow as offering
a way out of a chase in which he had grown to take
less than no interest.   Besides, he really was winded,
and when we got up I could barely get him into a
canter; and I saw no more of the run.   Meanwhile
Kermit and Tarlton raced alongside the wounded
bull, one on each flank, and started him toward camp,
which was about five miles from where the hunt be-

gan. Two or three times he came to a standstill, and turned first toward one and then toward the other of his pursuers, almost as if he meditated a charge; but they shouted at him and he resumed his flight. They brought him within three hundred yards of camp, and then Kermit leaped off and finished him.

This bull was a fine specimen, colored almost exactly like the giraffes of the Athi and Sotik, but with much more horn development. I doubt whether this five-horned kind is more than a local race. The bulls have been described as very dark; but the one thus shot, a big and old master bull, was unusually light, and in the herd there were individuals of every shade, much the darkest being a rather small cow. Indeed, in none of the varieties of giraffe did we find that the old bulls were markedly darker than the others; many of them were dark, but some of the biggest were light-colored, and the darkest individuals in a herd were often cows. Giraffes, by the way, do sometimes lie down to sleep, but not often.*

In order that Heller might take care of the giraffe

* This is just one of the points as to which no one observer should dogmatize or try to lay down general laws with no exceptions. Moreover, the personal equation of even the most honest observer must always be taken into account in considering not merely matters like this, but even such things as measurements. For example, Neuman, in his " Elephant Hunting," gives measurements of the height of both elephants and Grevy's zebra; our measurements made the elephants taller, and the big zebras less tall, than he found them. Measurements of the lengths of lions, made by different observers, are for this reason rarely of much value for purposes of comparison.

skin we had to spend a couple of days where we were
then camped. The tents were pitched near a spring
of good water, beside a slight valley in which there
were marshy spots and reed beds. The country was
rolling, and covered with fine grass, unfortunately
so tall as to afford secure cover for lions. There
were stretches bare of trees, and other stretches with
a sparse, scattered growth of low thorns or of the
big, glossy-leaved bush which I have spoken of as
the African jessamine because of the singularly sweet
and jessamine-like fragrance of its flowers. Most
of these bushes were in full bloom, as they had been
six months before on the Athi and three months before near Kenia; some bore berries, of which it is
said that the wild elephant herds are fond.

It is hard to lay down general rules as to the
blossoming times of plants or breeding times of animals in equatorial Africa. Before we left the Uasin
Gishu table-land some of the hartebeest cows' appeared with new-born calves. Some of the acacias
had put forth their small, globular, yellow blossoms, just as the acacias on the Athi plains were
doing in the previous May. The blue lupins were
flowering, for it is a cool, pleasant country.

Our camp here was attractive, and Kermit and
I took advantage of our leisure to fill out the series
of specimens of the big hartebeest and the oribi
which Heller needed for the National Museum. The
flesh of the oribis was reserved for our own table;

that of the kongonis—which had been duly hallalled by the Moslems among our gun-bearers—was turned over to what might be called the officers' mess of the safari proper, the headman, cooks, tent boys, gun-bearers, and saises; while of course the skinners and porters who happened to be out with us when any animal was slain got their share of the meat. We also killed two more hyenas; one, a dog, weighed one hundred and twenty pounds, being smaller than those Heller had trapped while skinning the first bull elephant I shot in the Kenia forest.

Good Ali, my tent boy, kept bowls of the sweet-scented jessamine on our dining-table; now that there were four of us together again we used the dining-tent, which I had discarded on the Guaso Nyero trip. Bakhari had been rather worn down by the work on the Guaso Nyero, and in his place I had taken Kongoni, a Wakamba, with filed teeth, like my second gun-bearer, Gouvimali, but a Moslem— although his Moslemism did not go very deep. Kongoni was the best gun-bearer I had yet had, very willing, and excellent both at seeing and tracking game. Kermit's two gun-bearers were Juma Yohari, a coal-black Swahili Moslem, and Kassitura, a Christian negro from Uganda. Both of them were as eager to do everything for Kermit as mine were to render me any service great or small; and in addition they were capital men for their special work. Juma was always smiling and happy, and was a high

favorite among his fellows; at lunch, when we had
any, if I gave my own followers some of the chocolate, or whatever else it was that I had put in my
saddle pocket, I always noticed that they called up
Yohari to share it. He it was who would receive
the colored cards from my companions' tobacco
pouches, or from the packages of chocolate, and
after puzzling over them until he could himself
identify the brilliantly colored ladies, gentlemen,
little girls, and wild beasts, would volubly explain
them to the others. Kassitura, quite as efficient and
hard-working, was a huge, solemn black man, as
faithful and uncomplaining a soul as I ever met.
Kermit had picked him out from among the porters
to carry his camera, and had then promoted him to
be gun-bearer. In his place he had taken as camera
bearer an equally powerful porter, a heathen 'Mnu-
wazi named Mali. His tent boy had gone crooked;
and one evening some months later after a long and
trying march he found Mali, whose performance of
his new duties he had been closely watching, the
only man up; and Mali, always willing, turned in
of his own accord to help get Kermit's tent in shape;
so Kermit suddenly told him he would promote him
to be tent boy. At first Mali did not quite understand; then he pondered a moment or two, and suddenly leaped into the air exclaiming in Swahili,
" Now I am a big man." And he faithfully strove
to justify his promotion. In similar fashion Ker-

mit picked out on the Nairobi race-track a Kikuyu
sais named Magi, and brought him out with us.
Magi turned out the best sais in the safari; and besides doing his own duty so well he was always
exceedingly interested in everything that concerned
his own Bwana, Kermit, or me—from the proper
arrangement of our sunpads to the success of our
shooting.

From the giraffe camp we went two days' journey
to the 'Nzoi River. Until this Uasin Gishu trip we
had been on waters which either vanished in the
desert or else flowed into the Indian Ocean. Now
we had crossed the divide, and were on the Nile
side of the watershed. The 'Nzoi, a rapid muddy
river, passing south of Mount Elgon, empties into
the Victoria Nyanza. Our route to its bank led
across a rolling country, covered by a dense growth
of tall grass, and in most places by open thorn scrub,
while here and there, in the shallow valleys or
depressions, were swamps. There were lions, and
at night we heard them; but in such long grass it
was wellnigh hopeless to look for them. Evidently
troops of elephants occasionally visited these plains,
for the tops of the little thorn-trees were torn off
and browsed down by the mighty brutes. How
they can tear off and swallow such prickly dainties
as these thorn branches, armored with needle-
pointed spikes, is a mystery. Tarlton told me that
he had seen an elephant, while feeding greedily on

the young top of a thorn-tree, prick its trunk until it uttered a little scream or whine of pain; and it then in a fit of pettishness revenged itself by wrecking the thorn-tree.

Game abounded on the plains. We saw a couple of herds of giraffes. The hartebeests were the most plentiful and the least shy; time after time a small herd loitered until we were within a hundred yards before cantering away. Once or twice we saw topi among them; and often there were mixed herds of zebras and hartebeests. Oribi were common, and sometimes uttered a peculiar squealing whistle when they first saw us. The reedbuck also whistled, but their whistle was entirely distinct. It was astonishing how close the reedbuck lay. Again and again we put them up within a few feet of us from patches of reeds or hollows in the long grass. A much more singular habit is the way in which they share these retreats with dangerous wild beasts; a trait common also to the cover-loving bushbuck. From one of the patches of reeds in which Kermit and I shot two hyenas a reedbuck doe immediately afterward took flight. She had been reposing peacefully during the day within fifty yards of several hyenas! Tarlton had more than once found both reedbuck and bushbuck in comparatively small patches of cover which also held lions.

It is, by the way, a little difficult to know what

names to use in distinguishing between the sexes cf
African game.   The trouble is one which obtains in
all new countries, where the settlers have to name
new beasts; and is, of course, primarily due to the
fact that the terms already found in the language
originally applied only to domestic animals and to
European beasts of the chase. Africanders,
whether Dutch or English, speak of all antelope, of
either sex, as " buck." Then they call the males
and females of the larger kinds bulls and cows, just
as Americans do when they speak of moose, wapiti,
and caribou; and the males and females of the
smaller kinds they usually speak of as rams and
ewes.

While on safari to the 'Nzoi I was even more interested in honey birds which led us to honey than
I was in the game.   Before starting for Africa John
Burroughs had especially charged me to look personally into this extraordinary habit of the honey
bird; a habit so extraordinary that he was inclined
to disbelieve the reality of its existence.   But it un-
questionably does exist.   Every experienced hunter
and every native who lives in the wilderness has
again and again been an eyewitness of it.   Kermit,
in addition to his experience in the Sotik, had been
led by a honey bird to honey in a rock, near Lake
Hannington.   Once while I was tracking game a
honey bird made his appearance, chattering loudly
and flying beside us; I let two of the porters follow

it, and it led them to honey. On the morning of the day we reached the 'Nzoi, a honey bird appeared beside the safari, behaving in the same manner. Some of the men begged to be allowed to follow it; while they were talking to me the honey bird flew to a big tree fifty yards off, and called loudly as it flitted to and fro in the branches; and sure enough there was honey in the tree. I let some of the men stay to get the honey; but they found little except comb filled with grubs. Some of this was put aside for the bird, which ate the grubs. The natives believe that misfortune will follow any failure on their part to leave the honey bird its share of the booty. They also insist that sometimes the honey bird will lead a man to a serpent or wild beast; and sure enough Dr. Mearns was once thus led up to a rhinoceros. While camped on the 'Nzoi the honey birds were almost a nuisance; they were very common, and were continually accompanying us as we hunted, flying from tree to tree, and never ceasing their harsh chatter. Several times we followed birds, which in each case led us to bee trees, and then perched quietly by until the gun-bearers and porters (Gouvimali shone on such occasions) got out the honey—which we found excellent eating by the way.

Our camp here was in a beautiful country, and game, for the most part Uganda kob and singsing waterbuck, often fed in sight of the tents. The kob is a small short-haired waterbuck, with slightly different horns. It is a chunky antelope, with a golden-red coat; I weighed one old buck which I shot and it tipped the beam at two hundred and twenty pounds; Kermit killed a bigger one, weighing two hundred and forty pounds, but its horns were poorer. In their habits the kob somewhat resemble impalla, the does being found in bands of twenty or thirty with a single master buck; and they sometimes make great impalla-like bounds. They fed, at all hours of the day, in the flats near the river, and along the edges of the swamps, and were not very wary. They never tried to hide, and were always easily seen; in utter contrast to the close-lying, skulking, bohor reedbuck, which lay like a rabbit in the long grass or reeds. The kob, on the contrary, were always anxious themselves to see round about, and, like waterbuck and hartebeest, frequently used the ant-heaps as lookout stations. It was a pretty sight to see a herd of the bright red creatures clustered on a big ant-hill, all the necks outstretched, and all the ears thrown forward. The females are hornless. By the middle of November we noticed an occasional new-born calf.

The handsome, shaggy-coated, singsing waterbuck had much the same habits as the kob. Like the kob they fed at all hours of the day; but they were more wary and more apt to be found in country where there were a good many bushes or small, trees. Waterbuck and kob sometimes associated together.

The best singsing bull I got I owed to Tarlton's good eyesight and skill in tracking and stalking. The herd of which he was master bull were shy, and took the alarm just as we first saw them. Tarlton followed their trail for a couple of miles, and then stalked them to an inch, by the dexterous use of a couple of bushes and an ant-hill; the ant-hill being reached after a two hundred yards' crawl, first on all-fours and then flat on the ground, which resulted in my getting a good off-hand shot at a hundred and eighty yards. At this time, about the middle of November, some of the cows had new-born calves. One day I shot a hartebeest bull, with horns twenty-four inches long, as it stood on the top of an ant-heap. On going up to it we noticed something behind a little bush, sixty yards off. We were puzzled what it could be, but finally made out a waterbuck cow; and a minute or two later away she bounded to safety, followed by a wee calf. The porters much appreciated the flesh of the waterbuck. We did not. It is the poorest eating of African antelope—and among the big antelope only the eland is good as a steady diet.

One day we drove a big swamp, putting a hundred porters across it in line, while Kermit and I walked a little ahead of them along the edges, he on one side and I on the other. I shot a couple of bushbuck, a ewe and a young ram; and after the drive was over he shot a female leopard as she stood on the side of an ant-hill.

There were a number of both reedbuck and bushbuck in the swamp. The reedbuck were all ewes, which we did not want. There were one or two big bushbuck rams, but they broke back through the beaters; and so did two bushbuck ewes and one reedbuck ewe, one of the bushbuck ewes actually knocking down a beater. They usually either cleared out while the beaters were still half a mile distant, or else waited until they were almost trodden on. The bushbuck rams were very dark colored; the hornless ewes, and the young, were a brilliant red, the belly, the under side and edges of the conspicuous fluffy tail, and a few dim spots on the cheeks and flanks, being white. Although these buck frequent thick cover, forest, or swamp, and trust for their safety to hiding, and to eluding observation by their stealthy, skulking ways, their coloration has not the smallest protective value, being on the contrary very conspicuous in both sexes, but especially in the females and young, who most need protection. Bushbuck utter a loud bark. The hooves of those we shot were very long, as is often the case with water-loving, marsh-frequenting species. There is a curious collar-like space around the neck on which there is no hair. Although if anything smaller than our white-tail deer, the bushbuck is a vicious and redoubtable fighter, and will charge a man without hesitation.

The last day we were at the 'Nzoi the porters petitioned for one ample meal of meat; and we shot a dozen buck for them—kongoni, kob, and singsing. One of the latter, a very fine bull, fairly charged Kermit and his gun-bearer when they got within a few yards of it, as it lay wounded. This bull grunted loudly as he charged; the grunt of an oryx under similar circumstances is almost a growl. On this day both Kermit and I were led to bee trees by honey birds and took some of the honey for lunch. Kermit stayed after his boys had left the tree, so as to see exactly what the honey bird did. The boys had smoked out the bees, and when they left the tree was still smoking. Throughout the process the honey bird had stayed quietly in a neighboring tree, occasionally uttering a single bubbling cluck. As soon as the boys left, it flew straight for the smoking bee tree, uttering a long trill, utterly different from the chattering noise made while trying to attract the attention of the men and lead them to the tree; and not only did it eat the grubs, but it also ate the bees that were stupefied by the smoke.

Next day we moved camp to the edge of a swamp about five miles from the river. Near the tents was one of the trees which, not knowing its real name, we called " sausage tree"; the seeds or fruits are encased in a kind of hard gourd, the size of a giant sausage, which swings loosely at the end of a long tendril. The swamp was half or three-quarters of a mile across, with one or two ponds in the middle, from which we shot ducks. Francolins—delicious eating, as the ducks were also—uttered their grating calls near by; while oribi and hartebeest were usually to be seen from the tents. The hartebeest, by the way, in its three forms, is much the commonest game animal of East Africa.

A few miles beyond this swamp we suddenly came on a small herd of elephants in the open. There were eight cows and two calves, and they were moving slowly, feeding on the thorny tops of the scattered mimosas, and of other bushes which were thornless. The eyesight of elephants is very bad; I doubt whether they see more clearly than a rather near-sighted man; and we walked up to within seventy yards of these, slight though the cover was, so that Kermit could try to photograph them. We did not need to kill another cow for the National Museum, and so after we had looked at the huge, interesting creatures as long as we wished, we croaked and whistled, and they moved off with leisurely indifference. There is always a fascination about watching elephants; they are such giants, they are so intelligent—much more so than any other game, except perhaps the lion, whose intelligence has a very sinister bent—and they look so odd with their great ears flapping and their trunks lifting and curling. Elephants are rarely absolutely still for any length of time; now and then they flap an ear, or

their bodies sway slightly, while at intervals they
utter curious internal rumblings, or trumpet gently.
These were feeding on saplings of the mimosas and
other trees, apparently caring nothing for the thorns
of the former; they would tear off branches, big or
little, or snap a trunk short off if the whim seized
them. They swallowed the leaves and twigs of
these trees; but I have known them merely chew and
spit out the stems of certain bushes.

After leaving the elephants we were on our way
back to camp when we saw a white man in the trail
ahead; and on coming nearer whom should it prove
to be but Carl Akeley, who was out on a trip for
the American Museum of Natural History in New
York. We went with him to his camp, where we
found Mrs. Akeley, Clark, who was assisting him.
and Messrs. McCutcheon and Stevenson who were
along on a hunting trip. They were old friends and
I was very glad to see them. McCutcheon, the cartoonist, had been at a farewell lunch given me by
Robert Collier just before I left New York, and at
the lunch we had been talking much of George Ade,
and the first question I put to him was, "*Where* is
George Ade?" for if one unexpectedly meets an
American cartoonist on a hunting trip in mid-Africa
there seems no reason why one should not also see
his crony, an American playwright. A year previously Mr. and Mrs. Akeley had lunched with me
at the White House, and we had talked over our

proposed African trips. Akeley, an old African wanderer, was going out with the especial purpose of getting a group of elephants for the American Museum, and was anxious that I should shoot one or two of them for him. I had told him that I certainly would if it were a possibility; and on learning that we had just seen a herd of cows he felt—as I did—that the chance had come for me to fulfil my promise. So we decided that he should camp with us that night, and that next morning we would start with a light outfit to see whether we could not overtake the herd.

An amusing incident occurred that evening. After dark some of the porters went through the reeds to get water from the pond in the middle of the swamp. I was sitting in my tent when a loud yelling and screaming rose from the swamp, and in rushed Kongoni to say that one of the men, while drawing water, had been seized by a lion. Snatching up a rifle I was off at a run for the swamp, calling for lanterns; Kermit and Tarlton joined me, the lanterns were brought, and we reached the meadow of short marsh grass which surrounded the high reeds in the middle. No sooner were we on this meadow than there were loud snortings in the darkness ahead of us, and then the sound of a heavy animal galloping across our front. It now developed that there was no lion in the case at all, but that the porters had been chased by a hippo. I should not have supposed that a hippo would live in such a small, isolated swamp; but there he was on the meadow in front of me, invisible, but snorting, and galloping to and fro. Evidently he was much interested in the lights, and we thought he might charge us; but he did not, retreating slowly as we advanced, until he plunged into the little pond. Hippos are sometimes dangerous at night, and so we waded through the swamp until we came to the pool at which the porters filled their buckets, and stood guard over them until they were through; while the hippo, unseen in the darkness, came closer to us, snorting and plunging—possibly from wrath and insolence, but more probably from mere curiosity.

Next morning Akeley, Tarlton, Kermit, and I started on our elephant hunt. We were travelling light. I took nothing but my bedding, wash kit, spare socks, and slippers, all in a roll of waterproof canvas. We went to where we had seen the herd and then took up the trail, Kongoni and two or three other gun-bearers walking ahead as trackers. They did their work well. The elephants had not been in the least alarmed. Where they had walked in single file it was easy to follow their trail; but the trackers had hard work puzzling it out where the animals had scattered out and loitered along feeding. The trail led up and down hills and through open thorn scrub, and it crossed and recrossed the wooded watercourses in the bottoms of the valleys.

At last, after going some ten miles we came on sign where the elephants had fed that morning, and four or five miles further on we overtook them. That we did not scare them into flight was due to Tarlton. The trail went nearly across wind; the trackers were leading us swiftly along it, when suddenly Tarlton heard a low trumpet ahead and to the right hand. We at once doubled back, left the horses, and advanced toward where the noise indicated that the herd was standing.

In a couple of minutes we sighted them. It was just noon. There were six cows, and two well-grown calves—these last being quite big enough to shift for themselves or to be awkward antagonists for any man of whom they could get hold. They stood in a clump, each occasionally shifting its position or lazily flapping an ear; and now and then one would break off a branch with its trunk, tuck it into its mouth, and withdraw it stripped of its leaves. The wind blew fair, we were careful to make no noise, and with ordinary caution we had nothing to fear from their eyesight. The ground was neither forest nor bare plain; it was covered with long grass and a scattered open growth of small scantily leaved trees, chiefly mimosas, but including some trees covered with gorgeous orange-red flowers. After careful scrutiny we advanced behind an ant-hill to within sixty yards, and I stepped forward for the shot.

Akeley wished two cows and a calf. Of the two

best cows one had rather thick, worn tusks; those
of the other were smaller, but better shaped. The
latter stood half facing me, and I put the bullet from
the right barrel of the Holland through her lungs,
and fired the left barrel for the heart of the other.
Tarlton, and then Akeley and Kermit followed suit.
At once the herd started diagonally past us, but half
halted and faced toward us when only twenty-five
yards distant, an unwounded cow beginning to advance with her great ears cocked at right angles to
her head; and Tarlton called "Look out; they are
coming for us." At such a distance a charge from
half a dozen elephant is a serious thing; I put a bullet into the forehead of the advancing cow, causing
her to lurch heavily forward to her knees; and then
we all fired. The heavy rifles were too much even
for such big beasts, and round they spun and rushed
off. As they turned I dropped the second cow I had
wounded with a shot in the brain, and the cow that
had started to charge also fell, though it needed two
or three more shots to keep it down as it struggled
to rise. The cow at which I had first fired kept on
with the rest of the herd, but fell dead before going
a hundred yards. After we had turned the herd
Kermit with his Winchester killed a bull calf, necessary to complete the museum group; we had been
unable to kill it before because we were too busy
stopping the charge of the cows. I was sorry to
have to shoot the third cow, but with elephant start-

ing to charge at twenty-five yards the risk is too great, and the need of instant action too imperative, to allow of any hesitation.

We pitched camp a hundred yards from the elephants, and Akeley, working like a demon, and assisted by Tarlton, had the skins off the two biggest cows and the calf by the time night fell; I walked out and shot an oribi for supper. Soon after dark the hyenas began to gather at the carcasses and to quarrel among themselves as they gorged. Toward morning a lion came near and uttered a kind of booming, long-drawn moan, an ominous and menacing sound. The hyenas answered with an extraordinary chorus of yelling, howling, laughing, and chuckling, as weird a volume of noise as any to which I ever listened. At dawn we stole down to the carcasses in the faint hope of a shot at the lion. However, he was not there; but as we came toward one carcass a hyena raised its head seemingly from beside the elephant's belly, and I brained it with the little Springfield. On walking up it appeared that I need not have shot at all. The hyena, which was swollen with elephant meat, had gotten inside the huge body, and had then bitten a hole through the abdominal wall of tough muscle and thrust his head through. The wedge-shaped head had slipped through the hole all right, but the muscle had then contracted, and the hyena was fairly caught, with its body inside the elephant's belly, and its head thrust out through the hole. We took several photos of the beast in its queer trap.

After breakfast we rode back to our camp by the swamp. Akeley and Clark were working hard at the elephant skins; but Mrs. Akeley, Stevenson, and McCutcheon took lunch with us at our camp. They had been having a very successful hunt; Mrs. Akeley had to her credit a fine maned lion and a bull elephant with enormous tusks. This was the first safari we had met while we were out in the field; though in Nairobi, and once or twice at outlying bomas, we had met men about to start on, or returning from, expeditions; and as we marched into Meru we encountered the safari of an old friend, William Lord Smith—" Tiger " Smith—who, with Messrs. Brooks and Allen, were on a trip which was partly a hunting trip and partly a scientific trip undertaken on behalf of the Cambridge Museum.

From the 'Nzoi we made a couple days' march to Lake Sergoi, which we had passed on our way out; a reed-fringed pond, surrounded by rocky hills which marked about the limit to which the Boer and English settlers who were taking up the country had spread. All along our route we encountered herds of game; sometimes the herd would be of only one species; at other times we would come across a great mixed herd, the red hartebeest always predominating; while among them might be zebras, showing silvery white or dark gray in the distance, topis with beautifully colored coats, and even waterbuck. We shot what hartebeests, topis, and oribis were needed for food. All over the uplands we came on the remains of a race of which even the memory has long since vanished. These remains consist of large, nearly circular walls of stones, which are sometimes roughly squared. A few of these circular enclosures contain more than one chamber. Many of them, at least, are not cattle kraals, being too small, and built round hollows; the walls are so low that by themselves they could not serve for shelter or defence, and must probably have been used as supports for roofs of timber or skins. They were certainly built by people who were in some respects more advanced than the savage tribes who now dwell in the land; but the grass grows thick on the earth mounds into which the ancient stone walls are slowly crumbling, and not a trace of the builders remains. Barbarians they doubtless were; but they have been engulfed in the black oblivion of a lower barbarism, and not the smallest tradition lingers to tell of their craft or their cruelty, their industry or prowess, or to give us the least hint as to the race from which they sprang.

We had with us an ox wagon, with the regulation span of sixteen oxen, the driver being a young Colonial Englishman from South Africa—for the Dutch and English Africanders are the best ox-wagon drivers in the world. On the way back to

Sergoi he lost his oxen, which were probably run off by some savages from the mountains; so at Sergoi we had to hire another ox wagon, the South African who drove it being a Dutchman named Botha. Sergoi was as yet the limit of settlement; but it was evident that the whole Uasin Gishu country would soon be occupied. Already many Boers from South Africa, and a number of English Africanders, had come in; and no better pioneers exist to-day than these South Africans, both Dutch and English. Both are so good that I earnestly hope they will become indissolubly welded into one people; and the Dutch Boer has the supreme merit of preferring the country to the town and of bringing his wife and children—plenty of children—with him to settle on the land. The homemaker is the only type of settler of permanent value; and the cool, healthy, fertile Uasin Gishu region is an ideal land for the right kind of pioneer home-maker, whether he hopes to make his living by raising stock or by growing crops.

At Sergoi Lake there is a store kept by Mr. Kirke, a South African of Scotch blood. With a kind courtesy which I cannot too highly appreciate he, with the equally cordial help of another settler, Mr. Skally—also a South African, but of Irish birth— and of the District Commissioner, Mr. Corbett, had arranged for a party of Nandi warriors to come over and show me how they hunted the lion. Two

Dutch farmers, Boers, from the neighborhood, had also come; they were Messrs. Mouton and Jordaan, fine fellows both, the former having served with De Wet during the war. Mr. and Mrs. Corbett—who were hospitality itself—had also come to see the sport; and so had Captain Chapman, an English army officer who was taking a rest after several years' service in Northern Nigeria.

The Nandi are a warlike pastoral tribe, close kin to the Masai in blood and tongue, in weapons and in manner of life. They have long been accustomed to kill with the spear lions which become man-eaters or which molest their cattle overmuch; and the peace which British rule has imposed upon them—a peace so welcome to the weaker, so irksome to the predatory, tribes—has left lion killing one of the few pursuits in which glory can be won by a young warrior. When it was told them that if they wished they could come to hunt lions at Sergoi eight hundred warriors volunteered, and much heartburning was caused in choosing the sixty or seventy who were allowed the privilege. They stipulated, however, that they should not be used merely as beaters, but should kill the lion themselves, and refused to come unless with this understanding.

The day before we reached Sergoi they had gone out, and had killed a lion and lioness; the beasts were put up from a small covert and despatched with the heavy throwing spears on the instant, before

they offered, or indeed had the chance to offer, any
resistance. The day after our arrival there was
mist and cold rain, and we found no lions. Next
day, November 20th, we were successful.

We started immediately after breakfast. Kirke,
Skally, Mouton, Jordaan, Mr. and Mrs. Corbett,
Captain Chapman, and our party were on horseback; of course we carried our rifles, but our duty
was merely to round up the lion and hold him, if he
went off so far in advance that even the Nandi runners could not overtake him. We intended to beat
the country toward some shallow, swampy valleys
twelve miles distant.

In an hour we overtook the Nandi warriors, who
were advancing across the rolling, grassy plains in
a long line, with intervals of six or eight yards between the men. They were splendid savages, stark
naked, lithe as panthers, the muscles rippling under
their smooth dark skins; all their lives they had
lived on nothing but animal food, milk, blood, and
flesh, and they were fit for any fatigue or danger.
Their faces were proud, cruel, fearless; as they ran
they moved with long springy strides. Their head-
dresses were fantastic; they carried ox-hide shields
painted with strange devices; and each bore in his
right hand the formidable war spear, used both for
stabbing and for throwing at close quarters. The
narrow spear heads of soft iron were burnished till
they shone like silver; they were four feet long, and

the point and edges were razor sharp. The wooden haft appeared for but a few inches; the long butt was also of iron, ending in a spike, so that the spear looked almost solid metal. Yet each sinewy warrior carried his heavy weapon as if it were a toy, twirling it till it glinted in the sun rays. Herds of game, red hartebeests and striped zebra and wild swine, fled right and left before the advance of the line.

It was noon before we reached a wide, shallow valley, with beds of rushes here and there in the middle, and on either side high grass and dwarfed and scattered thorn-trees. Down this we beat for a couple of miles. Then, suddenly, a maned lion rose a quarter of a mile ahead of the line and galloped off through the high grass to the right; and all of us on horseback tore after him.

He was a magnificent beast, with a black and tawny mane; in his prime, teeth and claws perfect, with mighty thews, and savage heart. He was lying near a hartebeest on which he had been feasting; his life had been one unbroken career of rapine and violence; and now the maned master of the wilderness, the terror that stalked by night, the grim lord of slaughter, was to meet his doom at the hands of the only foes who dared molest him.

It was a mile before we brought him to bay. Then the Dutch farmer, Mouton, who had not even a rifle, but who rode foremost, was almost on him;

he halted and turned under a low thorn-tree, and we galloped past him to the opposite side, to hold him until the spearmen could come. It was a sore temptation to shoot him; but of course we could not break faith with our Nandi friends. We were only some sixty yards from him, and we watched him with our rifles ready, lest he should charge either us, or the first two or three spearmen, before their companions arrived.

One by one the spearmen came up, at a run, and gradually began to form a ring around him. Each, when he came near enough, crouched behind his shield, his spear in his right hand, his fierce, eager face peering over the shield rim. As man followed man, the lion rose to his feet. His mane bristled, his tail lashed, he held his head low, the upper lip now drooping over the jaws, now drawn up so as to show the gleam of the long fangs. He faced first one way and then another, and never ceased to utter his murderous grunting roars. It was a wild sight; the ring of spearmen, intent, silent, bent on blood, and in the centre the great man-killing beast, his thunderous wrath growing ever more dangerous.

At last the tense ring was complete, and the spearmen rose and closed in. The lion looked quickly from side to side, saw where the line was thinnest, and charged at his topmost speed. The crowded moment began. With shields held steady, and quivering spears poised, the men in front braced

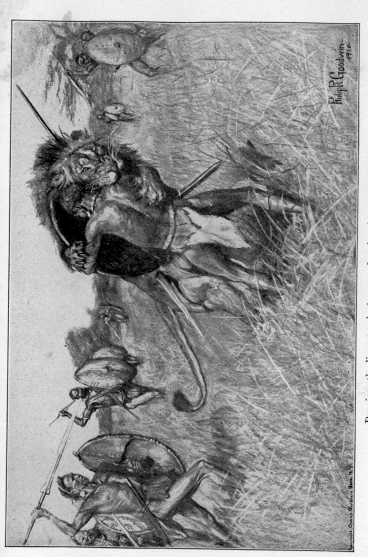

Rearing, the lion struck the man, bearing down the shield.

Drawn by Philip R. Goodwin from photographs and from descriptions furnished by Mr. Roosevelt.

themselves for the rush and the shock; and from either hand the warriors sprang forward to take their foe in flank. Bounding ahead of his fellows, the leader reached throwing distance; the long spear flickered and plunged; as the lion felt the wound he half turned, and then flung himself on the man in front. The warrior threw his spear; it drove deep into the life, for entering at one shoulder it came out of the opposite flank, near the thigh, a yard of steel through the great body. Rearing, the lion struck the man, bearing down the shield, his back arched; and for a moment he slaked his fury with fang and talon. But on the instant I saw another spear driven clear through his body from side to side; and as the lion turned again the bright spear blades darting toward him were flashes of white flame. The end had come. He seized another man, who stabbed him and wrenched loose. As he fell he gripped a spear head in his jaws with such tremendous force that he bent it double. Then the warriors were round and over him, stabbing and shouting, wild with furious exultation.

From the moment when he charged until his death I doubt whether ten seconds had elapsed, perhaps less; but what a ten seconds! The first half dozen spears had done the work. Three of the spear blades had gone clear through the body, the points projecting several inches; and these, and one or two others, including the one he had seized in his jaws, had been twisted out of shape in the terrible death struggle.

We at once attended to the two wounded men. Treating their wounds with antiseptic was painful, and so, while the operation was in progress, I told them, through Kirke, that I would give each a heifer. A Nandi prizes his cattle rather more than his wives; and each sufferer smiled broadly at the news, and forgot all about the pain of his wounds.

Then the warriors, raising their shields above their heads, and chanting the deep-toned victory song, marched with a slow, dancing step around the dead body of the lion; and this savage dance of triumph ended a scene of as fierce interest and excitement as I ever hope to see.

The Nandi marched back by themselves, carrying the two wounded men on their shields. We rode to camp by a roundabout way, on the chance that we might see another lion. The afternoon waned and we cast long shadows before us as we rode across the vast lonely plain. The game stared at us as we passed; a cold wind blew in our faces, and the tall grass waved ceaselessly; the sun set behind a sullen cloud bank; and then, just at nightfall, the tents glimmered white through the dusk.

Tarlton's partner, Newland—also an Australian, and as fine a fellow as Tarlton himself—once had a rather eerie adventure with a man-eating lion. He was camped near Kilimakiu, and after nightfall the alarm was raised that a lion was near by.   He came out of his tent, more wood was thrown on the fire, and he heard footsteps retreating, but could not make out whether they were those of a lion or a hyena.   Going back to his tent he lay down on his bed with his face turned toward the tent wall.   Just as he was falling to sleep the canvas was pushed almost into his face by the head of some creature outside; immediately afterward he heard the sound of a heavy animal galloping, and then the scream of one of his porters whom the lion had seized and was dragging off into the darkness.   Rushing out with his rifle he fired toward the sounds, shooting high; the lion let go his hold and made off, and the man ultimately recovered.

It has been said that lions are monogamous and that they mate for life.   If this were so they would almost always be found in pairs, a lion and a lioness. They are sometimes so found; but it is much more common to come across a lioness and her cubs, an old lion with several lionesses and their young (for they are often polygamous), a single lion or lioness, or a couple of lions or lionesses, or a small troop, either all lions or all lionesses, or of mixed sexes. These facts are not compatible with the romantic theory in question.

We tried to get the Nandi to stay with us for a few days and beat for lions; but this they refused to do, unless they were also to kill them; and I did

not care to assist as a mere spectator at any more
lion hunts, no matter how exciting—though to do
so once was well worth while. So we moved on by
ourselves, camping in likely places. In the swamps,
living among the reeds, were big handsome cuckoos,
which ate mice. Our first camp was by a stream
bordered by trees like clove-trees; at evening multitudes of yellow-billed pigeons flew up its course.
They were feeding on olives, and were good for the
table; and so were the yellow-billed mallards, which
were found in the occasional pools. Everything we
shot at this time went into the pot—except a hyena.
The stomachs of the reedbuck and oribi contained
nothing but grass; but the stomachs of the duikers
were filled with berries from a plant which looked
like the deadly nightshade. On the burned ground,
by the way, the oribi, which were very plentiful, behaved precisely like tommies, except that they did
not go in as large troops; they made no effort to
hide as they do in thick grass; and as duikers, stein-
bucks, and reedbucks always do. We saw, but
could not get a shot at, one topi with a white or
blazed face, like a South African blesbok. While
beating one swamp a lion appeared for an instant at
its edge, a hundred and fifty yards off. I got a snap
shot, and ought to have hit him, but didn't. We
tried our best to get him out of the swamp, finally
burning all of it that was not too wet; but we never
saw him again.

We recrossed the high hill country, through mists and driving rains, and were back at Londiani on the last day of November. Here, with genuine regret, we said good-bye to our safari; for we were about to leave East Africa, and could only take a few of our personal attendants with us into Uganda and the Nile Valley. I was really sorry to see the last of the big, strong, good-natured porters. They had been with us over seven months, and had always behaved well—though this, of course, was mainly owing to Cuninghame's and Tarlton's management. We had not lost a single man by death. One had been tossed by a rhino, one clawed by a leopard, and several had been sent to hospital for dysentery, small-pox, or fever; but none had died. While on the Guaso Nyero trip we had run into a narrow belt of the dreaded tsetse fly, whose bite is fatal to domestic animals. Five of our horses were bitten, and four of them died, two not until we were on the Uasin Gishu; the fifth, my zebra-shaped brown, although very sick, ultimately recovered, to the astonishment of the experts. Only three of our horses lasted in such shape that we could ride them in to Londiani; one of them being Tranquillity, and another Kermit's white pony, Huan Daw, who was always dancing and curvetting, and whom in consequence the saises had christened " merodadi," the dandy.

The first ten days of December I spent at Njoro,

on the edge of the Mau escarpment, with Lord Delamere.   It is a beautiful farming country; and Lord
Delamere is a practical and successful farmer, and
the most useful settler, from the stand-point of the
all-round interests of the country, in British East
Africa.   Incidentally, the home ranch was most attractive—especially the library, the room containing
Lady Delamere's books.   Delamere had been himself a noted big-game hunter, his bag including fifty-
two lions; but instead of continuing to be a mere
sportsman, he turned his attention to stock-raising
and wheat-growing, and became a leader in the work
of taming the wilderness, of conquering for civilization the world's waste spaces.   No career can be
better worth following.

During his hunting years Delamere had met with
many strange adventures.   One of the lions he shot
mauled him, breaking his leg, and also mauling his
two Somali gun-bearers.   The lion then crawled off
into some bushes fifty yards away, and camp was
pitched where the wounded men were lying.   Soon
after nightfall the hyenas assembled in numbers and
attacked, killed, and ate the mortally wounded lion,
the noise made by the combatants being ear-rending.
On another occasion he had heard a leopard attack
some baboons in the rocks, a tremendous row following as the big dog baboons hastened to the assistance of the one who had been seized and drove off
the leopard.   That evening a leopard, evidently the

same one, very thin and hungry, came into camp and was shot; it was frightfully bitten, the injuries being such as only baboons inflict, and would unquestionably have died of its wounds. The leopard wherever possible takes his kill up a tree, showing extraordinary strength in the performance of this feat. It is undoubtedly due to fear of interference from hyenas. The 'Ndorobo said that no single hyena would meddle with a leopard, but that three or four would without hesitation rob it of its prey. Some years before this time, while hunting north of Kenia Lord Delamere had met a Dr. Kolb, who was killed by a rhino immediately afterward. Dr. Kolb was fond of rhinoceros liver, and killed scores of the animals for food; but finally a cow, with a half-grown calf, which he had wounded charged him and thrust her horn right through the middle of his body.

We spent several days vainly hunting bongo in the dense mountain forests, with half a dozen 'Ndorobo. These were true 'Ndorobo, who never cultivate the ground, living in the deep forests on wild honey and game. It has been said that they hunt but little, and only elephant and rhino; but this is not correct as regards the 'Ndorobo in question. They were all clad in short cloaks of the skin of the tree hyrax; hyrax, monkey, bongo, and forest hog, the only game of the dense, cool, wet forest, were all habitually killed by them. They also occasionally

killed rhino and buffalo, finding the former, because
it must occasionally be attacked in the open, the
more dangerous of the two; twice Delamere had
come across small communities of 'Ndorobo literally
starving because the strong man, the chief hunter,
the breadwinner, had been killed by a rhino which he
had attacked. The headman of those with us, who
was named Mel-el-lek, had himself been fearfully
injured by a wounded buffalo; and the father of another one who was with us had been killed by baboons which had rallied to the aid of one which he
was trying to kill with his knobkerry. Usually they
did not venture to meddle with the lions which they
found on the edge of the forest, or with the leopards
which occasionally dwelt in the deep woods; but
once Melellek killed a leopard with a poisoned arrow
from a tree, and once a whole party of them attacked and killed with their poisoned arrows a lion
which had slain a cow buffalo near the forest. On
another occasion a lion in its turn killed two of their
hunters. In fact they were living just as palæo-
lithic man lived in Europe, ages ago.

Their arms were bows and arrows, the arrows
being carried in skin quivers, and the bows, which
were strung with zebra gut, being swathed in strips
of hide. When resting they often stood on one leg,
like storks. Their eyesight was marvellous, and
they were extremely skilful alike in tracking and in
seeing game. They threaded their way through the

forest noiselessly and at speed, and were extraordinary climbers. They were continually climbing trees to get at the hyrax, and once when a big black and white Colobus monkey which I had shot lodged in the top of a giant cedar one of them ascended and brought it down with matter-of-course indifference. He cut down a sapling, twenty-five feet long, with the stub of a stout branch left on as a hook, and for a rope used a section of vine which he broke and twisted into flexibility. Then, festooned with all his belongings, he made the ascent. There was a tall olive, sixty or eighty feet high, close to the cedar, and up this he went. From its topmost branches, where only a monkey or a 'Ndorobo could have felt at home, he reached his sapling over to the lowest limb of the giant cedar, and hooked it on; and then crawled across on this dizzy bridge. Up he went, got the monkey, recrossed the bridge, and climbed down again, quite unconcerned.

The big black and white monkeys ate nothing but leaves, and usually trusted for safety to ascending into the very tops of the tallest cedars. Occasionally they would come in a flying leap down to the ground, or to a neighboring tree; when on the ground they merely dashed toward another tree, being less agile than the ordinary monkeys, whether in the tree tops or on solid earth. They are strikingly handsome and conspicuous creatures. Their bold coloration has been spoken of as " protective "; but it is protective only to town-bred eyes. A non-expert finds any object, of no matter what color, difficult to make out when hidden among the branches at the top of a tall tree; but the black and white coloration of this monkey has not the slightest protective value of any kind. On the contrary, it is calculated at once to attract the eye. The 'Ndorobo were a unit in saying that these monkeys were much more easy to see than their less brightly colored kinsfolk who dwell in the same forests; and this was my own experience.

When camped in these high forests the woods after nightfall were vocal with the croaking and wailing of the tree hyraxes. They are squat, woolly, funny things, and to my great amusement I found that most of the settlers called them " Teddy bears." They are purely arboreal and nocturnal creatures, living in hollows high up in the big trees, by preference in the cedars. At night they are very noisy, the call consisting of an opening series of batrachian-like croaks, followed by a succession of quavering wails—eerie sounds enough, as they come out of the black stillness of the midnight. They are preyed on now and then by big owls and by leopards, and the white-tailed mongoose is their especial foe, following them everywhere among the tree tops. This mongoose is both terrestrial and arboreal in habits, and is hated by the 'Ndorobo because it robs their honey buckets.

The bongo and the giant hog were the big game of these deep forests, where a tangle of undergrowth filled the spaces between the trunks of the cedar, the olive, and the yew or yellow-wood, while where the bamboos grew they usually choked out all other plants.   Delamere had killed several giant hogs with his half-breed hounds; but on this occasion the hounds would not follow them.   On three days we came across bongo; once a solitary bull, on both the other occasions herds.   We never saw them, although we heard the solitary bull crash off through the bamboos; for they are very wary and elusive, being incessantly followed by the 'Ndorobo.   They are as large as native bullocks, with handsomely striped skins, and both sexes carry horns.   On each of the three days we followed them all day long, and it was interesting to trace so much as we could of their habits.   Their trails are deeply beaten, and converge toward the watercourses, which run between the steep, forest-clad spurs of the mountains.   They do not graze, but browse, cropping the leaves, flowers, and twigs of various shrubs, and eating thistles; they are said to eat bark, but this our 'Ndorobo denied.   They are also said to be nocturnal, feeding at night, and lying up in the daytime; but this was certainly not the case with those we came across. Both of the herds, which we followed patiently and cautiously for hours without alarming them, were feeding as they moved slowly along.   One herd lay down for a few hours at noon; the other kept feeding until mid-afternoon, when we alarmed it; and the animals then went straight up the mountain over the rimrock. It was cold rainy weather, and the dark of the moon, which may perhaps have had something to do with the bongo being on the move and feeding during the day; but the 'Ndorobo said that they never fed at night—I of course know nothing about this personally. Leopards catch the young bongo and giant hog, but dare not meddle with those that are full-grown. The forest which they frequent is so dense, so well-nigh impenetrable, that half the time no man can follow their trails save by bending and crawling, and cannot make out an object twenty yards ahead. It is extraordinary to see the places through which the bongo pass, and which are their chosen haunts.

While Lord Delamere and I were hunting in vain Kermit was more fortunate. He was the guest of Barclay Cole, Delamere's brother-in-law. They took eight porters and went into the forest accompanied by four 'Ndorobo. They marched straight up to the bamboo and yellow-wood forest near the top of the Mau escarpment. They spent five days hunting. The procedure was simply to find the trail of a herd, to follow it through the tangled woods as rapidly and noiselessly as possible until it was overtaken, and then to try to get a shot at the first patch of reddish hide of which they got a glimpse—for they never saw more than such a patch, and then only for a moment. The first day Kermit, firing at such a patch, knocked over the animal; but it rose and the tracks were so confused that even the keen eyes of the wild men could not pick out the right one. Next day they again got into a herd; this time Kermit was the first to see the game—all that was visible being a patch of reddish, the size of a man's two hands, with a white stripe across it. Firing he killed the animal; but it proved to be only half grown. Even the 'Ndorobo now thought it useless to follow the herd; but Kermit took one of them and started in pursuit. After a couple of hours' trailing the herd was again overtaken, and again Kermit got a glimpse of the animals. He hit two; and selecting the trail with most blood they followed it for three or four miles, until Kermit overtook and finished off the wounded bongo, a fine cow.

Kermit always found them lying up during the middle of the day and feeding in the morning and afternoon; otherwise his observations of their habits coincided with mine.

The next ten days Kermit spent in a trip to the coast, near Mombasa, for sable—the most beautiful antelope next to the koodoo. The cows and bulls are red, the very old bulls (of the typical form) jet black, all with white bellies; like the roan, both sexes carry scimitar-shaped horns, but longer than the roans. He was alone with his two gun-bearers, and

some Swahili porters; he acted as headman himself.
They marched from Mombasa, being ferried across
the harbor of Kilindini in a dhow, and then going
some fifteen miles south. Next day they marched
about ten miles to a Nyika village, where they arrived just in the middle of a funeral dance which
was being held in honor of a chief's son who had
died. Kermit was much amused to find that this
death dance had more life and go to it than any dance
he had yet seen, and the music—the dirge music—
had such swing and vivacity that it almost reminded
him of a comic opera. The dancers wore tied round
their legs queer little wickerwork baskets, with beans
inside, which rattled in the rhythm of their dancing.
Camp was pitched under a huge baobab-tree, in sight
of the Indian Ocean; but in the middle of the night
the ants swarmed in and drove everybody out; and
next day, while Kermit was hunting, camp was
shifted on about an hour's march to a little grove of
trees by a brook. It was a well-watered country,
very hilly, with palm-bordered streams in each valley. These wild palms bore ivory nuts, the fruit
tasting something like an apple. Each village had a
grove of cocoanut palms, and Kermit found the cool
cocoanut milk delicious after the return from a long
day's hunting.

Each morning he was off before daylight, and
rarely returned until after nightfall; and tired
though he was he enjoyed to the full the walks

campward in the bright moonlight among the palm
groves beside the rushing streams, while the cicadas
cried like katydids at home. The grass was long.
The weather was very hot, and almost every day
there were drenching thunder-storms, and the dews
were exceedingly heavy, so that Kermit was wet
almost all the time, although he kept in first-rate
health. There were not many sable and they were
shy. About nine or ten o'clock they would stop
feeding, and leave their pasture grounds of long
grass, taking refuge in some grove of trees and
thick bushes, not coming out again until nearly five
o'clock.

On the second day's hunting Juma spied a little
band of sable just entering a grove. A long and
careful stalk brought the hunters to the grove, but
after reaching it they at first saw nothing of the
game. Then Kermit caught a glimpse of a head,
fired, and brought down the beast in its tracks. It
proved to be a bull, just changing from the red to
the black coat; the horns were fair—in this northern
form they never reach the length of those borne by
the sable bulls of South Africa. He also killed a
cow, not fully grown. He therefore still needed a
full-grown cow, which he obtained three days later;
this animal when wounded was very savage, and
tried to charge.

We now went to Nairobi, where Cuninghame,
Tarlton, and the three naturalists were already pre-

paring for the Uganda trip and shipping the stuff hitherto collected. Working like beavers we got everything ready—including additions to the Pigskin Library, which included, among others, Cervantes, Goethe's "Faust," Molière, Pascal, Montaigne, St. Simon, Darwin's "Voyage of the Beagle," and Huxley's "Essays"—and on December 18th started for Lake Victoria Nyanza.

CHAPTER XIII

UGANDA, AND THE GREAT NYANZA LAKES

WHEN we left Nairobi it was with real regret that we said good-by to the many friends who had been so kind to us; officials, private citizens, almost every one we had met —including Sir Percy Girouard, the new governor. At Kijabe the men and women from the American mission—and the children too—were down at the station to wish us good luck; and at Nakuru the settlers from the neighborhood gathered on the platform to give us a farewell cheer. The following morning we reached Kisumu on Lake Victoria Nyanza. It is in the Kavirondo country, where the natives, both men and women, as a rule go absolutely naked, although they are peaceable and industrious. In the native market they had brought in baskets, iron spade heads, and food, to sell to the native and Indian traders who had their booths round about; the meat market, under the trees, was especially interesting.

At noon we embarked in a smart little steamer, to cross the lake. Twenty-four hours later we landed at Entebbe, the seat of the English Governor of Uganda. Throughout our passage the wind hardly ruffled the smooth surface of the lake. As we steamed away from the eastern shore the mountains behind us and on our right hand rose harsh and barren, yet with a kind of forbidding beauty. Dark clouds hung over the land we had left, and a rainbow stretched across their front. At nightfall, as the red sunset faded, the lonely waters of the vast inland sea stretched, ocean-like, west and south into a shoreless gloom. Then the darkness deepened, the tropic stars blazed overhead, and the light of the half moon drowned in silver the embers of the sunset.

Next morning we steamed along and across the equator; the last time we were to cross it, for thenceforth our course lay northward. We passed by many islands, green with meadow and forest, beautiful in the bright sunshine, but empty with the emptiness of death. A decade previously these islands were thronged with tribes of fisher folk; their villages studded the shores, and their long canoes, planks held together with fibre, furrowed the surface of the lake. Then, from out of the depths of the Congo forest came the dreadful scourge of the sleeping sickness, and smote the doomed peoples who dwelt beside the Victorian Nile, and on the coasts of the Nyanza Lakes and in the lands between. Its agent was a biting fly, brother to the tsetse whose bite is fatal to domestic animals. This fly dwells in forests, beside lakes and rivers; and wherever it

dwells after the sleeping sickness came it was found
that man could not live. In this country, between,
and along the shores of, the great lakes, two hundred
thousand people died in slow torment, before the
hard-taxed wisdom and skill of medical science and
governmental administration could work any better-
ment whatever in the situation. Men still die by
thousands, and the disease is slowly spreading into
fresh districts. But it has proved possible to keep
it within limits in the regions already affected; yet
only by absolutely abandoning certain districts, and
by clearing all the forest and brush in tracts which
serve as barriers to the fly, and which permit passage
through the infected belts. On the western shores
of Victoria Nyanza, and in the islands adjacent
thereto, the ravages of the pestilence were such, the
mortality it caused was so appalling, that the Government was finally forced to deport all the survivors
inland, to forbid all residence beside or fishing in the
lake, and with this end in view to destroy the villages and the fishing fleets of the people. The teeming lake fish were formerly a main source of food
supply to all who dwelt near by; but this has now
been cut off, and the myriads of fish are left to themselves, to the hosts of water birds, and to the monstrous man-eating crocodiles of the lake, on whose
blood the fly also feeds, and whence it is supposed
by some that it draws the germs so deadly to human
kind.

When we landed there was nothing in the hot, laughing, tropical beauty of the land to suggest the grisly horror that brooded so near. In green luxuriance the earth lay under a cloudless sky, yielding her increase to the sun's burning caresses, and men and women were living their lives and doing their work well and gallantly.

At Entebbe we stayed with the acting-Governor, Mr. Boyle, at Kampalla with the District Commissioner, Mr. Knowles; both of them veteran administrators, and the latter also a mighty hunter; and both of them showed us every courtesy, and treated us with all possible kindness. Entebbe is a pretty little town of English residents, chiefly officials; with well-kept roads, a golf course, tennis courts, and an attractive club house. The whole place is bowered in flowers, on tree, bush, and vine, of every hue— masses of lilac, purple, yellow, blue, and fiery crimson. Kampalla is the native town, where the little King of Uganda, a boy, lives, and his chiefs of state, and where the native council meets; and it is the head-quarters of the missions, both Church of England and Roman Catholic.

Kampalla is an interesting place; and so is all Uganda. The first explorers who penetrated thither, half a century ago, found in this heathen state, of almost pure negroes, a veritable semi-civilization, or advanced barbarism, comparable to that of the little 'Arab-negro or Berber-negro sultanates strung along

the southern edge of the Sahara, and contrasting
sharply with the weltering savagery which surrounded it, and which stretched away without a
break for many hundreds of miles in every direction. The people were industrious tillers of the soil,
who owned sheep, goats, and some cattle; they wore
decent clothing, and hence were styled " womanish "
by the savages of the Upper Nile region, who prided
themselves on the nakedness of their men as a proof
of manliness; they were unusually intelligent and
ceremoniously courteous; and, most singular of all,
although the monarch was a cruel despot, of the
usual African (whether Mohammedan or heathen)
type, there were certain excellent governmental cus-
toms, of binding observance, which in the aggregate might almost be called an unwritten constitu-
tion. Alone among the natives of tropical Africa
the people of Uganda have proved very accessible
to Christian teaching, so that the creed of Christianity is now dominant among them. For their good
fortune, England has established a protectorate over
them. Most wisely the English Government officials, and as a rule the missionaries, have bent
their energies to developing them along their own
lines, in government, dress, and ways of life, constantly striving to better them and bring them forward, but not twisting them aside from their natural line of development, nor wrenching them loose
from what was good in their past, by attempting

the impossible task of turning an entire native population into black Englishmen at one stroke.

The problem set to the governing caste in Uganda is totally different from that which offers itself in British East Africa. The highlands of East Africa form a white man's country, and the prime need is to build up a large, healthy population of true white settlers, white home-makers, who shall take the land as an inheritance for their children's children. Uganda can never be this kind of white man's country; and although planters and merchants of the right type can undoubtedly do well there—to the advantage of the country as well as of themselves—it must remain essentially a black man's country, and the chief task of the officials of the intrusive and masterful race must be to bring forward the natives, to train them, and above all to help them train themselves, so that they may advance in industry, in learning, in morality, in capacity for self-government—for it is idle to talk of " giving " a people self-government; the gift of the forms, when the inward spirit is lacking, is mere folly; all that can be done is patiently to help a people acquire the necessary qualities,—social, moral, intellectual, industrial, and lastly political— and meanwhile to exercise for their benefit, with justice, sympathy, and firmness, the governing ability which as yet they themselves lack. The widely spread rule of a strong European race in lands like

Africa gives, as one incident thereof, the chance for
nascent cultures, nascent semi-civilizations, to develop without fear of being overwhelmed in the surrounding gulfs of savagery; and this aside from the
direct stimulus to development conferred by the consciously and unconsciously exercised influence of the
white man, wherein there is much of evil, but much
more of ultimate good. In any region of wide-
spread savagery, the chances for the growth of each
self-produced civilization are necessarily small, because each little centre of effort toward this end is
always exposed to destruction from the neighboring
masses of pure savagery; and therefore progress is
often immensely accelerated by outside invasion and
control. In Africa the control and guidance is needed as much in the things of the spirit as in the things
of the body. Those who complain of or rail at missionary work in Africa, and who confine themselves
to pointing out the undoubtedly too numerous errors
of the missionaries and shortcomings of their flocks,
would do well to consider that even if the light
which has been let in is but feeble and gray it has
at least dispelled a worse than Stygian darkness. As
soon as native African religions—practically none
of which have hitherto evolved any substantial
ethical basis—develop beyond the most primitive
stage they tend, notably in middle and western Africa, to grow into malign creeds of unspeakable
cruelty and immorality, with a bestial and revolting

ritual and ceremonial. Even a poorly taught and imperfectly understood Christianity, with its underlying foundation of justice and mercy, represents an immeasurable advance on such a creed.

Where, as in Uganda, the people are intelligent and the missionaries unite disinterestedness and zeal with common sense, the result is astounding. The majority of the people of Uganda are now Christian, Protestant or Catholic; and many thousands among them are sincerely Christian and show their Christianity in practical fashion by putting conduct above ceremonial and dogma. Most fortunately, Protestant and Catholic seem now to be growing to work in charity together, and to show rivalry only in healthy effort against the common foe; there is certainly enough evil in the world to offer a target at which all good men can direct their shafts, without expending them on one another.

We visited the Church of England Mission, where we were received by Bishop Tucker, and the two Catholic Missions, where we were received by Bishops Hanlon and Streicher; we went through the churches and saw the schools with the pupils actually at work. In all the missions we were received with American and British flags and listened to the children singing the " Star-spangled Banner." The Church of England Mission has been at work for a quarter of a century; what has been accomplished by Bishop Tucker and those associated with him

makes one of the most interesting chapters in all
recent missionary history; I saw the high-school,
where the sons of the chiefs are being trained in
large numbers for their future duties, and I was especially struck by the admirable Medical Mission,
and by the handsome Cathedral, built by the native
Christians themselves without outside assistance in
either money or labor. At dinner at Mr. Knowles',
Bishop Tucker gave us exceedingly interesting details of his past experiences in Uganda, and of the
progress of the missionary work. He had been
much amused by an American missionary who had
urged him to visit America, saying that he would
" find the latch-string outside the door "; to an
American who knows the country districts well the
expression seems so natural that I had never even
realized that it was an Americanism.

At Bishop Hanlon's Mission, where I lunched
with the bishop, there was a friend, Mother Paul,
an American; before I left America I had promised
that I would surely see her, and look into the work
which she, and the sisters associated with her, were
doing. It was delightful seeing her; she not merely
spoke my language but my neighborhood dialect.
She informed me that she had just received a message of good will for me in a letter from two of
" the finest "—of course I felt at home when in mid-
Africa, under the equator, I received in such fashion
a message from two of the men who had served un-

der me in the New York police.* She had been
teaching her pupils to sing some lines of the " Star-
spangled Banner," in English, in my especial honor;
and of course, had been obliged in writing it out, to
use spelling far more purely phonetic than I had
ever dreamed of using. The first lines ran as follows: (Some of our word sounds have no equiva-
lent in Uganda.)

"O se ka nyu si bai di   mo   nseli laiti
(O say can you see by the morn's † early light)

Wati so pulauli wi eli adi twayi laiti   silasi
       giremi "
(What so proudly we hailed at the twilight's last
       gleaming.)

After having taught the children the first verse
in this manner Mother Paul said that she stopped to
avoid brain fever.

In addition to scholastic exercises Mother Paul
and her associates were training their school children in all kinds of industrial work, taking especial
pains to develop those industries that were natural
to them and would be of use when they returned to

* For the benefit of those who do not live in the neighborhood of New York I may explain that all good, or typical,
New Yorkers invariably speak of their police force as "the
finest"; and if any one desires to know what a "good" or
"typical" New Yorker is, I shall add, on the authority of
either Brander Matthews or the late H. C. Bunner—I forget
which—that when he isn't a Southerner or of Irish or German
descent he is usually a man born out West of New England
parentage.
† *sic.*

their own homes. Both at Bishop Hanlon's mission, and at Bishop Streicher's, the Mission of the White Fathers—originally a French organization, which has established churches and schools in almost all parts of Africa—the fathers were teaching the native men to cultivate coffee, and various fruits and vegetables.

I called on the little king, who is being well trained by his English tutor—few tutors perform more exacting or responsible duties—and whose comfortable house was furnished in English fashion. I met his native advisers, shrewd, powerful-looking men; and went into the Council Chamber, where I was greeted by the council, substantial looking men, well dressed in the native fashion, and representing all the districts of the kingdom. When we visited the king it was after dark, and we were received by smart-looking black soldiers in ordinary khaki uniform, while accompanying them were other attendants dressed in the old-time native fashion; men with flaming torches, and others with the big Uganda drums which they beat to an accompaniment of wild cries. These drums are characteristic of Uganda; each chief has one, and beats upon it his own peculiar tattoo. The king, and all other people of consequence, white, Indian, or native, went round in rickshaws, one man pulling in the shafts and three others pushing behind. The rickshaw men ran well, and sang all the time, the man in the

shafts serving as shanty-man, while the three behind
repeated in chorus every second or two a kind of
clanging note; and this went on without a break,
hour after hour. The natives looked well and were
dressed well; the men in long flowing garments of
white, the women usually in brown cloth made in
the old native style out of the bark of the bark cloth
tree. The clothes of the chiefs were tastefully or-
namented. All the people, gentle and simple, were
very polite and ceremonious both to one another
and to strangers. Now and then we met parties of
Sikh soldiers, tall, bearded, fine-looking men with
turbans; and there were Indian and Swahili and even
Arab and Persian traders.

The houses had mud walls and thatched roofs.
The gardens were surrounded by braided cane
fences. In the gardens and along the streets were
many trees; among them bark cloth trees, from
which the bark is stripped every year for cloth; great
incense trees, the sweet scented gum oozing through
wounds in the bark; and date palms, in the fronds
of which hung the nests of the golden weaver birds,
now breeding. White cow herons, tamer than barn-
yard fowls, accompanied the cattle, perching on
their backs, or walking beside them. Beautiful
kavirondo cranes came familiarly round the houses.
It was all strange and attractive. Birds sang everywhere. The air was heavy with the fragrance of
flowers of many colors; the whole place was a riot

of lush growing plants. Every day there were terrific thunder storms. At Kampalla three men had been killed by lightning within six weeks; a year or two before our host, Knowles, had been struck by lightning and knocked senseless, a huge zigzag mark being left across his body, and the links of his gold watch chain being fused; it was many months before he completely recovered.

Knowles arranged a situtunga hunt for us. The situtunga is closely related to the bushbuck but is bigger, with very long hoofs, and shaggy hair like a waterbuck. It is exclusively a beast of the marshes, making its home in the thick reedbeds, where the water is deep; and it is exceedingly shy, so that very few white men have shot, or even seen, it. Its long hoofs enable it to go over the most treacherous ground, and it swims well; in many of its haunts, in the thick papyrus, the water is waist deep on a man. Through the papyrus, and the reeds and marsh grass, it makes well-beaten paths. Where it is in any danger of molestation it is never seen abroad in the daytime, venturing from the safe cover of the high reeds only at night; but fifty miles inland, in the marsh grass on the edge of a big papyrus swamp, Kermit caught a glimpse of half a dozen feeding in the open, knee-deep in water, long after sunrise. On the hunt in question a patch of marsh was driven by a hundred natives, while the guns were strung along the likely passes which led to another patch of marsh. A fine situtunga buck came to Kermit's post, and he killed it as it bolted away. It had stolen up so quietly through the long marsh grass that he only saw it when it was directly on him. Its stomach contained not grass, but the leaves and twig tips of a shrub which grows in and alongside of the marshes.

The day after this hunt our safari started on its march north-westward to Lake Albert Nyanza. We had taken with us from East Africa our gun-bearers, tent boys, and the men whom the naturalists had trained as skinners. The porters were men of Uganda; the askaris were from the constabulary, and widely different races were represented among them, but all had been drilled into soldierly uniformity. The porters were well-clad, well-behaved, fine-looking men, and did their work better than the "shenzis," the wild Meru of Kikiu tribesmen, whom we had occasionally employed in East Africa; but they were not the equals of the regular East African porters. I think this was largely because of their inferior food, for they ate chiefly yams and plantains; in other words inferior sweet potatoes and bananas. They were quite as fond of singing as the East African porters, and in addition were cheered on the march by drum and fife; several men had fifes, and one carried nothing but one of the big Uganda drums, which he usually bore at the head of the safari, marching in company with the flag-

The situtunga shot by Kermit Roosevelt at Kampalla.

From a photograph by Edmund Heller.

bearer. Every hour or two the men would halt, often beside one of the queer little wicker-work booths in which native hucksters disposed of their wares by the roadside.

Along the road we often met wayfarers; once or twice bullock carts; more often men carrying rolls of hides or long bales of cotton on their heads; or a set of Bahima herdsmen, with clear-cut features, guarding their herds of huge-horned Angola cattle. All greeted us most courteously, frequently crouching or kneeling, as is their custom when they salute a superior; and we were scrupulous to acknowledge their salutes, and to return their greetings in the native fashion, with words of courtesy and long drawn e-h-h-s and a-a-h-s. Along the line of march the chiefs had made preparations to receive us. Each afternoon, as we came to the spot where we were to camp for the night, we found a cleared space strewed with straw and surrounded by a plaited reed fence. Within this space cane houses, with thatched roofs of coarse grass, had been erected, some for our stores, one for a kitchen, one, which was always decked with flowers, as a rest-house for ourselves; the latter with open sides, the roof upheld by cane pillars, so that it was cool and comfortable, and afforded a welcome shelter either from the burning sun if the weather was clear, or from the pelting, driving tropical storms if there was rain. The moon was almost full when we left

Kampalla, and night after night it lent a half unearthly beauty to the tropical landscape.

Sometimes in the evenings the mosquitoes bothered us; more often they did not; but in any event we slept well under our nettings. Usually at each camp we found either the head chief of the district, or a sub-chief, with presents; eggs, chickens, sheep, once or twice a bullock, always pineapples and bananas. The chief was always well dressed in flowing robes, and usually welcomed us with dignity and courtesy (sometimes, however, permitting the courtesy to assume the form of servility) ; and we would have him in to tea, where he was sure to enjoy the bread and jam. Sometimes he came in a rickshaw, sometimes in a kind of wickerwork palanquin, sometimes on foot. When we left his territory we made him a return gift.

We avoided all old camping grounds, because of the spirillum tick. This dangerous fever tick is one of the insect scourges of Uganda, for its bite brings on a virulent spirillum fever which lasts intermittently for months, and may be accompanied by partial paralysis. It is common on old camping grounds, and in native villages. The malarial mosquitoes also abound in places; and repeated attacks of malaria pave the way for black water fever, which is often fatal.

The first day's march from Kampalla led us through shambas, the fields of sweet potatoes and plantations of bananas being separated by hedges or by cane fences. Then for two or three days we passed over low hills and through swampy valleys, the whole landscape covered by a sea of elephant grass, the close-growing, coarse blades more than twice the height of a man on horseback. Here and there it was dotted with groves of strange trees; in these groves monkeys of various kinds—some black, some red-tailed, some auburn—chattered as they raced away among the branches; there were brilliant rollers and bee-eaters; little green and yellow parrots, and gray parrots with red tails; and many colored butterflies. Once or twice we saw the handsome, fierce, short-tailed eagle, the bateleur eagle, and scared one from a reedbuck fawn it had killed. Among the common birds there were black drongos, and musical bush shrikes; small black magpies with brown tails; white-headed kites and slate-colored sparrow-hawks; palm swifts, big hornbills; blue and mottled kingfishers, which never went near the water, and had their upper mandibles red and their under ones black; barbets, with swollen, saw-toothed bills, their plumage iridescent purple above and red below; bulbuls, also dark purple above and red below, which whistled and bubbled incessantly as they hopped among the thick bushes, behaving much like our own yellow-breasted chats; and a multitude of other birds, beautiful or fantastic. There were striped squirrels too, reminding us of the big Rocky Mountain chipmunk or Say's chipmunk, but with smaller ears and a longer tail.

Christmas day we passed on the march. There is not much use in trying to celebrate Christmas unless there are small folks to hang up their stockings on Christmas Eve, to rush gleefully in at dawn next morning to open the stockings, and after breakfast to wait in hopping expectancy until their elders throw open the doors of the room in which the big presents are arranged, those for each child on a separate table.

Forty miles from the coast the elephant grass began to disappear. The hills became somewhat higher, there were thorn-trees, and stately royal palms of great height, their stems swollen and bulging at the top, near the fronds. Parasitic ferns, with leaves as large as cabbage leaves, grew on the branches of the acacias. One kind of tree sent down from its branches to the ground roots which grew into thick trunks. There were wide, shallow marshes, and although the grass was tall it was no longer above a man's head. Kermit and I usually got two or three hours' hunting each day. We killed singsing waterbuck, bushbuck, and bohor reedbuck. The reedbuck differed slightly from those of East Africa; in places they were plentiful, and they were not wary. We also killed several harte-beests; a variety of the Jackson's hartebeest, being more highly colored, with black markings. I killed a very handsome harnessed bushbuck ram. It was rather bigger than a good-sized white-tail buck, its brilliant red coat beautifully marked with rows of white spots, its twisted black horns sharp and polished. It seemed to stand about half way between the dark-colored bushbuck rams of East and South Africa and the beautifully marked harnessed antelope rams of the west coast forests. The ewes and young rams showed the harness markings even more plainly; and, as with all bushbuck, were of small size compared to the old rams. These bushbuck were found in tall grass, where the ground was wet, instead of in the thick bush where their East African kinsfolk spend the daytime.

At the bushbuck camp we met a number of porters returning from the Congo, where they had been with an elephant poacher named Busherri—at least that was as near the name as we could make out. He had gone into the Congo to get ivory, by shooting and trading; but the wild forest people had attacked him, and had killed him and seven of his followers, and the others were straggling homeward. In Kampalla we had met an elephant hunter named Quin who had recently lost his right arm in an encounter with a wounded tusker. Near one camp the head chief pointed out two places, now overgrown with jungle, where little villages had stood less than a year before. In each case elephants had taken to feeding at night in the shambas, and had steadily grown bolder and bolder until the natives, their crops ruined by the depredations and their lives in danger, had abandoned the struggle, and shifted to some new place in the wilderness.

We were soon to meet elephant ourselves. The morning of the 28th was rainy; we struck camp rather late, and the march was long, so that it was mid-afternoon when Kermit and I reached our new camping place. Soon afterward word was brought us that some elephants were near by; we were told that the beasts were in the habit of devastating the shambas, and were bold and truculent, having killed a man who had tried to interfere with them. Kermit and I at once started after them, just as the last of the safari came in, accompanied by Cuninghame, who could not go with us as he was recovering from a bout of fever.

In half an hour we came on fresh sign, and began to work cautiously along it. Our guide, a wild-looking savage with a blunt spear, went first, followed by my gun-bearer, Kongoni, who is excellent on spoor; then I came, followed by Kermit, and by the other gun-bearers. The country was covered with tall grass, and studded with numerous patches of jungle and small forest. In a few minutes we heard the elephants, four or five of them, feeding in thick jungle where the vines that hung in tangled masses from the trees and that draped the bushes made dark caves of greenery. It was difficult to find any space clear enough to see thirty yards ahead. Fortunately there was no wind whatever. We picked out the spoor of a big bull and for an hour and a half we followed it, Kongoni usually in the lead. Two or three times, as we threaded our way among the bushes, as noiselessly as possible, we caught glimpses of gray, shadowy bulks, but only for a second at a time, and never with sufficient distinctness to shoot. The elephants were feeding, tearing down the branches of a rather large-leafed tree with bark like that of a scrub oak and big pods containing beans; evidently these beans were a favorite food. They fed in circles and zigzags, but toward camp, until they were not much more than half a mile from it, and the noise made by the porters in talking and gathering wood was plainly audible; but the elephants paid no heed to it, being evidently too much accustomed to the natives to have much fear of man. We continually heard them breaking branches, and making rumbling or squeaking sounds. They then fed slowly along in the opposite direction, and got into rather more open country; and we followed faster in the big footprints of the bull we had selected. Suddenly in an open glade Kongoni crouched and beckoned to me, and through a bush I caught the loom of the tusker. But at that instant he either heard us, saw us, or caught a whiff of our wind, and without a moment's hesitation he himself assumed the offensive. With his huge ears cocked at right angles to his head, and his trunk hanging down, he charged full tilt at us, coming steadily, silently, and at a great pace, his feet swishing through the long grass; and a formidable monster he looked. At forty yards I fired the right barrel of the Holland into his head, and though I missed the brain the shock dazed him and brought him to an instant halt. Immediately Kermit put a bullet from the Winchester into his head; as he wheeled I gave him the second barrel between the neck and shoulder, through his ear; and Kermit gave him three more shots before he slewed round and disappeared. There were not many minutes of daylight left, and we followed hard on his trail, Kongoni leading. At first there was only an occasional gout of dark blood; but soon we found splashes of red froth from the lungs; then we came to where he had fallen, and then we heard him crashing among the branches in thick jungle to the right. In we went after him, through the gathering gloom, Kongoni leading and I close behind, with the rifle ready for instant action; for though his strength was evidently fast failing, he was also evidently in a savage temper, anxious to wreak his vengeance before he died. On we went, following the bloody trail through the dim, cavernous windings in the dark, vine-covered jungle; we heard him smash the branches but a few yards ahead, and fall and rise; and stealing forward Kermit and I slipped up to within a dozen feet of him as he stood on the other side of some small twisted trees, hung with a mat of creepers. I put a bullet into his heart, Kermit fired; each of us fired again on the instant; the mighty bull threw up his trunk, crashed over backward, and lay dead on his side among the bushes. A fine sight he was, a sight to gladden any hunter's heart, as he lay in the twilight, a giant in death.

At once we trotted back to camp, reaching it as darkness fell; and next morning all of us came out to the carcass. He was full grown, and was ten feet nine inches high. The tusks were rather short, but thick, and weighed a hundred and ten pounds the pair. Out of the trunk we made excellent soup.

Several times while following the trail of this big bull we could tell he was close by the strong elephant smell. Most game animals have a peculiar scent, often strong enough for the species to be readily recognizable before it is seen, if in forest or jungle. On the open plains, of course, one rarely gets close enough to an animal to smell it before seeing it; but I once smelled a herd of hartebeest, when the wind was blowing strongly from them, although they were out of sight over a gentle rise. Waterbuck have a very strong smell. Buffalo smell very much like domestic cattle, but old bulls are rank. More than once, in forest, my nostrils have

warned me before my eyes that I was getting near
the quarry whose spoor I was on.

After leaving the elephant camp we journeyed
through country for the most part covered with an
open forest growth. The trees were chiefly acacias.
Among them were interspersed huge candelabra euphorbias, all in bloom, and now and then one of the
brilliant red flowering trees, which never seem to
carry many leaves at the same time with their
gaudy blossoms. At one place for miles the open
forest was composed of the pod-bearing, thick-leafed
trees on which we had found the elephants feeding;
their bark and manner of growth gave them somewhat the look of jack-oaks; where they made up
the forest, growing well apart from one another, it
reminded us of the cross-timbers of Texas and Ok-
lahoma. The grass was everywhere three or four
feet high; here and there were patches of the cane-
like elephant grass, fifteen feet high.

It was pleasant to stride along the road in the
early mornings, followed by the safari, and we saw
many a glorious sunrise. But as noon approached
it grew very hot, under the glare of the brazen
equatorial sun, and we were always glad when we
approached our new camp, with its grass-strewn
ground, its wickerwork fence, and cool, open rest
house. The local sub-chief and his elders were usually drawn up to receive me at the gate, bowing,
clapping their hands, and uttering their long-drawn

e-h-h-s; and often banana saplings or branches would be stuck in the ground to form avenues of approach, and the fence and rest-house might be decorated with flowers of many kinds. Sometimes we were met with music, on instruments of one string, of three strings, of ten strings—rudimentary fiddles and harps; and there was a much more complicated instrument, big and cumbrous, made of bars of wood placed on two banana stems, the bars being struck with a hammer, as if they were keys; its tones were deep and good. Along the road we did not see habitations or people; but continually there led away from it, twisting through the tall grass and the bush jungles, native paths, the earth beaten brown and hard by countless bare feet; and these, crossing and recrossing in a network, led to plantation after plantation of bananas and sweet potatoes, and clusters of thatched huts.

In the afternoon, as the sun began to get well beyond the meridian, we usually sallied forth to hunt, under the guidance of some native who had come in to tell us where he had seen game that morning. The jungle was so thick in places and the grass was everywhere so long, that without such guidance there was little successful hunting to be done in only two or three hours. We might come back with a buck, or with two or three guinea-fowl, or with nothing.

There were a good many poisonous snakes; I

killed a big puff-adder with thirteen eggs inside it; and we also killed a squat, short-tailed viper, beautifully mottled, not eighteen inches long, but with a wide, flat head and a girth of body out of all proportion to its length; and another very poisonous and vicious snake, apparently of colubrine type, long and slender. The birds were an unceasing pleasure. White wagtails and yellow wagtails walked familiarly about us within a few feet, wherever we halted and when we were in camp. Long-tailed, crested colys, with all four of their red toes pointed forward, clung to the sides of the big fruits at which they picked. White-headed swallows caught flies and gnats by our heads. There were large plantain-eaters; and birds like small jays with yellow wattles round the eyes. There were boat-tailed birds, in color iridescent green and purple, which looked like our grakles, but were kin to the bulbuls; and another bird, related to the shrikes, with bristly feathers on the rump, which was colored like a red-winged blackbird, black with red shoulders. Vultures were not plentiful, but the yellow-billed kites, true camp scavengers, were common and tame, screaming as they circled overhead, and catching bits of meat which were thrown in the air for them. The shrews and mice which the naturalists trapped around each camping place were kin to the species we had already obtained in East Africa, but in most cases there was a fairly well-marked difference; the

jerbilles for instance had shorter tails, more like ordinary rats. Frogs with queer voices abounded in
the marshes. Among the ants was one arboreal
kind which made huge nests, shaped like beehives or
rather like big gray bells, in the trees. Near the
lake, by the way, there were Goliath beetles, as large
as small rats.

Ten days from Kampalla we crossed the little
Kafu River, the black, smooth current twisting
quickly along between beds of plumed papyrus.
Beyond it we entered the native kingdom of Unyoro. It is part of the British protectorate of
Uganda, but is separate from the native kingdom of
Uganda, though its people in ethnic type and social
development seem much the same. We halted for a
day at Hoima, a spread-out little native town, pleasantly situated among hills, and surrounded by plantations of cotton, plantains, yams, millet, and beans.
It is the capital of Unyoro, where the king lives, as
well as three or four English officials, and Episcopa-
lian and Roman Catholic missionaries. The king,
accompanied by his prime minister and by the English commissioner, called on me, and I gave him five
o'clock tea; he is a Christian, as are most of his
chiefs and headmen, and they are sending their children to the mission schools.

A heron, about the size of our night heron but
with a longer neck, and with a curiously crow-like
voice, strolled about among the native houses at

Hoima; and the kites almost brushed us with their wings as they swooped down for morsels of food. The cheerful, confiding little wagtails crossed the threshold of the rest-house in which we sat. Black and white crows and vultures came around camp; and handsome, dark hawks, with white on their wings and tails, and with long, conspicuous crests, perched upright on the trees. There were many kinds of doves; one pretty little fellow was but six inches long. At night the jackals wailed with shrill woe among the gardens.

From Hoima we entered a country covered with the tall, rank elephant grass. It was traversed by papyrus-bordered streams, and broken by patches of forest. The date-palms grew tall, and among the trees were some with orange-red flowers like trumpet flowers, growing in grape-shaped clusters; and both the flowers and the seed-pods into which they turned stood straight up in rows above the leafy tops of the trees that bore them.

The first evening, as we sat in the cool, open cane rest-house, word was brought us that an elephant was close at hand. We found him after ten minutes' walk; a young bull, with very small tusks, not worth shooting. For three-quarters of an hour we watched him, strolling about and feeding, just on the edge of a wall of high elephant grass. Although we were in plain sight, ninety yards off, and sometimes moved about, he never saw us; for an elephant's eyes are very bad. He was feeding on some thick, luscious grass, in the usual leisurely elephant fashion, plucking a big tuft, waving it nonchalantly about in his trunk, and finally tucking it into his mouth; pausing to rub his side against a tree, or to sway to and fro as he stood; and continually waving his tail and half cocking his ears.

At noon on January 5th, 1910, we reached Butiaba, a sandpit and marsh on the shores of Lake Albert Nyanza. We had marched about one hundred and sixty miles from Lake Victoria. We camped on the sandy beach by the edge of the beautiful lake, looking across its waters to the mountains that walled in the opposite shore. At mid-day the whole landscape trembled in the white, glaring heat; as the afternoon waned a wind blew off the lake, and the west kindled in ruddy splendor as the sun went down.

At Butiaba we took boats to go down the Nile to the Lado country. The head of the water transportation service in Uganda, Captain Hutchinson, R.N.R., met us, having most kindly decided to take charge of our flotilla himself. Captain Hutchinson was a mighty hunter, and had met with one most extraordinary experience while elephant hunting; in Uganda the number of hunters who have been killed or injured by elephants and buffaloes is large. He wounded a big bull in the head, and followed it for three days. The wound was serious and on the fourth day he overtook the elephant. It charged as soon as it saw him. He hit it twice in the head with his .450 double-barrel as it came on, but neither stopped nor turned it; his second rifle, a double 8 bore, failed to act; and the elephant seized him in its trunk. It brandished him to and fro in the air several times, and then planting him on the ground knelt and stabbed at him with its tusks. Grasping one of its forelegs he pulled himself between them in time to avoid the blow; and as it rose he managed to seize a hind leg and clung to it. But the tusker reached round and plucked him off with its trunk, and once more brandished him high in the air, swinging him violently about. He fainted from pain and dizziness. When he came to he was lying on the ground; one of his attendants had stabbed the elephant with a spear, whereupon the animal had dropped the white man, vainly tried to catch his new assailant, and had then gone off for some three miles and died. Hutchinson was frightfully bruised and strained, and it was six months before he recovered.

CHAPTER XIV

THE GREAT RHINOCEROS OF THE LADO

THE region of which I speak is a dreary region in Libya, by the borders of the river Zaire. And there is no quiet there nor silence. The waters of the river have a saffron hue, and for many miles on either side of the river's oozy bed is a pale desert of gigantic water-lilies . . . and I stood in the morass among the tall lilies and the lilies sighed one unto the other in the solemnity of their desolation. And all at once the moon arose through the thin ghastly mist, and was crimson in color. . . . And the man looked out upon the dreary river Zaire, and upon the yellow ghastly waters, and upon the pale legions of the water-lilies. . . . Then I went down into the recess of the morass, and waded afar in among the wilderness of the lilies, and called unto the hippopotami which dwelt among the fens in the recesses of the morass." I was reading Poe, on the banks of the Upper Nile; and surely his " fable " does deserve to rank with the "tales in the volumes of the Magi—in the ironbound, melancholy volumes of the Magi."

We had come down through the second of the great Nyanza lakes. As we sailed northward, its

waters stretched behind us beyond the ken of vision,
to where they were fed by streams from the Mountains of the Moon. On our left hand rose the
frowning ranges on the other side of which the
Congo forest lies like a shroud over the land. On
our right we passed the mouth of the Victorian Nile,
alive with monstrous crocodiles, and its banks barren
of human life because of the swarms of the fly whose
bite brings the torment which ends in death. As
night fell we entered the White Nile, and steamed
and drifted down the mighty stream. Its current
swirled in long curves between endless ranks of
plumed papyrus. White and blue and red, the float-
ing water-lilies covered the lagoons and the still inlets among the reeds; and here and there the lotus
lifted its leaves and flowers stiffly above the surface.
The brilliant tropic stars made lanes of light on the
lapping water as we ran on through the night. The
river horses roared from the reedbeds, and snorted
and plunged beside the boat, and crocodiles slipped
sullenly into the river as we glided by. Toward
morning a mist arose and through it the crescent of
the dying moon shone red and lurid. Then the sun
flamed aloft and soon the African landscape, vast,
lonely, mysterious, stretched on every side in a shim-
mering glare of heat and light; and ahead of us the
great, strange river went twisting away into the distance.

At midnight we had stopped at the station of

Koba, where we were warmly received by the district commissioner, and where we met half a dozen of the professional elephant hunters, who for the most part make their money, at hazard of their lives, by poaching ivory in the Congo. They are a hardbit set, these elephant poachers; there are few careers more adventurous, or fraught with more peril, or which make heavier demands upon the daring, the endurance, and the physical hardihood of those who follow them. Elephant hunters face death at every turn, from fever, from the assaults of warlike native tribes, from their conflicts with their giant quarry; and the unending strain on their health and strength is tremendous.

At noon the following day we stopped at the deserted station of Wadelai, still in British territory. There have been outposts of white mastery on the Upper Nile for many years, but some of them are now abandoned, for as yet there has been no successful attempt at such development of the region as would alone mean permanency of occupation. The natives whom we saw offered a sharp contrast to those of Uganda; we were again back among wild savages. Near the landing at Wadelai was a group of thatched huts surrounded by a fence; there were small fields of mealies and beans, cultivated by the women, and a few cattle and goats; while big wickerwork fish-traps showed that the river also offered a means of livelihood. Both men and women were practically naked; some of the women entirely so except for a few beads. Here we were joined by an elephant hunter, Quentin Grogan, who was to show us the haunts of the great square mouthed rhinoceros, the so-called white rhinoceros, of the Lado, the only kind of African heavy game which we had not yet obtained. We were allowed to hunt in the Lado, owing to the considerate courtesy of the Belgian Government, for which I was sincerely grateful.

After leaving Wadelai we again went downstream. The river flowed through immense beds of papyrus. Beyond these on either side were rolling plains gradually rising in the distance into hills or low mountains. The plains were covered with high grass, dry and withered; and the smoke here and there showed that the natives, according to their custom, were now burning it. There was no forest; but scattered over the plains were trees, generally thorns, but other kinds also, among them palms and euphorbias.

The following morning, forty-eight hours after leaving Butiaba, on Lake Albert Nyanza, we disembarked from the little flotilla which had carried us—a crazy little steam launch, two sail-boats, and two big row-boats. We made our camp close to the river's edge, on the Lado side, in a thin grove of scattered thorn-trees. The grass grew rank and tall all about us. Our tents were pitched, and the grass huts of the porters built, on a kind of promontory, the main stream running past one side, while on the other was a bay. The nights were hot, and the days burning; the mosquitoes came with darkness, sometimes necessitating our putting on head nets and gloves in the evenings, and they would have made sleep impossible if we had not had mosquito biers. Nevertheless it was a very pleasant camp, and we thoroughly enjoyed it. It was a wild, lonely country, and we saw no human beings except an occasional party of naked savages armed with bows and poisoned arrows. Game was plentiful, and a hunter always enjoys a permanent camp in a good game country; for while the expedition is marching, his movements must largely be regulated by those of the safari, whereas at a permanent camp he is foot-loose.

There was an abundance of animal life, big and little, about our camp. In the reeds, and among the water-lilies of the bay, there were crocodiles, monitor lizards six feet long, and many water birds—herons, flocks of beautiful white egrets, clamorous spur-winged plover, sacred ibis, noisy purple ibis, saddle-billed storks, and lily trotters which ran lightly over the lily pads. There were cormorants and snake birds. Fish eagles screamed as they circled around; very handsome birds, the head, neck, tail, breast, and forepart of the back white, the rest of the plumage black and rich chestnut. There was a queer little eagle owl with inflamed red eyelids.

The black and red bulbuls sang noisily. There were many kingfishers, some no larger than chippy sparrows, and many of them brilliantly colored; some had, and others had not, the regular kingfisher voice; and while some dwelt by the river bank and caught fish, others did not come near the water and lived on insects. There were paradise flycatchers with long, wavy white tails; and olive-green pigeons with yellow bellies. Red-headed, red-tailed lizards ran swiftly up and down the trees. The most extraordinary birds were the nightjars; the cocks carried in each wing one very long, waving plume, the pliable quill being twice the length of the bird's body and tail, and bare except for a patch of dark feather webbing at the end. The two big, dark plume tips were very conspicuous, trailing behind the bird as it flew, and so riveting the observer's attention as to make the bird itself almost escape notice. When seen flying, the first impression conveyed was of two large, dark moths or butterflies fluttering rapidly through the air; it was with a positive effort of the eye that I fixed the actual bird. The big slate and yellow bats were more interesting still. There were several kinds of bats at this camp; a small dark kind that appeared only when night had fallen and flew very near the ground all night long, and a somewhat larger one, lighter beneath, which appeared late in the evening and flew higher in the air. Both of these had the ordinary bat habits of continuous, swallow-like flight. But the habits of the slate and yellow bats were utterly different. They were very abundant, hanging in the thinly leaved acacias around the tents, and, as everywhere else, were crepuscular, indeed to a large extent actually diurnal, in habit. They saw well and flew well by daylight, passing the time hanging from twigs. They became active before sunset. In catching insects they behaved not like swallows but like flycatchers. Except that they perched upside down so to speak, that is, that they hung from the twigs instead of sitting on them, their conduct was precisely that of a phœbe bird or a wood peewee. Each bat hung from its twig until it espied a passing insect, when it swooped down upon it, and after a short flight returned with its booty to the same perch or went on to a new one close by; and it kept twitching its long ears as it hung head downward devouring its prey.

There were no native villages in our immediate neighborhood, and the game was not shy. There were many buck: waterbuck, kob, hartebeest, bushbuck, reedbuck, oribi, and duiker. Every day or two Kermit or I would shoot a buck for the camp. We generally went out together with our gunbearers, Kermit striding along in front, with short trousers and leggings, his knees bare. Sometimes only one of us would go out. The kob and waterbuck were usually found in bands, and were perhaps the commonest of all. The buck seemed to have no settled time for feeding. Two oribi which I shot were feeding right in the open, just at noon, utterly indifferent to the heat. There were hippo both in the bay and in the river. All night long we could hear them splashing, snorting, and grunting; they were very noisy, sometimes uttering a strange, long-drawn bellow, a little like the exhaust of a giant steampipe, once or twice whinnying or neighing; but usually making a succession of grunts, or bubbling squeals through the nostrils. The long grass was traversed in all directions by elephant trails, and there was much fresh sign of the huge beasts—their dung, and the wrecked trees on which they had been feeding; and there was sign of buffalo also. In middle Africa, thanks to wise legislation, and to the very limited size of the areas open to true settlement, there has been no such reckless, wholesale slaughter of big game as that which has brought the once wonderful big game fauna of South Africa to the verge of extinction. In certain small areas of middle Africa, of course, it has gone; but as a whole it has not much diminished, some species have actually increased, and none is in danger of immediate extinction, unless it be the white rhinoceros. During the last decade, for instance, the buffalo have been recovering their lost ground throughout the Lado, Uganda, and British East Africa, having multiplied many times over. During the same period, in the same region, the elephant have not greatly diminished in aggregate numbers, although the number of bulls carrying big ivory has been very much reduced; indeed the reproductive capacity of the herds has probably been very little impaired, the energies of the hunters having been almost exclusively directed to the killing of the bulls with tusks weighing over thirty pounds apiece; and the really big tuskers, which are most eagerly sought after, are almost always past their prime, and no longer associate with the herd.

But this does not apply to the great beast which was the object of our coming to the Lado, the square-mouthed or, as it is sometimes miscalled, the white, rhinoceros. Africa is a huge continent, and many species of the big mammals inhabiting it are spread over a vast surface; and some of them offer strange problems for inquiry in the discontinuity of their distribution. The most extraordinary instance of this discontinuity is that offered by the distribution of the square-mouthed rhinoceros. It is almost as if our bison had never been known within historic times except in Texas and Ecuador. This great rhinoceros was formerly plentiful in South Africa south of the Zambesi, where it has been completely exterminated except for a score or so of individuals on a game reserve. North of the Zambesi it was and is utterly unknown, save that during the last ten years it has been found to exist in several localities on the left bank of the Upper Nile, close to the river, and covering a north and south extension of about two hundred miles. Even in this narrow ribbon of territory the square-mouthed rhinoceros is found only in certain localities, and although there has not hitherto been much slaughter of the mighty beast, it would certainly be well if all killing of it were prohibited until careful inquiry has been made as to its numbers and exact distribution. It is a curious animal, on the average distinctly larger than, and utterly different from, the ordinary African rhinoceros. The spinal processes of the dorsal vertebræ are so developed as to make a very prominent hump over the withers, while forward of this is a still higher and more prominent fleshy hump on the neck. The huge, misshapen head differs in all respects as widely from the head of the common or so-called black rhinoceros as the head of a moose differs from that of a wapiti.

The morning after making camp we started on a rhinoceros hunt. At this time in this neighborhood, the rhinoceros seemed to spend the heat of the day in sleep, and to feed in the morning and evening, and perhaps throughout the night; and to drink in the evening and morning, usually at some bay or inlet of the river. In the morning they walked away from the water for an hour or two, until they came to a place which suited them for the day's sleep. Unlike the ordinary rhinoceros, the square-mouthed rhinoceros feeds exclusively on grass. Its dung is very different; we only occasionally saw it deposited in heaps, according to the custom of its more common cousin. The big, sluggish beast seems fond of nosing the ant-hills of red earth, both with its horn and with its square muzzle; it may be that it licks them for some saline substance. It is apparently of less solitary nature than the prehensile-lipped rhino, frequently going in parties of four or five or half a dozen individuals.

We did not get an early start. Hour after hour we plodded on, under the burning sun, through the tall, tangled grass, which was often higher than our heads. Continually we crossed the trails of elephant and more rarely of rhinoceros, but the hard, sun-baked earth and stiff, tinder-dry long grass made it a matter of extreme difficulty to tell if a trail was fresh, or to follow it. Finally, Kermit and his gun-bearer, Kassitura, discovered some unquestionably fresh footprints which those of us who were in front had passed over. Immediately we took the trail, Kongoni and Kassitura acting as trackers, while Kermit and I followed at their heels. Once or twice the two trackers were puzzled, but they were never entirely at fault; and after half an hour Kassitura suddenly pointed toward a thorn-tree about sixty yards off. Mounting a low ant-hill I saw rather dimly through the long grass a big gray bulk, near the foot of the tree; it was a rhinoceros lying asleep

on its side, looking like an enormous pig. It heard
something and raised itself on its forelegs, in a sitting posture, the big ears thrown forward. I fired
for the chest, and the heavy Holland bullet knocked
it clean off its feet. Squealing loudly it rose again,
but it was clearly done for, and it never got ten
yards from where it had been lying.

At the shot four other rhino rose. One bolted
to the right, two others ran to the left. Firing
through the grass Kermit wounded a bull and followed it for a long distance, but could not overtake
it; ten days later,* however, he found the carcass,
and saved the skull and horns. Meanwhile I killed a
calf, which was needed for the museum; the rhino
I had already shot was a full-grown cow, doubtless
the calf's mother. As the rhino rose I was struck
by their likeness to the picture of the white
rhino in Cornwallis Harris's folio of the big game
of South Africa seventy years ago. They were totally different in look from the common rhino, seeming to stand higher and to be shorter in proportion
to their height, while the hump and the huge, ungainly, square-mouthed head added to the dissimi-
larity. The common rhino is in color a very dark
slate gray; these were a rather lighter slate gray;
but this was probably a mere individual peculiarity,
for the best observers say that they are of the same

* Kermit on this occasion was using the double-barrelled
rifle which had been most kindly lent him for the trip by Mr.
John Jay White, of New York.

hue. The muzzle is broad and square, and the upper lip without a vestige of the curved, prehensile development which makes the upper lip of a common rhino look like the hook of a turtle's beak. The stomachs contained nothing but grass; it is a grazing, not a browsing animal.

There were some white egrets—not, as is usually the case with both rhinos and elephants, the cow heron, but the slender, black-legged, yellow-toed egret—on the rhinos, and the bodies and heads of both the cow and calf looked as though they had been splashed with streaks of whitewash. One of the egrets returned after the shooting and perched on the dead body of the calf.

The heat was intense, and our gun-bearers at once began skinning the animals, lest they should spoil; and that afternoon Cuninghame and Heller came out from camp with tents, food, and water, and Heller cared for the skins on the spot, taking thirty-six hours for the job. The second night he was visited by a party of lions, which were after the rhinoceros meat and came within fifteen feet of the tents.

On the same night that Heller was visited by the lions we had to fight fire in the main camp. At noon we noticed two fires come toward us, and could soon hear their roaring. The tall, thick grass was like tinder; and if we let the fires reach camp we were certain to lose everything we had. So Loring, Mearns, Kermit, and I, who were in camp, got out the porters and cut a lane around our tents and goods; and then started a back fire, section after section, from the other side of this lane. We kept every one ready, with branches and wet gunny-sacks, and lit each section in turn, so that we could readily beat out the flames at any point where they threatened. The air was still, and soon after nightfall our back fire had burnt fifty or a hundred yards away from camp, and the danger was practically over. Shortly afterward one of the fires against which we were guarding came over a low hill-crest into view, beyond the line of our back fire. It was a fine sight to see the long line of leaping, wavering flames advance toward one another. An hour or two passed before they met, half a mile from camp. Wherever they came together there would be a moment's spurt of roaring, crackling fire, and then it would vanish, leaving at that point a blank in the circle of flame. Gradually the blanks in the lines extended, until the fire thus burnt itself out, and darkness succeeded the bright red glare.

The fires continued to burn in our neighborhood for a couple of days. Finally one evening the great beds of papyrus across the bay caught fire. After nightfall it was splendid to see the line of flames, leaping fifty feet into the air as they worked across the serried masses of tall papyrus. When they came toward the water they kindled the surface of the bay into a ruddy glare, while above them the crimson smoke clouds drifted slowly to leeward. The fire did not die out until toward morning; and then, behind it, we heard the grand booming chorus of a party of lions. They were full fed, and roaring as they went to their day beds; each would utter a succession of roars which grew louder and louder until they fairly thundered, and then died gradually away, until they ended in a succession of sighs and grunts.

As the fires burned to and fro across the country birds of many kinds came to the edge of the flames to pick up the insects which were driven out. There were marabou storks, kites, hawks, ground hornbills, and flocks of beautiful egrets and cow herons, which stalked sedately through the grass, and now and then turned a small tree nearly white by all perching in it. The little bank swallows came in myriads; exactly the same, by the way, as our familiar home friends, for the bank swallow is the most widely distributed of all birds. The most conspicuous attendants of the fires, however, were the bee-eaters the largest and handsomest we had yet seen, their plumage, every shade of blended red and rose, varied with brilliant blue and green. The fires seemed to bother the bigger animals hardly at all. The game did not shift their haunts, or do more than move in quiet leisurely fashion out of the line of advance of the flames. I saw two oribi which had found a patch of short grass that split the fire, feeding thereon, entirely undisturbed, although the flames were crackling by some fifty yards on each side of them. Even the mice and shrews did not suffer much, probably because they went into holes. Shrews, by the way, were very plentiful, and Loring trapped four kinds, two of them new. It was always a surprise to me to find these tiny shrews swarming in Equatorial Africa just as they swarm in Arctic America.

In a little patch of country not far from this camp there were a few sleeping-sickness fly, and one or two of us were bitten, but, seemingly, the fly were not infected, although at this very time eight men were dying of sleeping sickness at Wadelai where we had stopped. There were also some ordinary tsetse fly, which caused us uneasiness about our mule. We had brought four little mules through Uganda, riding them occasionally on safari; and had taken one across into the Lado, while the other three, with the bulk of the porters, marched on the opposite bank of the Nile from Koba, and were to join us at Nimule.

It was Kermit's turn for the next rhino; and by good luck it was a bull, giving us a complete group of bull, cow, and calf for the National Museum. We got it as we had gotten our first two. Marching through likely country—burnt, this time—we came across the tracks of three rhino, two big and one small, and followed them through the black ashes. It was an intricate and difficult piece of tracking, for the trail wound hither and thither and was criss-crossed by others; but Kongoni and Kassitura gradually untangled the maze, found where the beasts had drunk at a small pool that morning, and then led us to where they were lying asleep under some thorn-trees. It was about eleven o'clock. As the bull rose Kermit gave him a fatal shot with his beloved Winchester. He galloped full speed toward us, not charging, but in a mad panic of terror and bewilderment; and with a bullet from the Holland I brought him down in his tracks only a few yards away. The cow went off at a gallop. The calf, a big creature, half grown, hung about for some time, and came up quite close, but was finally frightened away by shouting and hand-clapping. Some cow herons were round these rhino; and the head and body of the bull looked as if it had been splashed with whitewash.

It was an old bull, with a short, stubby, worn-down horn. It was probably no heavier than a big ordinary rhino bull such as we had shot on the Sotik, and its horns were no larger, and the front and rear ones were of the same proportions relatively to each other. But the misshapen head was much larger, and the height seemed greater because of the curious hump. This fleshy hump is not over the high dorsal vertebræ, but just forward of them, on the neck itself, and has no connection with the spinal column. The square-mouthed rhinoceros of

South Africa is always described as being very much bigger than the common prehensile-lipped African rhinoceros, and as carrying much longer horns. But the square-mouthed rhinos we saw and killed in the Lado did not differ from the common kind in size and horn development as much as we had been led to expect; although on an average they were undoubtedly larger, and with bigger horns, yet there was in both respects overlapping, the bigger prehensile-lipped rhinos equalling or surpassing the smaller individuals of the other kind. The huge, square-muzzled head, and the hump, gave the Lado rhino an utterly different look, however, and its habits are also in some important respects different. Our gun-bearers were all East Africans, who had never before been in the Lado. They had been very sceptical when told that the rhinos were different from those they knew, remarking that "all rhinos were the same"; and the first sight of the spoor merely confirmed them in their belief; but they at once recognized the dung as being different; and when the first animal was down they examined it eagerly and proclaimed it as a rhinoceros with a hump, like their own native cattle, and with the mouth of a hippopotamus.

On the way to camp, after the death of this bull rhino, I shot a waterbuck bull with finer horns than any I had yet obtained. Herds of waterbuck and of kob stared tamely at me as I walked along; whereas a little party of hartebeest were wild and shy. On other occasions I have seen this conduct exactly reversed, the hartebeest being tame, and the waterbuck and kob shy. Heller, as usual, came out and camped by this rhino, to handle the skin and skeleton. In the middle of the night a leopard got caught in one of his small steel traps, which he had set out with a light drag. The beast made a terrific row and went off with the trap and drag. It was only caught by one toe; a hyena similarly caught would have wrenched itself loose; but the leopard, though a far braver and more dangerous beast, has less fortitude under pain than a hyena. Heller tracked it up in the morning, and shot it as, hampered by the trap and drag, it charged the porters.

On the ashes of the fresh burn the footprints of the game showed almost as distinctly as on snow. One morning we saw where a herd of elephant, cows and calves, had come down the night before to drink at a big bay of the Nile, three or four miles north of our camp. Numerous hippo tracks showed that during the darkness these beasts wandered freely a mile or two inland. They often wandered back of our camp at night. Always beside these night trails we found withered remnants of water cabbage and other aquatic plants which they had carried inland with them; I suppose accidentally on their backs. On several occasions where we could only make out scrapes on the ground the hippo trails puzzled us, being so far inland that we thought they might be those of rhinos; until we would come on some patch of ashes or of soft soil where we could trace the four toe marks. The rhino has but three toes, the one in the middle being very big; it belongs, with the tapir and horse, to the group of ungulates which tends to develop one digit of each foot at the expense of all the others; a group which in a long-past geological age was the predominant ungulate group of the world. The hippo, on the contrary, belongs with such cloven-hoofed creatures as the cow and pig, in the group of ungulates which has developed equally two main digits in each foot; a group much more numerously represented than the other in the world of to-day.

As the hippos grew familiar with the camp they became bolder and more venturesome after nightfall. They grunted and brayed to one another throughout the night, splashed and wallowed among the reeds, and came close to the tents during their dry-land rambles in the darkness. One night, in addition to the hippo chorus, we heard the roaring of lions and the trumpeting of elephants. We were indeed in the heart of the African wilderness.

Early in the morning after this concert we started for a day's rhino hunt, Heller and Cuninghame having just finished the preparation, and transport to camp, of the skin of Kermit's bull. Loring, who had not hitherto seen either elephant or rhino alive, went with us; and by good luck he saw both.

A couple of miles from camp we were crossing a wide, flat, swampy valley in which the coarse grass grew as tall as our heads. Here and there were kob, which leaped up on the ant-hills to get a clear view of us. Suddenly our attention was attracted by the movements of a big flock of cow herons in front of us, and then watching sharply we caught a glimpse of some elephants, about four hundred yards off. We now climbed an ant-hill ourselves, and inspected the elephants, to see if among them were any big-tusked bulls. There were no bulls, however; the little herd consisted of five cows and four calves, which were marching across a patch of burnt ground ahead of us, accompanied by about fifty white cow herons. We stood where we were until they had passed; we did not wish to get too close, lest they might charge us and force us to shoot in self-defence. They walked in unhurried confidence, and yet were watchful, continually cocking their ears and raising and curling their trunks. One dropped behind and looked fixedly in our direction, probably having heard us talking; then with head aloft and tail stiffly erect it hastened after the others, presenting an absurd likeness to a baboon. The four calves played friskily about, especially a very comical little pink fellow which accompanied the leading cow. Meanwhile a few of the white herons rode on

their backs, but most of the flock stalked sedately
alongside through the burnt grass, catching the
grasshoppers which were disturbed by the great feet.
When, however, the herd reached the tall grass all
the herons flew up and perched on the backs and
heads of their friends; even the pink calf carried
one.   Half a mile inside the edge of the tall grass
the elephants stopped for the day beside a clump of
bushes; and there they stood, the white birds clustered on their dark bodies.   At the time we could
distinctly hear the Doctor's shot-gun, as he collected
birds near camp; the reports did not disturb the elephants, and when we walked on we left them standing unconcernedly in the grass.

A couple of hours later, as we followed an elephant path, we came to where it was crossed by the
spoor of two rhino.   Our gun-bearers took up the
trail, over the burnt ground, while Kermit and I
followed immediately behind them.   The trail wound
about, and was not always easy to disentangle, but
after a mile or two we saw the beasts.   They were
standing among bushes and patches of rank, unburned grass; it was just ten o'clock, and they were
evidently preparing to lie down for the day.   As
they stood they kept twitching their big ears; both
rhino and elephant are perpetually annoyed, as are
most game, by biting flies, large and small.   We
got up very close, Kermit with his camera and I
with the heavy rifle.   Too little is known of these

northern square-mouthed rhino for us to be sure
that they are not lingering slowly toward extinction;
and, lest this should be the case, we were not willing
to kill any merely for trophies; while, on the other
hand, we deemed it really important to get good
groups for the National Museum in Washington and
the American Museum in New York, and a head for
the National Collection of Heads and Horns which
was started by Mr. Hornaday, the director of the
Bronx Zoological Park. Moreover Kermit and
Loring desired to get some photos of the animals
while they were alive.

Things did not go well this time, however. The
rhinos saw us before either Kermit or Loring could
get a good picture. As they wheeled I fired hastily
into the chest of one, but not quite in the middle,
and away they dashed—for they do not seem as
truculent as the common rhino. We followed them.
After an hour the trails separated; Cuninghame
went on one, but failed to overtake the animal, and
we did not see him until we reached camp late that
afternoon.

Meanwhile our own gun-bearers followed the
bloody spoor of the rhino I had hit, Kermit and I
close behind, and Loring with us. The rhino had
gone straight off at a gallop, and the trail offered
little difficulty, so we walked fast. A couple of
hours passed. The sun was now high and the heat
intense as we walked over the burned ground. The

scattered trees bore such scanty foliage as to cast hardly any shade. The rhino galloped strongly and without faltering; but there was a good deal of blood on the trail. At last, after we had gone seven or eight miles, Kiboko the skinner, who was acting as my gun-bearer, pointed toward a small thorn-tree; and beside it I saw the rhino standing with drooping head. It had been fatally hit, and if undisturbed would probably never have moved from where it was standing; and we finished it off forthwith. It was a cow, and before dying it ran round and round in a circle, in the manner of the common rhino.

Loring stayed to superintend the skinning and bringing in of the head and feet, and slabs of hide. Meanwhile Kermit and I, with our gun-bearers, went off with a "shenzi," a wild native who had just come in with the news that he knew where another rhino was lying, a few miles away. While bound thither we passed numbers of oribi, and went close to a herd of waterbuck which stared at us with stupid tameness; a single hartebeest was with them. When we reached the spot there was the rhino, sure enough, under a little tree, sleeping on his belly, his legs doubled up, and his head flat on the ground. Unfortunately the grass was long, so that it was almost impossible to photograph him. However, Kermit tried to get his picture from an ant-hill fifty yards distant, and then, Kermit with his camera and I with my rifle, we walked up to within about

We walked up to within about twenty yards

From a photograph, copyright, by Kermit Roosevelt.

twenty yards. At this point we halted, and on the instant the rhino jumped to his feet with surprising agility and trotted a few yards out from under the tree. It was a huge bull, with a fair horn; much the biggest bull we had yet seen; and with head up and action high, the sun glinting on his slate hide and bringing out his enormous bulk, he was indeed a fine sight. I waited a moment for Kermit to snap him. Unfortunately the waving grass spoiled the picture. Then I fired right and left into his body, behind the shoulders, and down he went. In color he seemed of exactly the same shade as the common rhino, but he was taller and heavier, being six feet high. He carried a stout horn, a little over two feet long; the girth at the base was very great.

Leaving the gun-bearers (with all our water) to skin the mighty beast, Kermit and I started for camp; and as we were rather late Kermit struck out at a great pace in front, while I followed on the little ambling mule. On our way in we passed the elephants, still standing where we had left them in the morning, with the white cow herons flying and walking around and over them. Heller and Cuninghame at once went out to camp by the skin and take care of it, and to bring back the skeleton. We had been out about eleven hours without food; we were very dirty from the ashes on the burnt ground; we had triumphed; and we were thoroughly happy as we took our baths and ate our hearty dinner.

It was amusing to look at our three naturalists and compare them with the conventional pictures of men of science and learning—especially men of science and learning in the wilderness—drawn by the novelists a century ago. Nowadays the field naturalist—who is usually at all points superior to the mere closet naturalist—follows a profession as full of hazard and interest as that of the explorer or of the big-game hunter in the remote wilderness. He penetrates to all the out-of-the-way nooks and corners of the earth; he is schooled to the performance of very hard work, to the endurance of fatigue and hardship, to encountering all kinds of risks, and to grappling with every conceivable emergency. In consequence he is exceedingly competent, resourceful, and self-reliant, and the man of all others to trust in a tight place.

Around this camp there were no ravens or crows; but multitudes of kites, almost as tame as sparrows, circled among the tents, uttering their wailing cries, and lit on the little trees near by or waddled about on the ground near the cook fires. Numerous vultures, many marabou storks, and a single fish eagle, came to the carcasses set for them outside the camp by Loring; and he took pictures of them. The handsome fish eagle looked altogether out of place among the foul carrion-feeding throng; on the ground the vultures made way for him respectfully enough, but they resented his presence, and now and then two or three would unite to mob him while on the wing.

We wished for another cow rhino, so as to have a bull and a cow both for the National Museum at Washington, and for the American Museum in New York; and Kermit was to shoot this. Accordingly he and I started off early one morning with Grogan —a man of about twenty-five, a good hunter and a capital fellow, with whom by this time we were great friends. It was much like our other hunts. We tramped through high grass across a big, swampy plain or broad valley between low rises of ground, until, on the opposite side, we struck a by-this-time familiar landmark, two tall royal palms, the only ones for some miles around. Here we turned into a broad elephant and rhinoceros path, worn deep and smooth by the generations of huge feet that had tramped it; for it led from the dry inland to a favorite drinking place on the Nile. Along this we walked until Kassitura made out the trail of two rhino crossing it at right angles. They were evidently feeding and seeking a noonday rest-ing place; in this country the square-mouthed rhi-noceros live on the grassy flats, sparsely covered with small thorn-trees, and only go into the high reeds on their way to drink. With Kassitura and Kongoni in the lead we followed the fresh trail for a mile or so, until we saw our quarry. The stupid beasts had smelt us, but were trotting to and fro

in a state of indecision and excitement, tails twisting
and ears cocked, uncertain what to do. At first we
thought they were a bull and a small cow; but they
proved to be a big cow with good horns, and a calf
which was nearly full grown. The wind and sun
were both exactly wrong, so Kermit could not take
any photos; and accordingly he shot the cow behind
the shoulder. Away both animals went, Kermit
tearing along behind, while Grogan and I followed.
After a sharp run of a mile and a half Kermit overtook them, and brought down the cow. The
younger one then trotted threateningly toward him.
He let it get within ten yards, trying to scare it;
as it kept coming on, and could of course easily kill
him, he then fired into its face, to one side, so as to
avoid inflicting a serious injury, and, turning, off
it went at a gallop. When I came up the cow had
raised itself on its forelegs, and he was taking its
picture. It had been wallowing, and its whole body
was covered with dry caked mud. It was exactly
the color of the common rhino, but a little larger
than any cow of the latter that we had killed. We
at once sent for Heller—who had been working
without intermission since we struck the Lado, and
liked it—and waited by the body until he appeared,
in mid-afternoon.

Here in the Lado we were in a wild, uninhabited
country, and for meat we depended entirely on our
rifles; nor was there any difficulty in obtaining all

we needed.   We only shot for meat, or for museum specimens—all the museum specimens being used for food too—and as the naturalists were as busy as they well could be, we found that, except when we were after rhinoceros, it was not necessary to hunt for more than half a day or thereabouts.   On one of these hunts, on which he shot a couple of buck, Kermit also killed a monitor lizard, and a crocodile ten feet long; it was a female, and contained fifty-two eggs, which, when scrambled, we ate and found good.

The morning after Kermit killed his cow rhino he and Grogan went off for the day to see if they could not get some live rhino photos.   Cuninghame started to join Heller at the temporary camp which we had made beside the dead rhino, in order to help him with the skin and skeletons.   Mearns and Loring were busy with birds, small beasts, and photographs.   So, as we were out of fresh meat, I walked away from camp to get some, followed by my gun-bearers, the little mule with its well-meaning and utterly ignorant shenzi sais, and a dozen porters.

We first went along the river brink to look for crocodiles.   In most places the bank was high and steep.   Wherever it was broken there was a drinking place, with leading down to it trails deeply rutted in the soil by the herds of giant game that had travelled them for untold years.   At this point the Nile was miles wide, and was divided into curving channels which here and there spread into lake-like expanses of still water. Along the edges of the river and between the winding channels and lagoons grew vast water-fields of papyrus, their sheets and bands of dark green breaking the burnished silver of the sunlit waters. Beyond the further bank rose steep, sharply peaked hills. The Tricolored fish eagles, striking to the eye because of their snow-white heads and breasts, screamed continually, a wild eerie sound. Cormorants and snake birds were perched on trees overhanging the water, and flew away, or plunged like stones into the stream, as I approached; herons of many kinds rose from the marshy edges of the bays and inlets; wattled and spur-winged plovers circled overhead; and I saw a party of hippopotami in a shallow on the other side of the nearest channel, their lazy bulks raised above water as they basked asleep in the sun. The semi-diurnal slate-and-yellow bats flitted from one scantily leaved tree to another, as I disturbed them. At the foot of a steep bluff, several yards from the water, a crocodile lay. I broke its neck with a soft-nosed bullet from the little Springfield; for the plated skin of a crocodile offers no resistance to a modern rifle. We dragged the ugly man-eater up the bank, and sent one of the porters back to camp to bring out enough men to carry the brute in bodily. It was a female, con-

taining thirty eggs. We did not find any crocodile's nest; but near camp, in digging a hole for the
disposal of refuse, we came on a clutch of a dozen
eggs of the monitor lizard. They were in sandy
loam, two feet and a half beneath the surface, without the vestige of a burrow leading to them. When
exposed to the sun, unlike the crocodile's eggs, they
soon burst. Evidently the young are hatched in the
cool earth and dig their way out.

We continued our walk and soon came on some
kob. At two hundred yards I got a fine buck,
though he went a quarter of a mile. Then, at a
hundred and fifty yards, I dropped a straw-colored
Nile hartebeest. Sending in the kob and hartebeest used up all our porters but two, and I mounted
the little mule and turned toward camp, having been
out three hours. Soon Gouvimali pointed out a big
bustard, marching away through the grass a hundred yards off. I dismounted, shot him through
the base of the neck, and remounted. Then Kongoni pointed out, some distance ahead, a bushbuck
ram, of the harnessed kind found in this part of
the Nile Valley. Hastily dismounting, and stealing rapidly from ant-heap to ant-heap, until I was
not much over a hundred yards from him, I gave
him a fatal shot; but the bullet was placed a little
too far back, and he could still go a considerable
distance. So far I had been shooting well; now,
pride had a fall. Immediately after the shot a diffi-

culty arose in the rear between the mule and the shenzi sais; they parted company, and the mule joined the shooting party in front, at a gallop. The bushbuck, which had halted with its head down, started off and I trotted after it, while the mule pursued an uncertain course between us; and I don't know which it annoyed most. I emptied my magazine twice, and partly a third time, before I finally killed the buck and scared the mule so that it started for camp. The bushbuck in this part of the Nile Valley did not live in dense forest, like those of East Africa, but among the scattered bushes and acacias. Those that I shot in the Lado had in their stomachs leaves, twig tips, and pods; one that Kermit shot, a fine buck, had been eating grass also. On the Uasin Gishu, in addition to leaves and a little grass, they had been feeding on the wild olives.

Our porters were not as a rule by any means the equals of those we had in East Africa, and we had some trouble because, as we did not know their names and faces, those who wished to shirk would go off in the bushes while their more willing comrades would be told off for the needed work. So Cuninghame determined to make each readily identifiable; and one day I found him sitting, in Rhadamanthus mood, at his table before his tent, while all the porters filed by, each in turn being decorated with a tag, conspicuously numbered, which was hung round his neck—the tags, by the way, being Smithsonian label cards, contributed by Dr. Mearns.

At last Kermit succeeded in getting some good white rhino pictures. He was out with his gun-bearers and Grogan. They had hunted steadily for nearly two days without seeing a rhino; then Kermit made out a big cow with a calf lying under a large tree, on a bare plain of short grass. Accompanied by Grogan, and by a gun-bearer carrying his rifle, while he himself carried his "naturalist's graphlex" camera, he got up to within fifty or sixty yards of the dull-witted beasts, and spent an hour cautiously manœuvring and taking photos. He got several photos of the cow and calf lying under the tree. Then something, probably the click of the camera, rendered them uneasy and they stood up. Soon the calf lay down again, while the cow continued standing on the other side of the tree, her head held down, the muzzle almost touching the ground, according to the custom of this species. After taking one or two more pictures Kermit edged in, so as to get better ones. Gradually the cow grew alarmed. She raised her head, as these animals always do when interested or excited, twisted her tail into a tight knot, and walked out from under the tree, followed by the calf; she and the calf stood stern to stern for a few seconds, and Kermit took another photo. By this time the cow had become both puzzled and irritated. Even with her dim eyes she could make out the men and the camera, and once or twice she threatened a charge, but thought better of it. Then she began to move off; but suddenly wheeled and charged, this time bent on mischief. She came on at a slashing trot, gradually increasing her pace, the huge, square lips shaking from side to side. Hoping that she would turn Kermit shouted loudly and waited before firing until she was only ten yards off. Then, with the Winchester, he put a bullet in between her neck and shoulder, a mortal wound. She halted and half wheeled, and Grogan gave her right and left, Kermit putting in a couple of additional bullets as she went off. A couple of hundred yards away she fell, rose again, staggered, fell again, and died. The calf, which was old enough to shift for itself, refused to leave the body, although Kermit and Grogan pelted it with sticks and clods. Finally a shot through the flesh of the buttocks sent it off in frantic haste. Kermit had only killed the cow because it was absolutely necessary in order to avoid an accident, and he was sorry for the necessity; but I was not, for it was a very fine specimen, with the front horn thirty-one inches long; being longer than any other we had gotten. The second horn was compressed laterally, exactly as with many black rhinos (although it is sometimes stated that this does not occur in the case of the white rhino). We preserved the head-skin and skull for the National Museum.

The flesh of this rhino, especially the hump, proved excellent. It is a singular thing that scientific writers seem almost to have overlooked, and never lay any stress upon, the existence of this neck hump. It is on the neck, forward of the long dorsal vertebra, and is very conspicuous in the living animal; and I am inclined to think that some inches of the exceptional height measurements attributed to South African white rhinos may be due to measuring to the top of this hump. I am also puzzled by what seems to be the great inferiority in horn development of these square-mouthed rhinos of the Lado to the square-mouthed or white rhinos of South Africa (and, by the way, I may mention that on the whole these Lado rhinos certainly looked lighter colored, when we came across them standing in the open, than did their prehensile-lipped East African brethren). We saw between thirty and forty square-mouthed rhinos in the Lado, and Kermit's cow had much the longest horn of any of them; and while they averaged much better horns than the black rhinos we had seen in East Africa, between one and two hundred in number, there were any number of exceptions on both sides. There are recorded measurements of white rhino horns from South Africa double as long as our longest from the Lado. Now this is, scientifically, a fact

Of some importance, but it is of no consequence
whatever when compared with the question as to
what, if any, the difference is between the average
horns; and this last fact is very difficult to ascertain,
largely because of the foolish obsession for " record " heads which seems to completely absorb so
many hunters who write. What we need at the
moment is more information about the average
South African heads. There are to be found among
most kinds of horn-bearing animals individuals
with horns of wholly exceptional size, just as among
all nations there are individuals of wholly exceptional height. But a comparison of these wholly
exceptional horns, although it has a certain value,
is, scientifically, much like a comparison of the
giants of different nations. A good head is of
course better than a poor one; and a special effort
to secure an exceptional head is sportsmanlike and
proper. But to let the desire for " record " heads,
to the exclusion of all else, become a craze, is absurd. The making of such a collection is in itself
not only proper but meritorious; all I object to is
the loss of all sense of proportion in connection
therewith. It is just as with philately, or heraldry,
or collecting the signatures of famous men. The
study of stamps, or of coats of arms, or the collecting of autographs, is an entirely legitimate amusement, and may be more than a mere amusement;
it is only when the student or collector allows him-

self utterly to misestimate the importance of his pursuit that it becomes ridiculous.

Cuninghame, Grogan, Heller, Kermit, and I now went off on a week's safari inland, travelling as light as possible. The first day's march brought us to the kraal of a local chief named Sururu. There were a few banana trees, and patches of scrawny cultivation, round the little cluster of huts, ringed with a thorn fence, through which led a low door; and the natives owned goats and chickens. Sururu himself wore a white sheet of cotton as a toga, and he owned a red fez and a pair of baggy blue breeches, which last he generally carried over his shoulder. His people were very scantily clad indeed, and a few of them, both men and women, wore absolutely nothing except a string of blue beads around the waist or neck. Their ears had not been pierced and stretched like so many East African savages, but their lower lips were pierced for wooden ornaments and quills. They brought us eggs and chickens, which we paid for with American cloth; this cloth, and some umbrellas, constituting our stock of trade goods, or gift goods, for the Nile.

The following day Sururu himself led us to our next camp, only a couple of hours away. It was a dry country of harsh grass, everywhere covered by a sparse growth of euphorbias and stunted thorns, which were never in sufficient numbers to make a forest, each little, wellnigh leafless tree, standing a dozen rods or so distant from its nearest fellow. Most of the grass had been burnt, and fires were still raging. Our camp was by a beautiful pond, covered with white and lilac water-lilies. We pitched our two tents on a bluff, under some large acacias that cast real shade. It was between two and three degrees north of the equator. The moon, the hot January moon of the mid-tropics, was at the full, and the nights were very lovely; the little sheet of water glimmered in the moon rays, and round about the dry landscape shone with a strange, spectral light.

Near the pond, just before camping, I shot a couple of young waterbuck bulls for food, and while we were pitching the tents a small herd of elephants —cows, young bulls, and calves, seemingly disturbed by a grass fire which was burning a little way off, came up within four hundred yards of us. At first we mistook one large cow for a bull, and running quickly from bush to bush, diagonally to its course, I got within sixty yards, and watched it pass at a quick shuffling walk, lifting and curling its trunk. The blindness of both elephant and rhino has never been sufficiently emphasized in books. Near camp was the bloody, broken skeleton of a young wart-hog boar, killed by a lion the previous night. There were a number of lions in the neighborhood, and they roared at intervals all night long.

Next morning, after Grogan and I had started from camp, when the sun had been up an hour, we heard one roar loudly less than a mile away. Running toward the place we tried to find the lion; but near by a small river ran through beds of reeds, and the fires had left many patches of tall, yellow, half-burned grass, so that it had ample cover, and our search was fruitless.

Near the pond were green parrots and brilliant wood hoopoos, rollers, and sunbirds; and buck of the ordinary kinds drank at it. A duiker which I shot for the table had been feeding on grass tips and on the stems and leaves of a small, low-growing plant.

After giving up the quest for the lion Grogan and I, with our gun-bearers, spent the day walking over the great dry flats of burnt grass land and sparse, withered forest. The heat grew intense as the sun rose higher and higher. Hour after hour we plodded on across vast level stretches, or up or down inclines so slight as hardly to be noticeable. The black dust of the burn rose in puffs beneath our feet; and now and then we saw dust devils, violent little whirlwinds, which darted right and left, raising to a height of many feet gray funnels of ashes and withered leaves. In places the coarse grass had half resisted the flames, and rose above our heads. Here and there bleached skulls of elephant and rhino, long dead, showed white against

the charred surface of the soil.   Everywhere, crossing and recrossing one another, were game trails,
some slightly marked, others broad and hard, and
beaten deep into the soil by the feet of the giant
creatures that had trodden them for ages.   The
elephants had been the chief road makers; but the
rhinoceros had travelled their trails, and also buffalo and buck.

There were elephant about, but only cows and
calves, and an occasional bull with very small tusks.
Of rhinoceros, all square-mouthed, we saw nine,
none carrying horns which made them worth shooting.   The first one I saw was in long grass.   My
attention was attracted by a row of white objects
moving at some speed through the top of the grass.
It took a second look before I made out that they
were cow herons perched on the back of a rhino.
This proved to be a bull, which joined a cow and a
calf.   None had decent horns, and we plodded on.
Soon we came to the trail of two others, and after
a couple of miles' tracking Kongoni pointed to two
gray bulks lying down under a tree.   I walked cautiously to within thirty yards.   They heard something, and up rose the two pig-like blinking creatures, who gradually became aware of my presence,
and retreated a few steps at a time, dull curiosity
continually overcoming an uneasiness which never
grew into fear. Tossing their stumpy-horned
heads, and twisting their tails into tight knots, they

ambled briskly from side to side, and were ten minutes in getting to a distance of a hundred yards.
Then our shenzi guide mentioned that there were
other rhinos close by, and we walked off to inspect
them.   In three hundred yards we came on them, a
cow and a well-grown calf. Sixty yards from them
was an ant-hill with little trees on it.   From this we
looked at them until some sound or other must have
made them uneasy, for up they got. The young
one seemed to have rather keener suspicions, although no more sense, than its mother, and after
a while grew so restless that it persuaded the cow
to go off with it.   But the still air gave no hint
of our whereabouts, and they walked straight toward us.   I did not wish to have to shoot one, and
so when they were within thirty yards we raised a
shout and away they cantered, heads tossing and
tails twisting.

Three hours later we saw another cow and calf.
By this time it was half-past three in the afternoon,
and the two animals had risen from their noonday
rest and were grazing busily, the great clumsy
heads sweeping the ground. Watching them forty
yards off it was some time before the cow raised
her head high enough for me to see that her horns
were not good.   Then they became suspicious, and
the cow stood motionless for several minutes, her
head held low. We moved quietly back, and at
last they either dimly saw us, or heard us, and stood

looking toward us, their big ears cocked forward. At this moment we stumbled on a rhino skull, bleached, but in such good preservation that we knew Heller would like it; and we loaded it on the porters that had followed us. All the time we were thus engaged the two rhinos, only a hundred yards off, were intently gazing in our direction, with foolish and bewildered solemnity; and there we left them, survivors from a long vanished world, standing alone in the parched desolation of the wilderness.

On another day Kermit saw ten rhino, none with more than ordinary horns. Five of them were in one party, and were much agitated by the approach of the men; they ran to and fro, their tails twisted into the usual pig-like curl, and from sheer nervous stupidity bade fair at one time to force the hunters to fire in self-defence. Finally, however, they all ran off. In the case of a couple of others a curious incident happened. When alarmed they failed to make out where the danger lay, and after running away a short distance they returned to a bush near by to look about. One remained standing, but the other deliberately sat down upon its haunches like a dog, staring ahead, Kermit meanwhile being busy with his camera. Two or three times I saw rhino, when roused from sleep, thus sit up on their haunches and look around before rising on all four legs; but this was the only time that any of us saw a rhino which was already standing assume such a position. No other kind of heavy game has this habit; and indeed, so far as I know, only one other hoofed animal, the white goat of the northern Rocky Mountains. In the case of the white goat, however, the attitude is far more often assumed, and in more extreme form; it is one of the characteristic traits of the queer goat-antelope, so many of whose ways and looks are peculiar to itself alone.

From the lily pond camp we went back to our camp outside Sururu's village. This was a very pleasant camp because while there, although the heat was intense in the daytime, the nights were cool and there were no mosquitoes. During our stay in the Lado it was generally necessary to wear head nets and gloves in the evenings and to go to bed at once after dinner, and then to lie under the mosquito bar with practically nothing on through the long hot night, sleeping or contentedly listening to the humming of the baffled myriads outside the net. At the Sururu camp, however, we could sit at a table in front of the tents, after supper—or dinner, whichever one chose to call it—and read by lamplight, in the still, cool, pleasant air; or walk up and down the hard, smooth elephant path which led by the tents, looking at the large red moon just risen, as it hung low over the horizon, or later, when, white and clear, it rode high in the heavens and flooded the land with its radiance.

There was a swamp close by, and we went through this the first afternoon in search of buffalo. We found plenty of sign; but the close-growing reeds were ten feet high, and even along the winding buffalo trails by which alone they could be penetrated it was impossible to see a dozen paces ahead. Inside the reeds it was nearly impossible to get to the buffalo, or at least to be sure to kill only a bull, which was all I wanted; and at this time when the moon was just past the full, these particular buffalo only came out into the open to feed at night, or very early in the morning and late in the evening. But Sururu said that there were other buffalo which lived away from the reeds, among the thorn-trees on the grassy flats and low hills; and he volunteered to bring me information about them on the morrow. Sure enough, shortly before eleven next morning, he turned up with the news that he had found a solitary bull only about five miles away. Grogan and I at once started back with him, accompanied by our gun-bearers. The country was just such as that in which we had hitherto found our rhinos; and there was fresh sign of rhino as well as buffalo. The thorny, scantily leaved trees were perhaps a little closer together than in most places, and there were a good many half-burned patches of tall grass. We passed a couple of ponds which must have been permanent, as water-lilies were growing in them; at one a buffalo had been drinking. It was half-past twelve when we reached the place where Sururu had seen the bull. We then advanced with the utmost caution as the wind was shifty, and although the cover was thin, it yet rendered it difficult to see a hundred yards in advance. At last we made out the bull, on his feet and feeding, although it was high noon. He was stern toward us, and while we were stealing toward him a puff of wind gave him our scent. At once he whipped around, gazed at us for a moment with outstretched head, and galloped off. I could not get a shot through the bushes, and after him we ran, Kongoni leading, with me at his heels. It was hot work running, for at this time the thermometer registered 102° in the shade. Fortunately the bull had little fear of man, and being curious, and rather truculent, he halted two or three times to look round. Finally, after we had run a mile and a half, he halted once too often, and I got a shot at him at eighty yards. The heavy bullet went home; I fired twice again as rapidly as possible, and the bull never moved from where he had stood. He was an old bull, as big as an East African buffalo bull; but his worn horns were smaller and rather different. This had rendered Kongoni uncertain whether he might not be a cow; and when we came up to the body he exclaimed with delight that it was a " duck "—Kongoni's invariable method of pronouncing " buck," the term he used to describe anything male, from a lion or an elephant to a bustard or a crocodile; "cow" being his expression for the female of these and all other creatures. As Gouvimali came running up to shake hands, his face wreathed in smiles, he exclaimed "G-o-o-d-e morning"; a phrase which he had picked up under the impression that it was a species of congratulation.

As always when I have killed buffalo I was struck by the massive bulk of the great bull as he lay in death, and by the evident and tremendous muscular power of his big-boned frame. He looked what he was, a formidable beast. Thirty porters had to be sent out to bring to camp the head, hide, and meat. We found, by the way, that his meat made excellent soup, his kidneys a good stew; while his tongue was delicious.

Next morning Kermit and I with the bulk of the safari walked back to our main camp, on the Nile, leaving Cuninghame and Heller where they were for a day, to take care of the buffalo skin. Each of us struck off across the country by himself, with his gun-bearers. After walking five or six miles I saw a big rhino three-quarters of a mile off. At this point the country was flat, the acacias very thinly scattered, and the grass completely burnt off, the green young blades sprouting; and there was no difficulty in making out, at the distance we did, the vast gray bulk of the rhino as it stood inertly under a tree. Drawing nearer we saw that it had a good horn, although not as good as Kermit's best; and approaching quietly to within forty yards I shot the beast.

At the main camp we found that Mearns had made a fine collection of birds in our absence; while Loring had taken a variety of excellent photos, of marabou, vultures, and kites feeding, and, above all, of a monitor lizard plundering the nest of a crocodile. The monitors were quite plentiful near camp. They are amphibious, carnivorous lizards of large size; they frequent the banks of the river, running well on the land, and sometimes even climbing trees, but taking to the water when alarmed. They feed on mice and rats, other lizards, eggs, and fish; the stomachs of those we caught generally contained fish, for they are expert swimmers. One morning Loring surprised a monitor which had just uncovered some crocodile eggs on a small sandy beach. The eggs, about thirty in number, were buried in rather shallow fashion, so that the monitor readily uncovered them. The monitor had one of the eggs transversely in its mouth, and, head erect, was marching off with it. As soon as it saw Loring it dropped the egg and scuttled into the reeds; in a few minutes it returned, took another egg, and walked off into the bushes, where it broke the shell, swallowed the yolk, and at once returned to the nest for another egg. Loring took me out to see the feat repeated, replenish-

ing the rifled nest with eggs taken from a crocodile
the Doctor had shot; and I was delighted to watch,
from our hiding place, the big lizard as he cautiously approached, seized an egg, and then retired
to cover with his booty. Kermit came on a monitor
plundering a crocodile's nest at the top of a steep
bank, while, funnily enough, a large crocodile lay
asleep at the foot of the bank only a few yards distant. As soon as it saw Kermit the monitor
dropped the egg it was carrying, ran up a slanting
tree which overhung the river, and dropped into the
water like a snake bird.

There was always something interesting to do or
to see at this camp. One afternoon I spent in the
boat. The papyrus along the channel rose like a
forest, thirty feet high, the close-growing stems
knit together by vines. As we drifted down, the
green wall was continually broken by openings,
through which side streams from the great river
rushed, swirling and winding, down narrow lanes
and under low archways, into the dim mysterious
heart of the vast reedbeds, where dwelt bird and
reptile and water beast. In a shallow bay we came
on two hippo cows with their calves, and a dozen
crocodiles. I shot one of the latter—as I always
do, when I get a chance—and it turned over and
over, lashing with its tail as it sank. A half-grown
hippo came up close by the boat and leaped nearly
clear of the water; and in another place I saw a

mother hippo swimming, with the young one resting half on its back.

Another day Kermit came on some black and white Colobus monkeys. Those we had shot east of the Rift Valley had long mantles, and more white than black in their coloring; west of the Rift Valley they had less white and less of the very long hair; and here on the Nile the change had gone still further in the same direction. On the west coast this kind of monkey is said to be entirely black. But we were not prepared for the complete change in habits. In East Africa the Colobus monkeys kept to the dense cool mountain forests, dwelt in the tops of the big trees, and rarely descended to the ground. Here, on the Nile, they lived in exactly such country as that affected by the smaller greenish-yellow monkeys, which we found along the Guaso Nyero for instance; country into which the East African Colobus never by any chance wandered. Moreover, instead of living in the tall timber, and never going on the ground except for a few yards, as in East Africa, here on the Nile they sought to escape danger by flight over the ground, in the scrub. Kermit found some in a grove of fairly big acacias, but they instantly dropped to the earth and galloped off among the dry, scattered bushes and small thorn-trees. Kermit also shot a twelve-foot crocodile in which he found the remains of a big heron.

One morning we saw from camp a herd of elephants in a piece of unburned swamp. It was a mile and a half away in a straight line, although we had to walk three miles to get there. There were between forty and fifty of them, a few big cows with calves, the rest half-grown and three-quarters-grown animals. Over a hundred white herons accompanied them. From an ant-hill to leeward we watched them standing by a mud hole in the swamp; evidently they now and then got a whiff from our camp, for they were continually lifting and curling their trunks. To see if by any chance there was a bull among them we moved them out of the swamp by shouting; the wind blew hard and as they moved away evidently smelled the camp strongly, for all their trunks went into the air; and off they went at a rapid pace, half of the herons riding on them, while the others hovered over and alongside, like a white cloud. Two days later the same herd again made its appearance.

Spur-winged plover were nesting near camp, and evidently distrusted the carrion feeders, for they attacked and drove off every kite or vulture that crossed what they considered the prohibited zone. They also harassed the marabous, but with more circumspection; for the big storks were short-tempered, and rather daunted the spurwings by the way they opened their enormous beaks at them. The fish eagles fed exclusively on fish, as far as we could tell, and there were piles of fish bones and heads

under their favorite perches. Once I saw one
plunge into the water, but it failed to catch anything. Another time, suddenly, and seemingly in
mere mischief, one attacked a purple heron which
was standing on a mud bank. The eagle swooped
down from a tree and knocked over the heron; and
when the astonished heron struggled to its feet and
attempted to fly off, the eagle made another swoop
and this time knocked it into the water. The heron
then edged into the papyrus, and the eagle paid it
no further attention.

In this camp we had to watch the white ants,
which strove to devour everything. They are nocturnal, and work in the daytime only under the tunnels of earth which they build over the surface of
the box, or whatever else it is, that they are devouring; they eat out everything, leaving this outside
shell of earth. We also saw a long column of the
dreaded driver ants. These are carnivorous; I
have seen both red and black species; they kill every
living thing in their path, and I have known them
at night drive all the men in a camp out into the
jungle to fight the mosquitoes unprotected until daylight. On another occasion, where a steamboat
was moored close to a bank, an ant column entered
the boat after nightfall, and kept complete posses-
sion of it for forty-eight hours. Fires, and boiling
water, offer the only effectual means of resistance.
The bees are at times as formidable; when their

nests are disturbed they will attack every one in
sight, driving all the crew of a boat overboard or
scattering a safari, and not infrequently killing men
and beasts of burden that are unable to reach some
place of safety.

The last afternoon, when the flotilla had called
to take us farther on our journey, we shot about
a dozen buck, to give the porters and sailors a feast,
which they had amply earned. All the meat did
not get into camp until after dark—one of the
sailors, unfortunately, falling out of a tree and
breaking his neck on the way in—and it was picturesque to see the rows of big antelope—hartebeest, kob, waterbuck—stretched in front of the
flaring fires, and the dark faces of the waiting
negroes, each deputed by some particular group of
gun-bearers, porters, or sailors to bring back its
share.

Next morning we embarked, and steamed and
drifted down the Nile; ourselves, our men, our belongings, and the spoils of the chase all huddled together under the torrid sun. Two or three times
we grounded on sand bars; but no damage was
done, and in twenty-six hours we reached Nimule.
We were no longer in healthy East Africa. Kermit and I had been in robust health throughout the
time we were in Uganda and the Lado; but all the
other white men of the party had suffered more or
less from dysentery, fever, and sun prostration

while in the Lado; some of the gun-bearers had been down with fever, one of them dying while we were in Uganda; and four of the porters who had marched from Koba to Nimule had died of dysentery—they were burying one when we arrived.

At Nimule we were as usual greeted with hospitable heartiness by the English officials, as well as by two or three elephant hunters. One of the latter, three days before, had been charged by an unwounded bull elephant. He fired both barrels into it as it came on, but it charged home, knocked him down, killed his gun-bearer, and made its escape into the forest. In the forlorn little graveyard at the station were the graves of two white men who had been killed by elephants. One of them, named Stoney, had been caught by a wounded bull, which stamped the life out of him and then literally dismembered him, tearing his arms from his body. In the African wilderness, when a man dies, his companion usually brings in something to show that he is dead, or some remnant of whatever it is that has destroyed him; the sailors whose companion was killed by falling out of the tree near our Lado camp, for instance, brought in the dead branch which had broken under his weight; and Stoney's gun-bearer marched back to Nimule carrying an arm of his dead master, and deposited his grewsome burden in the office of the district commissioner.

CHAPTER XV

DOWN THE NILE; THE GIANT ELAND

WE spent two or three days in Nimule, getting everything ready for the march north to Gondokoro.

By this time Kermit and I had grown really attached to our personal followers, whose devotion to us, and whose zeal for our success and welfare and comfort, had many times been made rather touchingly manifest; even their shortcomings were merely those of big, naughty children, and though they occasionally needed discipline, this was rare, whereas the amusement they gave us was unending. When we reached Nimule we were greeted with enthusiasm by Magi, Kermit's Kikuyu sais, who had been in charge of the mules which we did not take into the Lado. Magi was now acting as sais for me as well as for Kermit; and he came to Kermit to discuss the new dual relationship. " Now I am the sais of the Bwana Makuba, as well as of you, the Bwana Merodadi " (the Dandy Master, as for some inscrutable reason all the men now called Kermit) ; " well, then, you'll both have to take care of me," concluded the *rusé* Magi.

Whenever we reached one of these little stations

where there was an Indian trading store, we would
see that those of our followers who had been specially devoted to us—and this always included all
our immediate attendants—had a chance to obtain
the few little comforts and luxuries, tea, sugar, or
tobacco, for instance, which meant so much to
them. Usually Kermit would take them to the
store himself, for they were less wily than the Indian trader, and, moreover, in the excitement of
shopping occasionally purchased something for
which they really had no use. Kermit would march
his tail of followers into the store, give them time
to look around, and then make the first purchase
for the man who had the least coming to him; this
to avoid heartburnings, as the man was invariably
too much interested in what he had received to
scrutinize closely what the others were getting.
The purchase might be an article of clothing or a
knife, but usually took the form of tobacco, sugar,
and tea; in tobacco the man was offered his choice
between quality and quantity, that is, either a mod-
erate quantity of good cigarettes or a large amount
of trade tobacco. Funny little Juma Yohari, for
instance, one of Kermit's gun-bearers, usually went
in for quality, whereas his colleague Kassitura pre-
ferred quantity. Juma was a Zanzibari, a wiry
merry little grig of a man, loyal, hardworking,
fearless; Kassitura a huge Basoga negro, of guile-
less honesty and good faith, incapable of neglect-

ing his duty. Juma was rather the wit of the gun-bearers' mess, and Kassitura the musician, having a little native harp on which for hours at a time he would strum queer little melancholy tunes, to which he hummed an accompaniment in undertone.

All the natives we met, and the men in our employ, were fond of singing, sometimes simply improvised chants, sometimes sentences of three or four words repeated over and over again. The Uganda porters who were with us after we left Kampalla did not sing nearly as freely as our East African safari, although they depended much on the man who beat the drum, at the head of the marching column. The East African porters did every kind of work to an accompaniment of chanting. When for instance, after camp was pitched, a detail of men was sent out for wood—the " wood safari "—the men as they came back to camp with their loads never did anything so commonplace as each merely to deposit his burden at the proper spot. The first comers waited in the middle of the camp until all had assembled, and then marched in order to where the fire was to be made, all singing vigorously and stepping in time together. The leader, or shanty man, would call out " Kooni " (wood) ; and all the others would hum in unison " Kooni telli " (plenty of wood). " Kooni," again came the shout of the shanty man; and the answer would be " Kooni." " Kooni," from the shanty man; and this time all the rest would simply utter a long-drawn " Hum-m-m." " Kooni," again; and the answer would be " Kooni telli," with strong emphasis on the " telli." Then, if they saw me, the shanty man might vary by shouting that the wood was for the Bwana Makuba; and so it would continue until the loads were thrown down.

Often a man would improvise a song regarding any small incident which had just happened to him, or a thought which had occurred to him. Drifting down the Nile to Nimule Kermit and the three naturalists and sixty porters were packed in sardine fashion on one of the sail-boats. At nightfall one of the sailors, the helmsman, a Swahili from Mombasa, began to plan how he would write a letter to his people in Mombasa and give it to another sailor, a friend of his, who intended shortly to return thither. He crooned to himself as he crouched by the tiller, steering the boat, and gradually, as the moon shone on the swift, quiet water of the river, his crooning turned into a regular song. His voice was beautiful, and there was a wild meaningless refrain to each verse; the verses reciting how he intended to write this letter to those whom he had not seen for two years; how a friend would take it to them, so that the letter would be in Mombasa; but he, the man who wrote it, would for two years more be in the far-off wilderness.

On February 17th the long line of our laden

safari left Nimule on its ten days' march to Gondokoro. We went through a barren and thirsty land.
Our first camp was by a shallow, running river,
with a shaded pool in which we bathed. After that
we never came on running water, merely on dry
watercourses with pools here and there, some of the
pools being crowded with fish. Tall half-burnt
grass, and scattered, well-nigh leafless thorn scrub
covered the monotonous landscape, although we
could generally find some fairly leafy tree near
which to pitch the tents. The heat was great;
more than once the thermometer at noon rose to
112° in the shade—not real shade, however, but in
a stifling tent, or beneath a tree the foliage of which
let through at least a third of the sun rays. The
fiery heat of the ground so burnt and crippled the
feet of the porters that we had to start each day's
march very early.

At quarter of three in the morning the whistle
blew; we dressed and breakfasted while the tents
were taken down and the loads adjusted. Then off
we strode, through the hot starlit night, our backs
to the Southern Cross and our faces toward the
Great Bear; for we were marching northward and
homeward. The drum throbbed and muttered as
we walked, on and on, along the dim trail. At last
the stars began to pale, the gray east changed to
opal and amber and amethyst, the red splendor of
the sunrise flooded the world, and to the heat of

the night succeeded the more merciless heat of the
day. Higher and higher rose the sun. The sweat
streamed down our faces, and the bodies of the
black men glistened like oiled iron. We might
halt early in the forenoon, or we might have to
march until noon, according to the distance from
waterhole to waterhole.

Occasionally in the afternoons, and once when
we halted for a day to rest the porters, Kermit and
I would kill buck for the table—hartebeest, reedbuck, and oribi. I also killed a big red ground
monkey, with baboon-like habits; we had first seen
the species on the Uasin Gishu, and had tried in
vain to get it, for it was wary, never sought safety
in trees, and showed both speed and endurance in
running. Kermit killed a bull and a cow roan
antelope. These so-called horse antelope are fine
beasts, light roan in color, with high withers, rather
short curved horns, huge ears, and bold face markings. Usually we found them shy, but occasionally
very tame. They are the most truculent and dangerous of all antelope; this bull, when seemingly
on the point of death, rose like a flash when Kermit approached and charged him full tilt; Kermit
had to fire from the hip, luckily breaking the animal's neck.

On the same day Loring had an interesting experience with one of the small cormorants so common in this region. Previously, while visiting the

rapids of the Nile below Nimule, I had been struck by the comparative unwariness of these birds, one of them repeatedly landing on a rock a few yards away from me, and thence slipping unconcernedly into the swift water—and, by the way, it was entirely at home in the boiling rapids. But the conduct of Loring's bird was wholly exceptional. He was taking a swim in a pool when the bird lit beside him. It paid no more heed to the naked white man than it would have paid to a hippo, and although it would not allow itself to be actually touched, it merely moved a few feet out of his way when he approached it. Moreover it seemed to be on the lookout for enemies in the air, not in the water. It was continually glancing upward, and when a big hawk appeared, followed its movements with close attention. It stayed in and about the pool for many minutes before flying off. I suppose that certain eagles and hawks prey on cormorants; but I should also be inclined to think that crocodiles at least occasionally prey on them.

The very most attractive birds we met in middle Africa and along the Nile were the brave, cheery little wagtails. They wear trim black and white suits, when on the ground they walk instead of hopping, they have a merry, pleasing song, and they are as confiding and fearless as they are pretty. The natives never molest them, for they figure to advantage in the folklore of the various tribes.

They came round us at every halting place, entering the rest-houses in Uganda and sometimes even our tents, coming up within a few feet of us as we lay under trees, and boarding our boats on the Nile; and they would stroll about camp quite unconcernedly, in pairs, the male stopping every now and then to sing. Except the whiskey jacks and Hudsonian chickadees of the North Woods I never saw such tame little birds.

At Gondokoro we met the boat which the Sirdar, Major General Sir Reginald Wingate, had sent to take us down the Nile to Khartoum; for he, and all the Soudan officials—including especially Colonel Asser, Colonel Owen, Slatin Pasha, and Butler Bey—treated us with a courtesy for which I cannot too strongly express my appreciation. In the boat we were to have met an old friend and fellow countryman, Leigh Hunt; to our great regret he could not meet us, but he insisted on treating us as his guests, and on our way down the Nile we felt as if we were on the most comfortable kind of yachting trip; and everything was done for us by Captain Middleton, the Scotch engineer in charge.

Nor was our debt only to British officials and to American friends. At Gondokoro I was met by M. Ranquet, the Belgian Commandant of the Lado district and, both he and M. Massart, the Chef de Poste at Redjaf, were kindness itself, and aided us in every way.

From Gondokoro Kermit and I crossed to Redjaf, for an eight days' trip after the largest and handsomest, and one of the least known, of African antelopes, the giant eland. We went alone, because all the other white men of the party were down with dysentery or fever. We had with us sixty Uganda porters and a dozen mules sent us by the Sirdar, together with a couple of our little riding mules, which we used now and then for a couple of hours on safari, or in getting to the actual hunting ground. As always when only one or two of us went, or when the safari was short, we travelled light, with no dining-tent and nothing unnecessary in the way of baggage; the only impedimenta which we could not minimize were those connected with the preservation of the skins of the big animals, which, of course, were throughout our whole trip what necessitated the use of the bulk of the porters and other means of transportation employed.

From the neat little station of Redjaf, lying at the foot of the bold pyramidal hill of the same name, we marched two days west, stopping short of the river Koda, where we knew the game drank. Now and then we came on flower-bearing bushes, of marvellously sweet scent, like gardenias. It was the height of the dry season; the country was covered with coarse grass and a scrub growth of nearly leafless thorn-trees, usually growing rather wide apart, occasionally close enough together to look almost like a forest. There were a few palms, euphorbias, and very rarely scattered clumps of withered bamboo, and also bright green trees with rather thick leaves and bean pods, on which we afterward found that the eland fed.

The streams we crossed were dry torrent beds, sandy or rocky; in two or three of them were pools of stagnant water, while better water could be obtained by digging in the sand alongside. A couple of hours after reaching each camp everything was in order, and Ali had made a fire of some slivers of wood and boiled our tea; and our two meals, breakfast and dinner, were taken at a table in the open, under a tree.

We had with us seven black soldiers of the Belgian native troops, under a corporal; they came from every quarter of the Congo, but several of them could speak Swahili, the lingua franca of middle Africa, and so Kermit could talk freely with them. These black soldiers behaved excellently, and the attitude, both toward them and toward us, of the natives in the various villages we came across was totally incompatible with any theory that these natives had suffered from any maltreatment; they behaved just like the natives in British territory. There had to be the usual parleys with the chiefs of the villages to obtain food for the soldiers (we carried the posho for our own men), and ample payment was given for what was brought in; and in the only two cases where the natives thought themselves aggrieved by the soldiers, they at once brought the matter before us. One soldier had taken a big gourd of water when very thirsty; another, a knife from a man who was misbehaving himself. On careful inquiry, and delivering judgment in the spirit of Solomon, we decided that both soldiers had been justified by the provocation received; but as we were dealing with the misdeeds of mere big children, we gave the gourd back to its owner with a reprimand for having refused the water, and permitting the owner of the knife, whose offence had been more serious, to ransom his property by bringing in a chicken to the soldier who had it.

The natives lived in the usual pointed beehive huts in unfenced villages, with shambas lying about them; and they kept goats, chickens, and a few cattle. Our permanent camp was near such a village. It was interesting to pass through it at sunrise or sunset, when starting on or returning from a hunt. The hard, bare earth was swept clean. The doors in the low mud walls of the huts were but a couple of feet high and had to be entered on allfours; black pickaninnies scuttled into them in wild alarm as we passed. Skinny, haggard old men and women, almost naked, sat by the fires smoking long pipes; the younger men and women laughed and jested as they moved among the houses. One day, in the course of a long and fruitless hunt, we stopped to rest near such a village, at about two in the afternoon, having been walking hard since dawn. We—I and my gun-bearer, a black askari, a couple of porters, and a native guide—sat down under a big tree a hundred yards from the village. Soon the chief and several of his people came out to see us. The chief proudly wore a dirty jersey and a pair of drawers; a follower carried his spear and the little wooden stool of dignity on which he sat. There were a couple of warriors with him, one a man in a bark apron with an old breech-loading rifle, the other a stark-naked savage—not a rag on him—with a bow and arrows; a very powerfully built man with a ferocious and sinister face. Two women bore on their heads, as gifts for us, one a large earthenware jar of water, the other a basket of groundnuts. They were tall and well-shaped. One as her sole clothing wore a beaded cord around her waist, and a breechclout consisting of half a dozen long, thickly leaved, fresh sprays of a kind of vine; the other, instead of this vine breechclout, had hanging from her girdle in front a cluster of long-stemmed green leaves, and behind a bundle of long strings, carried like a horse's tail.

The weather was very hot, and the country, far and wide, was a waste of barren desolation. The flats of endless thorn scrub were broken by occasional low and rugged hills, and in the empty watercourses the pools were many miles apart. Yet there was a good deal of game. We saw buffalo, giraffe, and elephant; and on our way back to camp in the evenings we now and then killed a roan, hartebeest, or oribi. But the game we sought was the giant eland, and we never fired when there was the slightest chance of disturbing our quarry. They usually went in herds, but there were solitary bulls. We found that they drank at some pool in the Koda before dawn and then travelled many miles back into the parched interior, feeding as they went; and, after lying up for some hours about mid-day, again moved slowly off, feeding. They did not graze, but fed on the green leaves, and the bean pods of the tree of which I have already spoken and of another tree. One of their marked habits—shared in some degree by their forest cousin, the bongo—was breaking the higher branches with their horns, to get at the leaves; they thus broke branches two or three inches in diameter and seven or eight feet from the ground, the crash of the branches being a sound for which we continually listened as we followed the tracks of a herd. They were far more wary than roan, or hartebeest, or any of the other buck, and the country was such that it was difficult to see more than a couple of hundred yards ahead.

It took me three hard days' work before I got

my eland. Each day I left camp before sunrise and on the first two I came back after dark, while it always happened that at noon we were on a trail and could not stop. We would walk until we found tracks made that morning, and then the gun-bearers and the native guide would slowly follow them, hour after hour, under the burning sun. On the first day we saw nothing; on the next we got a moment's glimpse of an eland, trotting at the usual slashing gait; I had no chance to fire. By mid-afternoon on each day it was evident that further following of the trail we were on was useless, and we plodded campward, tired and thirsty. Gradually the merciless glare softened; then the sun sank crimson behind a chain of fantastically carved mountains in the distance; and the hues of the after-glow were drowned in the silver light of the moon, which was nearing the full.

On the third day we found the spoor of a single bull by eight o'clock. Hour after hour went by while the gun-bearers, even more eager than weary, puzzled out the trail. At half past twelve we knew we were close on the beast, and immediately afterward caught a glimpse of it. Taking advantage of every patch of cover I crawled toward it on all-fours, my rifle too hot for me to touch the barrel, while the blistering heat of the baked ground hurt my hands. At a little over a hundred yards I knelt and aimed at the noble beast; I could now plainly

see his huge bulk and great, massive horns, as he
stood under a tree. The pointed bullet from the
little Springfield hit a trifle too far back and up,
but made such a rip that he never got ten yards
from where he was standing; and great was my
pride as I stood over him, and examined his horns,
twisted almost like a koodoo's, and admired his
size, his finely modelled head and legs, and the
beauty of his coat.

Meanwhile, Kermit had killed two eland, a cow
on the first day, and on the second a bull even better than, although not quite so old as, mine.
Kermit could see game, and follow tracks, almost
as well as his gun-bearers, and in a long chase could
outrun them. On each day he struck the track of
a herd of eland, and after a while left his gun-
bearers and porters, and ran along the trail accompanied only by a native guide. The cow was killed
at two hundred yards with a shot from his Winchester. The bull yielded more excitement. He
was in a herd of about forty which Kermit had
followed for over five hours, toward the last accompanied only by the wild native; at one point the
eland had come upon a small party of elephant, and
trotted off at right angles to their former course
—Kermit following them after he had satisfied
himself that the elephants were cows and half-
grown animals. When he finally overtook the
eland, during the torrid heat of the early afternoon,

they were all lying down, in a place where the trees grew rather more thickly than usual.

Stalking as close as he dared he selected a big animal which he hoped was a bull, and fired three shots into it; however, it ran, and he then saw that it was a cow. As the rest of the herd jumped up he saw the form of the master bull looming above the others. They crossed his front at a slashing trot, the cows clustered round the great bull; but just as they came to a little opening, they opened somewhat, giving him a clear shot. Down went the bull on his head, rose, received another bullet, and came to a stand-still. This was the last bullet from the magazine; and now the mechanism of the rifle refused to work or to throw the empty shell out of the chamber. The faithful Winchester, which Kermit had used steadily for ten months, on foot and on horseback, which had suffered every kind of hard treatment and had killed every kind of game, without once failing, had at last given way under the strain. While Kermit was working desperately at the mechanism, the bull, which was standing looking at him within fifty yards, gradually recovered, moved off step by step, and broke into a slow trot. After it went Kermit as hard as he could go, still fussing with the rifle, which he finally opened, and refilled with five cartridges. Kermit could just about keep the eland in sight, running as hard as he was able; after a mile

or two it lay down, but rose as he came near, and
went off again, while he was so blown that though,
with four shots, he hit it twice he failed to kill it.
He now had but one bullet left, after which he
knew that the rifle would jam again; and it was
accordingly necessary to kill outright with the next
shot. He was just able to keep close to the bull
for a half mile, then it halted; and he killed it.
Leaving the shenzi by the carcass, he went off to
see about the wounded cow, but after an hour was
forced to give up the chase and return, so as to be
sure to save the bull's skin. The gun-bearers, and
another shenzi had by this time reached the dead
eland; they had only Kermit's canteen of water
among them. One of the shenzis was at once sent
to camp to bring back twenty porters, with rope,
and plenty of water; and, with parched mouths,
Kermit and the gun-bearers began to take off the
thick hide of the dead bull. Four hours later the
porters appeared with the ropes and the water; the
thirsty men drank gallons; the porters were loaded
with the hide, head, and meat; and they marched
back to camp by moonlight.

It was no easy job, in that climate, to care for
and save the three big skins; but we did it. On the
trip we had taken, besides our gun-bearers and tent
boys, Magi, the sais, and two of our East African
skinners, Kiboko and Merefu; they formed in the
safari a kind of chief-petty-officer's mess, so to

speak. They were all devoted to their duties, and they worked equally hard whether hunting or caring for the skins; the day Kermit killed his bull he and the gun-bearers and skinners, with Magi as a volunteer, worked until midnight at the hide. But they had any amount of meat, and we shared our sugar and tea with them. On the last evening there was nothing to do, and they sat in the brilliant moonlight in front of their tents, while Kassitura played his odd little harp. Kermit and I strolled over to listen; and at once Kassitura began to improvise a chant in my honor, reciting how the Bwana Makuba had come, how he was far from his own country, how he had just killed a giant eland, and so on and so on. Meanwhile, over many little fires strips of meat were drying on scaffolds of bent branches, and askaris and porters were gathered in groups, chatting and singing; while the mighty tree near which our tents were pitched cast a black shadow on the silver plain. Then the shenzis who had helped us came to receive their reward, and their hearts were gladdened with red cloth and salt, and for those whose services had been greatest there were special treasures in the shape of three green and white umbrellas. It was a pleasant ending to a successful hunt.

On our return to Gondokoro we found Cuninghame all right, although he had been obliged single-handed to do the work of getting our porters safely started on their return march to Kampalla, as well as getting all the skins and skeletons properly packed for shipment. Heller had also recovered, and had gone on a short trip during which he trapped a leopard and a serval at the same carcass, the leopard killing the serval. Dr. Mearns and Loring were both seriously sick; so was the district commissioner, kind Mr. Haddon. One day a German missionary dined with us; the next he was dead, of black water fever. An English sportsman whom we had met at Nimule had been brought in so sick that he was at death's door; Dr. Mearns took care of him, badly off though he himself was. We had brought with us a case of champagne for just such emergencies; this was the first time that we made use of it.

On the last day of February we started down the Nile, slipping easily along on the rapid current, which wound and twisted through stretches of reeds and marsh grass and papyrus. We halted at the attractive station of Lado for a good-bye breakfast with our kind Belgian friends, and that evening we dined at Mongalla with Colonel Owen, the Chief of the southernmost section of the Soudan. I was greatly interested in the Egyptian and Soudanese soldiers, and their service medals. Many of these medals showed that their owners had been in a dozen campaigns; some of the native officers and men (and also the Reis or native captain of

Mr. Roosevelt and Kermit Roosevelt with giant eland horns.

our boat, by the way) had served in the battles
which broke forever the Mahdi's cruel power; two
or three had been with Gordon. They were a fine-
looking set; and their obvious self-respect was a
good thing to see. That same afternoon I wit-
nessed a native dance, and was struck by the lack
of men of middle age; in all the tribes who were
touched by the blight of the Mahdist tyranny, with
its accompaniments of unspeakable horror, suffered
such slaughter of the then young men that the loss
has left its mark to this day. The English when
they destroyed Mahdism rendered a great service to
humanity; and their rule in the Soudan has been
astoundingly successful and beneficial from every
stand-point.*

We steamed onward down the Nile; sometimes
tying up to the bank at nightfall, sometimes steaming steadily through the night. We reached the
Sud, the vast papyrus marsh once so formidable a
barrier to all who would journey along the river;
and sunrise and sunset were beautiful over the endless, melancholy stretches of water reeds. In the
Sud the only tree seen was the water-loving am-
batch, light as cork. Occasionally we saw hippos
and crocodiles and a few water birds; and now and

* The despotism of Mahdist rule was so revolting, so vilely
cruel and hideous, that the worst despotism by men of European blood in recent times seems a model of humanity by
comparison; and yet there were nominal "anti-militarists"
and self-styled "apostles of peace" who did their feeble best
to prevent the destruction of this infamy.

then passed native villages, the tall, lean men and women stark naked, and their bodies daubed with mud, grease, and ashes to keep off the mosquitoes.

On March 4th we were steaming slowly along the reedy, water-soaked shores of Lake No, keeping a sharp lookout for the white-eared kob and especially for the handsome saddle-marked lechwe kob—which has been cursed with the foolishly inappropriate name of "Mrs. Gray's waterbuck."

Early in the morning we saw a herd of these saddle-marked lechwe in the long marsh grass and pushed the steamer's nose as near to the shore as possible. Then Cuninghame, keen-eyed Kongoni, and I started for what proved to be a five hours' tramp. The walking was hard; sometimes we were on dry land, but more often in water up to our ankles or knees, and occasionally floundering and wallowing up to our hips through stretches of reeds, water-lilies, green water, and foul black slime. Yet there were ant-hills in the marsh. Once or twice we caught a glimpse of the game in small patches of open ground covered with short grass; but almost always they kept to the high grass and reeds. There were with the herd two very old bucks, with a white saddle-shaped patch on the withers, the white extending up the back of the neck to the head; a mark of their being in full maturity, or past it, for on some of the males, at least, this coloration only begins to appear when they seem already to have attained their growth of horn and body, their teeth showing them to be five or six years old, while they are obviously in the prime of vigor and breeding capacity. Unfortunately, in the long grass it was impossible to single out these old bucks. Marking as well as we could the general direction of the herd we would steal toward it until we thought we were in the neighborhood, and then cautiously climb an ant-hill to look about. Nothing would be in sight. We would scan the ground in every direction; still nothing. Suddenly a dozen heads would pop up, just above the grass, two or three hundred yards off, and after a steady gaze would disappear; and some minutes later would again appear a quarter of a mile farther on. Usually they skulked off at a trot or canter, necks stretched level with the back; for they were great skulkers, and trusted chiefly to escaping observation and stealing away from danger unperceived. But occasionally they would break into a gallop, making lofty bounds, clear above the tops of the grass; and then they might go a long way before stopping. I never saw them leap on the ant-hills to look about, as is the custom of the common or Uganda kob. They were rather noisy; we heard them grunting continually, both when they were grazing and when they saw us.

At last, from an ant-hill, I saw dim outlines of two or three animals moving past a little over a hundred yards ahead. There was nothing to shoot at; but a moment afterward I saw a pair of horns through the grass tops, in such a position that it was evident the owner was looking at me. I guessed that he had been moving in the direction in which the others had gone, and I guessed at the position of the shoulder, and fired. The horns disappeared. Then I caught a glimpse, first of a doe, next of a buck, in full flight, each occasionally appearing for an instant in a great bound over the grass tops. I had no idea whether or not I had hit my buck; so Cuninghame stayed on the ant-heap to guide us, while Kongoni and I plunged into the long grass, as high as our heads. Sure enough, there was the buck, a youngish one, about four years old; my bullet had gone true. While we were looking at him we suddenly caught a momentary glimpse of two more of the herd rushing off to our right, and we heard another grunting and sneaking away, invisible, thirty yards or so to our left.

Half an hour afterward I shot another buck, at over a hundred and fifty yards, after much the same kind of experience. At this one I fired four times, hitting him with three bullets; three of the shots were taken when I could only see his horns and had to guess at the position of the body. This was a very big buck, with horns over twenty-nine inches long, but the saddle mark was yellow, with many whitish hairs, showing that he was about to assume the white saddle of advanced maturity. His stomach was full of the fine swamp grass.

These handsome antelopes come next to the situtunga as lovers of water and dwellers in the marshes. They are far more properly to be called "waterbuck" than are the present proprietors of that name, which, like the ordinary kob, though liking to be near streams, spend most of their time on dry plains and hill-sides. This saddle-marked antelope of the swamps has the hoofs very long and the whole foot flexible and spreading, so as to help it in passing over wet ground and soft mud; the pasterns behind are largely bare of hair. It seems to be much like the lechwe, a less handsome, but equally water-loving, antelope of southern Africa, which is put in the same genus with the waterbuck and kob.

That afternoon Dr. Mearns killed with his Winchester 30–40, on the wing, one of the most interesting birds we obtained on our whole trip, the whale-billed stork. It was an old male and its gizzard was full of the remains of small fish. The whalebill is a large wader, blackish-gray in color, slightly crested, with big feet and a huge, swollen bill; a queer-looking bird, with no near kinsfolk, and so interesting that nothing would have persuaded me to try to kill more than the four actually needed for the *public* (not private) museum to which our collections were going. It is of solitary habits and is found only in certain vast, lonely marshes of tropical Africa, where it is conspicuous by its extraordinary bill, dark coloration, and sluggishness of conduct, hunting sedately in the muddy shallows, or standing motionless for hours, surrounded by reed-beds or by long reaches of quaking and treacherous ooze.

Next morning while at breakfast on the breezy deck we spied another herd of the saddle-marked lechwe, in the marsh alongside; and Kermit landed and killed one, after deep wading, up to his chin in some places, and much hard work in the rank grass. This buck was interesting when compared with the two I had shot. He was apparently a little older than either, but not aged; on the contrary, in his prime, and fat. He had the white saddle-like mark on the withers, and the white back of the neck, well developed. Yet he was smaller than either of mine, and the horns much smaller; indeed they were seven inches shorter than my longest ones. It looks as if, in some animals at least, the full size of body and horns were reached before the white saddle markings are acquired. The horns of these saddle-mark lechwes are, relatively to the body, far longer and finer than in other species of the genus; just as is the case with the big East African gazelle when compared with other gazelles.

That afternoon, near the mouth of the Rohr, which runs into the Bahr el Ghazal, I landed and shot a good buck, of the Vaughn's kob; which is perhaps merely a subspecies of the white-eared kob. It is a handsome animal, handsomer than its close kinsman, the common or Uganda kob; although much less so than its associate, the saddle-marked lechwe. Its hooves are like those of the ordinary kobs and waterbucks, not in the least like those of the saddleback; so that although the does are colored alike, there is no chance of mistaking any lechwe doe for any true kob doe. We found these kobs in much drier ground than the saddlebacks, and therefore they were easier to get at. The one I shot was an old ram, accompanied by several ewes. We saw them from the boat, but they ran. Cuninghame and I, with Kongoni and Gouvimali, hunted for them in vain for a couple of hours. Then we met a savage, a very tall, lean Nuer. He was clad in a fawn skin, and carried two spears, one with a bright, sharp, broad-bladed head, the other narrow-headed with villainous barbs. His hair, much longer than that of a west coast negro, was tied back. As we came toward him he stood on one leg, with the other foot resting against it, and, raising his hand, with fingers extended, he motioned to us with what in civilized regions would be regarded as a gesture bidding us halt. But he meant it as a friendly greeting, and solemnly shook hands with all four of us, including the gun-bearers. By signs we made him understand that we were after game;

so was he; and he led us to the little herd of koɓ.
Kongoni, as usual, saw them before any one else.
From an ant-hill I could make out the buck's horns
and his white ears, which he was continually flapping at the biting flies that worried him; when he
lowered his head I could see nothing. Finally, he
looked fixedly at us; he was a hundred and fifty
yards off and I had to shoot standing on the peak of
the ant-heap, and aim through the grass, guessing
where his hidden body might be; and I missed him.
At the shot the does went off to the left, but he ran
to the right, once or twice leaping high; and when
he halted, at less than two hundred yards, although
I could still only see his horns, I knew where his
body was; and this time I killed him. We gave
most of the meat to the Nuer. He was an utterly
wild savage, and when Cuninghame suddenly lit a
match he was so frightened that it was all we could
do to keep him from bolting.

Kermit went on to try for a doe, but had bad
luck, twice killing a spike buck by mistake, and did
not get back to the boat until long after dark.

The following day we were in the mouth of the
Bahr el Ghazal. It ran sluggishly through immense marshes, which stretched back from the river
for miles on either hand, broken here and there by
flats of slightly higher land with thorn-trees. The
whale-billed storks were fairly common, and were
very conspicuous as they stood on the quaking sur-

face of the marsh, supported by their long-toed feet. After several fruitless stalks and much following through the thick marsh grass, sometimes up to our necks in water, I killed one with the Springfield at a distance of one hundred and thirty yards, and Kermit, after missing one standing, cut it down as it rose with his Winchester 30–40. These whale-bills had in their gizzards not only small fish but quite a number of the green blades of the marsh grass. The Arabs call them the "Father of the Shoe," and Europeans call them shoebills as well as whalebills. The Bahr el Ghazal was alive with water-fowl, saddle-bill storks, sacred and purple ibis, many kinds of herons, cormorants, plover, and pretty tree ducks which twittered instead of quacking. There were sweet-scented lotus water-lilies in the ponds. A party of waterbuck cows and calves let the steamer pass within fifty yards without running.

We went back to Lake No, where we met another steamer, with aboard it M. Solvé, a Belgian sportsman, a very successful hunter, whom we had already met at Lado; with him were his wife, his sister, and his brother-in-law, both of the last being as ardent in the chase, especially of dangerous game, as he was. His party had killed two whale-bills, one for the British Museum and one for the Congo Museum. They were a male and female who were near their nest, which contained two downy young; these were on M. Solvé's boat, where we saw them. The nest was right on the marsh water; the birds had bent the long blades of marsh grass into an interlacing foundation, and on this had piled grass which they had cut with their beaks. These beaks can give a formidable bite, by the way, as one of our sailors found to his cost when he rashly tried to pick up a wounded bird.

I was anxious to get a ewe of the saddle-back lechwe for the museum, and landed in the late afternoon, on seeing a herd. The swamp was so deep that it took an hour's very hard and fatiguing wading, forcing ourselves through the rank grass up to our shoulders in water before we got near them. The herd numbered about forty individuals; their broad trail showed where they had come through the swamp, and even through a papyrus bed; but we found them grazing on merely moist ground, where there were ant-hills in the long grass. As I crept up they saw me and greeted me with a chorus of croaking grunts; they are a very noisy buck. I shot a ewe, and away rushed the herd through the long grass, making a noise which could have been heard nearly a mile off, and splashing and bounding through the shallow lagoons; they halted, and again began grunting; and then off they rushed once more. The doe's stomach was filled with tender marsh grass. Meanwhile, Kermit killed, on drier ground, a youngish male of the white-eared kob.

Next morning we were up at the Bahr el Zeraf.
At ten we sighted from the boat several herds of
white-eared kob, and Kermit and I went in different
directions after them, getting four. The old rams
were very handsome animals with coats of a deep
rich brown that was almost black, and sharply con-
trasted black and white markings on their faces;
but it was interesting to see that many of the
younger rams, not yet in the fully adult pelage, had
horns as long as those of their elders. The young
rams and ewes were a light reddish-yellow, being
in color much like the ewes of the saddle-back
lechwe; and there was the usual disproportion in
size between the sexes. With each flock of ewes
and young rams there was ordinarily one old black
ram; and some of the old rams went by themselves.
The ground was so open that all my shots had to be
taken at long range. In habits they differed from
the saddle-back lechwes, for they were found on
dry land, often where the grass was quite short,
and went freely among the thorn-trees; they cared
for the neighborhood of water merely as ordinary
waterbuck or kob care for it.

Here we met another boat, with aboard it Sir
William Garstin, one of the men who have made
Egypt and the Soudan what they are to-day, and
who have thereby rendered an incalculable service
not only to England but to civilization.

We had now finished our hunting, save that once

or twice we landed to shoot a buck or some birds for the table. It was amusing to see how sharply the birds discriminated between the birds of prey which they feared and those which they regarded as harmless. We saw a flock of guinea-fowl strolling unconcernedly about at the foot of a tree in which a fish eagle was perched; and one evening Dr. Mearns saw some guinea-fowl go to roost in a bush in which two kites had already settled themselves for the night, the kites and the guineas perching amiably side by side.

We stopped at the mouth of the Sobat to visit the American Mission, and were most warmly and hospitably received by the missionaries, and were genuinely impressed by the faithful work they are doing, under such great difficulties and with such cheerfulness and courage. The Medical Mission was especially interesting. It formed an important part of the mission work; and not only were the natives round about treated, but those from far away also came in numbers. At the time of our visit there were about thirty patients, taking courses of treatment, who had come from distances varying from twenty-five miles to a hundred and fifty.

We steamed steadily down the Nile. Where the great river bent to the east we would sit in the shade on the forward deck during the late afternoon and look down the long glistening water-street in front of us, with its fringe of reedbed and marshy grassland and papyrus swamp, and the slightly higher dry land on which grew acacias and scattered palms. Along the river banks and inland were villages of Shilluks and other tribes, mostly cattle owners; some showing slight traces of improvement, others utter savages, tall, naked men, bearing bows and arrows.

Our Egyptian and Nubian crew recalled to my mind the crew of the dahabiah on which as a boy I had gone up the Egyptian Nile thirty-seven years before; especially when some piece of work was being done by the crew as they chanted in grunting chorus " Ya allah, ul allah." As we went down the Nile we kept seeing more and more of the birds which I remembered, one species after another appearing; familiar cow herons, crocodile plover, noisy spur-wing plover, black and white kingfishers, hoopoos, green bee-eaters, black and white chats, desert larks, and trumpeter bullfinches.

At night we sat on deck and watched the stars and the dark, lonely river. The swimming crocodiles and plunging hippos made whirls and wakes of feeble light that glimmered for a moment against the black water. The unseen birds of the marsh and the night called to one another in strange voices. Often there were grass fires, burning, leaping lines of red, the lurid glare in the sky above them making even more sombre the surrounding gloom.

As we steamed northward down the long stretch

of the Nile which ends at Khartoum, the wind blew in our faces, day after day, hard and steadily. Narrow reedbeds bordered the shore; there were grass flats and groves of acacias and palms, and farther down reaches of sandy desert. The health of our companions who had been suffering from fever and dysentery gradually improved; but the case of champagne, which we had first opened at Gondokoro, was of real service, for two members of the party were at times so sick that their situation was critical.

We reached Khartoum on the afternoon of March 14th, 1910, and Kermit and I parted from our comrades of the trip with real regret; during the year we spent together there had not been a jar, and my respect and liking for them had grown steadily. Moreover, it was a sad parting from our faithful black followers, whom we knew we should never see again. It had been an interesting and a happy year; though I was very glad to be once more with those who were dear to me, and to turn my face toward my own home and my own people.

Kermit's and my health throughout the trip had been excellent. He had been laid up for three days all told, and I for five. Kermit's three days were due, two to tick fever on the Kapiti Plains, one probably to the sun. Mine were all due to fever; but I think my fever had nothing to do with Africa at all, and was simply a recurrence of the fever I caught in the Santiago campaign, and which ever since has come on at long and irregular intervals for a day or two at a time. The couple of attacks I had in Africa were very slight; by no means as severe as one I had while bear hunting early one spring in the Rocky Mountains. One of these attacks came on under rather funny circumstances. It was at Lake Naivasha on the day I killed the hippo which charged the boat. We were in the steam launch and I began to feel badly, and knew I was in for a bout of fever. Just then we spied the hippo and went after it in the row-boat. I was anxious to hold back the attack until I got the hippo, as when shaking with a chill it is of course very difficult to take aim. I just succeeded, the excitement keeping me steady; and as soon as the hippo was dead I curled up in the boat and had my chill in peace and comfort.

There are differences of opinion as to whether any spiritous liquors should be drunk in the tropics. Personally I think that the less one has to do with them the better. Not liking whiskey I took a bottle of brandy for emergencies. Very early in the trip I decided that even when feverish or exhausted by a hard day's tramp, hot tea did me more good than brandy, and I handed the bottle over to Cuninghame. At Khartoum he produced it and asked what he should do with it, and I told him to put it in the steamer's stores; he did so, after finding out the amount that had been drunk, and informed me that I had taken just six ounces in eleven months.

LIST OF GAME SHOT WITH THE RIFLE DURING THE TRIP

	BY T. R.	BY K. R.
Lion	9	8
Leopard	—	3
Cheetah	—	7
Hyena	5	4
Elephant	8	3
Square-mouthed rhinoceros . . .	5	4
Hook-lipped rhinoceros	8	3
Hippopotamus	7	1
Wart-hog	8	4
Common zebra	15	4
Big or Grévy's zebra	5	5
Giraffe	7	2
Buffalo	6	4
Giant eland	1	2
Common eland	5	2
Bongo	—	2
Kudu	—	2
Situtunga	—	1
Bushbuck		
East African	2	4
Uganda harnessed	1	2
Nile harnessed	3	3
Sable	—	3
Roan	4	5
Oryx	10	3
Wildebeest	5	2

	BY T. R.	BY K. R.
Neumann's hartebeest	—	3
Coke's hartebeest	10	3
Big hartebeest		
Jackson's	14	7
Uganda	1	3
Nilotic	8	4
Topi	12	4
Common waterbuck	5	3
Singsing waterbuck	6	6
Common kob	10	6
Vaughn's kob	1	2
White-eared kob	3	2
Saddle-backed lechwe (Mrs. Gray's)	3	1
Bohor reedbuck	10	4
Chanler's buck	3	4
Impalla	7	5
Big gazelle		
Granti	5	3
Robertsi	4	6
Notata	8	1
Thomson's gazelle	11	9
Gerenuk	3	2
Klipspringer	1	3
Oribi	18	8
Duiker	3	2
Steinbuck	4	2
Dikdik	1	1
Baboon	—	3
Red ground monkey	1	—
Green monkey	—	1
Black and white monkey	5	4
Serval	—	1
Jackal	—	1

	BY T. R.	BY K. R.
Aardwolf	—	1
Rattel	—	1
Porcupine	—	2
Ostrich	2	—
Great bustard	4 (1 on wing)	3 (1 on wing)
Lesser bustard	1	1
Kavirondo crane	2 (on wing)	—
Flamingo	—	4
Whale-headed stork	1	1 (on wing)
Marabou	1	1
Saddle-billed stork	1 (on wing)	—
Ibis stork	2 (1 on wing)	—
Pelican	1	—
Guinea-fowl	5	5
Francolin	1	2
Fish eagle	—	1
Vulture	—	2
Crocodile	1	3
Monitor	—	1
Python	3	1
	296	216

Grand Total 512

In addition we killed, with the Fox shot-gun,
Egyptian geese, yellow-billed mallards, francolins,
spurfowl and sand grouse for the pot, and certain
other birds for specimens.

Kermit and I kept about a dozen trophies for ourselves; otherwise we shot nothing that was not used either as a museum specimen or for meat—usually for both purposes. We were in hunting grounds practically as good as any that have ever existed; but we did not kill a tenth, nor a hundredth part of what we might have killed had we been willing. The mere size of the bag indicates little as to a man's prowess as a hunter, and almost nothing as to the interest or value of his achievement.

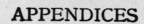

APPENDICES

APPENDIX A

I wish to thank Sir Edward Grey and Lord Crewe for the numerous courtesies extended to me by the British officials throughout the British possessions in Africa; and M. Renkin for the equal courtesy shown me by the Belgian officials in the Lado.

The scientific part of the expedition could not have been undertaken save for the generous assistance of Mr. Andrew Carnegie, Mr. Oscar Straus, Mr. Leigh Hunt, and certain others, to all of whom lovers of natural history are therefore deeply indebted.

I owe more than I can express to the thoughtful and unwearied consideration of Mr. F. C. Selous and Mr. E. N. Buxton, through whom my excellent outfit was obtained.

Mr. R. J. Cuninghame, assisted in East Africa by Mr. Leslie J. Tarlton, managed the expedition in the field; and no two better men for our purposes could have been found anywhere. I doubt if Mr. Cuninghame's equal in handling such an expedition as ours exists; I know no one else who combines as he does the qualities which make a first-class explorer, guide, hunter, field-naturalist and safari manager. Messrs. Newland and Tarlton, of Nairobi, did the actual work of providing and arranging for our whole journey in the most satisfactory manner.

APPENDIX B

THE following is a partial list of the small mammals obtained on the trip, except certain bats, shrews, and rodents which it is not possible to identify in the field; even some of these identifications are not final.

LIST OF SMALL MAMMALS

UNGULATA—HOOFED MAMMALS

Procavia mackinderi . . . Alpine Hyrax
Procavia brucei maculata . . Athi Rock Hyrax
Procavia (Dendrohyrax) bettoni . . . . Kikuyu Tree Hyrax
Procavia (Dendrohyrax) crawshayi . . . . . . Alpine Tree Hyrax

GLIRES—RODENTS

Heliosciurus keniæ . . . . Kenia Forest Squirrel
Paraxerus bæhmi emini . . Uganda Striped Squirrel
Paraxerus jacksoni . . . . Jackson Forest Squirrel
Paraxerus jacksoni capitis . Nairobi Forest Squirrel
Euxerus microdon fulvior . Kenia Ground Squirrel
Graphiurus raptor . . . . Kenia Dormouse
Graphiurus parvus . . . . Pygmy Dormouse
Lophiomys testudo . . . . Nandi Maned Rat
Tatera mombasæ . . . . Mombasa Gerbille
Tatera pothæ . . . . . Highland Gerbille
Tatera fallax . . . . . . Uganda Gerbille
Tatera varia . . . . . . Sotik Gerbille
Tatera emini . . . . . . Nile Gerbille

Tatera nigrita	Dusky Gerbille
Dipodillus harwoodi . . .	Pygmy Gerbille
Otomys irroratus orestes . .	Alpine Veldt Rat
Otomys irroratus tropicalis .	Masai Veldt Rat
Dendromus nigrifrons . . .	Black-fronted Tree Mouse
Dendromus insignis . . .	Greater Tree Mouse
Dendromus whytei pallescens	Athi Tree Mouse
Steatomys athi	East African Fat Mouse
Lophuromys ansorgei . . .	Uganda Harsh-furred Mouse
Lophuromys aquilus . . .	Masai Harsh-furred Mouse
Mus (Leggada) bellus . .	East African Pygmy Mouse
Mus (Leggada) gratus . . .	Uganda Pygmy Mouse
Mus (Leggada) sorellus . .	Elgon Pygmy Mouse
Mus (Leggada) triton murillus	Sooty Pygmy Mouse
Mus (Leggada) triton naivashæ	Naivasha Pygmy Mouse
Epimys hindei	Masai Bush Rat
Epimys endorobæ	Small-footed Forest Mouse
Epimys jacksoni	Uganda Forest Mouse
Epimys peromyscus	Large-footed Forest Mouse
Epimys hildebranti	Taita Multimammate Mouse
Epimys ugandæ	Uganda Multimam'te Mouse
Epimys panya	Masai Multimammate Mouse
Epimys nieventris ulæ . . .	Athi Rock Mouse
Zelotomys hildegardæ . . .	Broad-headed Bush Mouse
Thamnomys surdaster polionops	Athi Tree Rat
Thamnomys loringi	Masked Tree Rat
Œnomys hypoxanthus bacchante	Rusty-nosed Rat
Dasymus helukus	East African Swamp Rat
Acomys wilsoni	East African Spiny Mouse
Arvicanthis abyssinicus nairobæ	Athi Grass Rat
Arvicanthis abyssinicus rubescens	Uganda Grass Rat
Arvicanthis pulchellus massaicus	Spotted Grass Rat
Arvicanthis barbarus albolineatus	Striped Grass Rat
Arvicanthis pumilio diminutus	Pygmy Grass Rat
Arvicanthis dorsalis maculosus	Single Striped Grass Rat

Pelomys roosevelti . . . . Iridescent Creek Rat
Saccostomus umbriventer . . Sotik Pouched Rat
Saccostomus mearnsi . . . Swahili Pouched Rat
Tachyoryctes annectens . . Rift Valley Mole Rat
Tachyoryctes splendens ibeanus Nairobi Mole Rat
Tachyoryctes rex . . . . Alpine Mole Rat
Myoscalops kapiti . . . . Masai Blesmol
Pedetes surdaster . . . . East African Springhaas
Hystrix galeata . . . . . East African Porcupine
Lepus victoriæ . . . . . East African Hare

FERÆ—CARNIVORES

Hyæna striata schillingsi . . Masai Striped Hyæna
Hyæna crocuta germinans . . East African Spotted Hyæna
Proteles cristatus septentri-
onalis . . . . Somali Aard Wolf
Genetta bettoni . . . . . East African Genet
Crossarchus fasciatus macrurus Uganda Banded Mongoose
Mungos sanguienus ibeæ . . Kikuyu Lesser Mongoose
Mungos albicaudus ibeanus . Masai White-tailed Mongoose
Canis mesomelas . . . . Black-backed Jackal
Canis variegatus . . . . Silver-backed Jackal
Lycaon pictus lupinus . . . East African Hunting Dog
Otocyon virgatus . . . . Masai Great-eared Fox
Mellivora ratel . . . . . Cape Honey Badger

INSECTIVORA—INSECTIVORES

Nasilio brachyrhynchus dela-
merei . . . . Athi Lesser Elephant Shrew
Elephantulus pulcher . . . East African Elephant Shrew
Erinaceus albiventris . . . White-bellied Hedgehog
Crocidura flavescens myansæ . Giant Shrew
Crocidura alchemillæ . . . Alpine Shrew
Crocidura fumosa . . . . Dusky Shrew
Crocidura argentata fisheri . Veldt Shrew
Crocidura bicolor elgonius . Elgon Pygmy Shrew
Crocidura allex . . . . . Rift Valley Pygmy Shrew
Surdisorex noræ . . . . Short-tailed Shrew

CHIROPTERA—BATS

Scotophilus nigrita colias . .	Kikuyu Green Bat
Pipistrellus kuhlii fuscatus .	Naivasha Pygmy Bat
Nyctinomus hindei	Free-tailed Bat
Lavia frons	East African Great-eared Bat
Lavia frons affinis	Nile Great-eared Bat
Petalia thebaica	Nile Wrinkle-nosed Bat
Rhinolophus hildebrandti eloqueus	Elgon Horseshoe Bat
Hipposiderus caffer centralis .	Uganda Leaf-nosed Bat

PRIMATES—MONKEYS

Galago (Otolemur) lasiotis .	Mombasa Lemur
Papio ibeanus	East African Baboon
Cercocebus albigena johnstoni	Uganda Mangabey
Erythrocebus formosus . .	Uganda Patas Monkey
Cercopithecus ascanius schmidti	Uganda White-nosed Monkey
Cercopithecus pygerythrus johnstoni	Masai Green Monkey
Cercopithecus kolbi	Kikuyu Forest Green Monkey
Cercopithecus kolbi hindei . .	Kenia Forest Green Monkey
Colobus abyssinicus caudatus .	White-tailed Colobus Monkey
Colobus abyssinicus matschiei	Uganda Colobus Monkey
Colobus palliatus cottoni . .	Nile Colobus Monkey

LIST OF LARGE MAMMALS

UNGULATA—HOOFED MAMMALS

Diceros simus cottoni . . .	Nile Square-nosed Rhinoceros
Diceros bicornis	Black Rhinoceros
Equus burchelli granti . . .	Northern Burchell Zebra
Equus grevyi	Grevy Zebra
Hippopotamus amphibius . .	Nile Hippopotamus
Potamochœrus chœropotamus dæmonis	East African Bush Pig

Hylochœrus meinertzhageni .	East African Forest Hog
Phacochœrus œthiopicus massaicus	East African Wart Hog
Bos caffer radcliffei . . .	East African Buffalo
Bos œquinoctialis	Abyssinian Buffalo
Taurotragus oryx livingstonii	East African Eland
Taurotragus gigas	Giant Eland
Boocercus isaaci	East African Bongo
Strepsiceros strepsiceros . .	Greater Koodoo
Tragelaphus scriptus heywoodi	Aberdare Bushbuck
Tragelaphus scriptus dama .	Kavirondo Bushbuck
Tragelaphus scriptus bor . .	Nile Bushbuck
Limnotragus spekii	Uganda Situtunga
Ozanna roosevelti	Roosevelt Sable Antelope
Ozanna equinus langheldi . .	East African Roan Antelope
Ozanna equinus bakeri . . .	Nile Roan Antelope
Oryx beisa annectens . . .	East African Beisa
Gazella granti	Grant Gazelle
Gazella granti robertsi . . .	Nyanza Grant Gazelle
Gazella granti notata . . .	Boran Grant Gazelle
Gazella thomsoni	Thomson Gazelle
Lithocranius walleri . . .	Gerenuk Gazelle
Æpyceros melampus suara .	Impalla
Redunca fulvorufula chanleri	East African Rock Reedbuck
Redunca redunca wardi . .	Highland Bohor Reedbuck
Redunca redunca donaldsoni .	Uganda Bohor Reedbuck
Kobus kob thomasi	Kavirondo Kob
Kobus vaughani	Rufous White-eared Kob
Kobus leucotis	White-eared Kob
Kobus defassa ugandæ . . .	Uganda Defassa Waterbuck
Kobus defassa harnieri . . .	White Nile Defassa Waterbuck
Kobus ellipsiprymnus . . .	East African Waterbuck
Kobus maria	White-withered Waterbuck
Cephalophus abyssinicus hindei	Masailand Duikerbok
Cephalophus abyssinicus nyansæ	Kavirondo Duikerbok
Cephalophus ignifer . . .	Rufous Forest Duikerbok
Nototragus neumanni . . .	East African Steinbok

Ourebia montana	Abyssinian Oribi
Ourebia cottoni	Guas Ngishu Oribi
Rhynchotragus kirki hindei .	Masai Dikdik
Oreotragus schillingsi . . .	East African Klippspringer
Connochætes albojubatus . .	White-bearded Wildebeest
Damaliscus corrigum jimela .	East African Topi
Bubalis jacksoni	Jackson Hartebeest
Bubalis jacksoni insignis . .	Uganda Hartebeest
Bubalis cokei	Kongoni Hartebeest
Bubalis neumanni	Neumann Hartebeest
Bubalis lelwel niediecki . .	White Nile Hartebeest
Giraffa reticulata	Somali Giraffe
Giraffa camelopardalis tippelskirchi	Masailand Giraffe
Giraffa camelopardalis rothschildi	Five-horned Giraffe
Elephas africanus peeli . .	British E. African Elephant

FERÆ—CARNIVORES

Felis leo massaica	East African Lion
Felis pardus suahelica . . .	East African Leopard
Felis capensis hindei . . .	East African Serval Cat
Cynælurus jubatus guttatus .	African Cheetah

The following is a partial list of those species obtained by Heller concerning which he (and occasionally I) could make observations as to their life histories. In the comparisons with or allusions to our American species there is, I need hardly say, no implication of kinship; the differences are generally fundamental, and I speak of the American animals only for the purpose of securing a familiar standard of comparison. The central African fauna is of course much more nearly allied to that of Europe

than to that of North America, and were I familiar
with small European mammals, I should use them,
rather than the American, for purposes of illustra-
tion.

Heliosciurus keniæ (Kenia Forest Squirrel). Mount
Kenia, B. E. A. Heller shot one in a tree in the
heavy forest by our first elephant camp. In size and
actions like our gray squirrel. Shy.

Paraxerus jacksoni. Shot at same camp; common at
Nairobi and Kijabe, B. E. A. A little smaller than
our red squirrel; much less noisy and less vivacious in
action. Tamer than the larger squirrel, but much
shyer than our red squirrel or chickaree. Kept
among the bushes and lower limbs of the trees. Local
in distribution; found in pairs or small families.

Graphiurus parvus (Pygmy Dormouse). Everywhere in
B. E. A. in the forest; arboreal, often descending to
the ground at night, for they are strictly nocturnal.
Found in the woods fringing the rivers in the Sotik
and on the Athi Plains, but most common in the juniper forests of the higher levels. Spend the daytime
in crevices and hollows in the big trees. Build round,
ball-like nests of bark fibre and woolly or cottony
vegetable fibre. One of them placed in a hollow, four
inches across, in a stump, the entrance being five
feet above the ground. Caught in traps baited with
walnuts or peanuts.

Tatera pothæ Heller (n. s.) (Athi Gerbille). Common
on the Athi Plains, in open ground at the foot of the
hills. Live in short grass, not bush. Nocturnal.
Live in burrows, each burrow often possessing several
entrances, and sometimes several burrows, all inhabited by same animal, not communicating.

wood rat of California; almost the size of the wood
rat of the Eastern States.   Is a ground-loving species,
fond of bushes; in habits like the Mus panya; but
less widely distributed, and entering houses less freely.

Epimys peromyscus Heller (n. s.)   African White-footed
Mouse.   Externally strikingly like our white-footed
mouse.   Found in thick forest, along the edges of
the Rift Valley and on Mount Kenia.   Near our elephant camp Heller failed to trap any white-footed
mice in the open glades, even when the glades were
of small size, but caught them easily if the traps were
set only a few yards within the dense forest.   Evidently very abundant in the forest, but not venturing
at all into the open.   Strictly nocturnal.   Dwell under
logs and in decayed places around stumps, and the
trunks of big trees.

Epimys panya (East African House Mouse).   Common
in B. E. A., coming into the houses, and acting like a
house mouse, but twice the size.   Frequently came
into our camps, entering the tents.   Very common on
the edges of the forest and in brush country and long
grass, and among the shambas; not in the deep forests, except along streams, and not in the bare open
plains.   Nocturnal.   Found in the runways of *Otomys*
and *Arvicanthis*.   Does not seem to be a grass-feed-
ing species, like *Otomys;* eats grain, beans, etc.

Epimys nieventris ulae (Athi Rock Mouse).   On the Athi
Plains, in the Sotik, around Naivasha, and in the Rift
Valley.   Body only slightly larger than that of a
house mouse, but tail at least a third longer than the
head and body together.   Yellowish-brown above and
whitish beneath.   Never found except among rocks;
we always found it where there were cliffs or on
stony koppies.   Lives in crevices in the rocks and

along the ledges of the cliffs. Nocturnal. Caught in traps with nuts.

Zelotomys hildegardæ (Broad-headed Bush Mouse). Looks like a small-eared, broad-headed house mouse. Rather common on Athi Plains, in same localities with Uganda mouse, but rare, and seldom enters houses.

Thamnomys surdaster polionops (Longtailed Tree Mouse). Arboreal; more like a mouse than a rat. On the Athi Plains, in the Sotik and Rift Valley. Not found in heavy forest, but in the open acacia woods and in bushy country. Apparently lives much of the time on the ground, and builds no nests in the trees, but runs up and down them and among their branches freely. Nocturnal.

Thamnomys Loringi Heller (n. s.) (Masked Tree Rat). In the Rift Valley; common around Naivasha. Has a black ring around each eye, the color spreading over the nose like a mask. Arboreal and nocturnal. Much the habits of our neotoma, but do not build large nests. Build nests about six inches in diameter, made of sticks, placed in the branches of the thorn-trees; also in burrows near the bottom of the trunks; runways lead from the trees containing the nests to the burrows. Trapped on the ground and in traps set in notches of the trees.

Oenomys hypoxanthus bacchante (Rusty-nosed Rat). Found in same country as above, and with similar habits, but somewhat less arboreal. A handsome species.

Dasymus helukus Heller (n. s.) (Swamp Rat). In appearance much like the Alexandrian or roof rat, but with longer hair and shorter, much less conspicuous ears. Found all over the Athi Plains where there was brush, especially along stream beds. Nocturnal.

Arvicanthis abyssinicus nairobæ (Athi Grass Rat). The commonest mouse in B. E. A. on the plains. Out-numbers any other species. Found everywhere in grass and brush, but not in deep forest. Often lives in shallow burrows round the bases of thorn-trees, from which its well-marked runways radiate into the grass. Strictly diurnal. Often seen running about in bright sunlight. Never found in traps at night. A striped mouse that has lost its stripes, vestiges of which are occasionally found in the young.

Arvicanthis pulchellus masaicus (Nairobi Striped Mouse). Diurnal. Common on the Athi Plains and on the Sotik and in Rift Valley. Around Neri we often saw them running about through the shambas. Live in brush and cultivated fields. In pattern of coloration much like our thirteen-striped gopher.

Arvicanthis pumilio diminutus (Naivasha Striped Rat). Common in Rift Valley, and on the Aberdares and around Kenia. Sometimes occurs in company with Nairobi mouse, but less widely distributed; much more abundant where found, and ascends to much higher altitudes.

Pelomys roosevelti Heller (n. s.) About the size of our cotton rat, and with much the same build. Coarse, bristly hair; the dorsal coloration is golden yellow overlaid by long hairs with an olive iridescence; the under parts are silky white. It is a meadow mouse found at high altitudes, seven to nine thousand feet high; usually lives close to streams in heavy grass; through which it makes runways. Not common.

Saccostomus umbriventer (Sotik Pouched Rat). Heller trapped several on the Sotik at the base of the south-ernmost range of mountains we reached. Found in the longish grass along a dry creek bed. Trapped in their rather indistinct runways. The pockets or pouches are internal; not external as in our pocket mice.

Tachyroyctes splendens ibeanus (Nairobi Mole Rat). A mole rat of B. E. A. with general habits of above, but avoiding rocky places, and not generally found many miles out on the plains away from the forest. Rarely found in the bamboos—in spite of its name.

Myoscalops kapiti Heller (n. s.) (Kapiti Blesmole). On the Kapiti and Athi Plains and in the Sotik. Smaller than German East African form and no white occipital spot. A cinnamon wash on its silvery fur. Burrows like our pocket gophers, and has same squat look and general habits. Lives in rocky ground, where bamboo rat does not penetrate. It does not run just below the surface of the soil, as the pocket gopher does in winter. The blesmole's burrows are about a foot below the surface. Eats roots.

Pedetes surdaster (Springhaas). (See body of book.) One young at birth. A colony of four to eight open burrows, all inhabited by a single animal.

Hystrix galeata. (See body of book.) Heller found in stomach the remains of a root or tuber and seeds like those of the nightshade.

Lepus victoriæ. Generally distributed on plains; much the habits and look of a small jack-rabbit. Does not burrow.

Elephantulus pulcher (Elephant Shrew). Fairly common throughout B. E. A. in bush and on hills, not in deep forests or on bare plains. Often out at dusk, but generally nocturnal. A gravid female contained a single embryo. One in a trap had its mouth full of partly masticated brown ants. A gentle thing, without the fierceness of the true shrews. Trapped in the runways of arvicanthis.

Erinaceus albiventris (Hedgehog). Fairly common in the Sotik. In certain places under trees Heller found accumulations of their spiny skins, as if some bird of prey had been feeding on them.

Crocidura fisheri. The common shrew of the Athi Plains and the Sotik in the Rift Valley. Largely diurnal. Males quite yellowish, females smoky brown. Generally trapped in runways of arvicanthis. Pregnant females contained three to five embryos, usually four. Not found in heavy forest or swamp.

Crocidura fumosa (Dusky Shrew). A darker form found in the rush swamps and sedgy places of the same region. Number of young usually three. Diurnal. Occasional in forests.

Crocidura alchemillæ Heller (n. s.). Aberdare shrew; a diurnal form, occurring above timber line on the Aberdare; perhaps identical with the foregoing.*

Crocidura allex. A pygmy shrew, taken at Naivasha.

* *Crocidura alchemillæ*, new species (Heller). Type from the summit of the Aberdare Range; altitude, 10,500 feet; British East Africa; adult male, number 163,087, U. S. Nat. Mus.; collected by Edmund Heller, October 17, 1909; original number, 1177.

Allied to *fumosa* of Mount Kenia, but coloration much darker, everywhere clove brown, the underparts but slightly lighter in shade; feet somewhat lighter sepia brown but much darker than in *fumosa;* hair at base slaty-black. Hair long and heavy, on back 6 to 7 mm. long; considerably longer than in *fumosa*. Musk glands on sides of body clothed with short brownish hairs, the glands producing an oily odor very similar to that of a petrel. Skull somewhat smaller than *fumosa* with relatively smaller teeth.

Measurements: Head and body, 90; tail, 55; hind foot, 15.3. Skull: Condylo-incisive length, 21; mastoid breadth, 9.7; upper tooth row (alveoli), 8.3.

This species is an inhabitant of the dense beds of *Alchemilla* which clothe the alpine moorland of the Aberdare Range.

Crocidura nyansæ. Very big for a shrew. Chiefly in
the high country, near watercourses; found round the
edge of the forest, at Kenia and Kijabe. A fierce,
carnivorous creature, preying on small rodents as
well as insects; habitually ate mice, rats, or shrews
which it found in the traps, and would then come
back and itself be readily trapped.

Surdisorex noræ. A shrew in shape not unlike our mole
shrew. On the high, cold, wet Aberdare plateau.
Diurnal.

Scotophilus migrita colias. Common at Nairobi; flying
among the tree tops in the evenings. Greenish back,
with metallic glint; belly sulphur. Has the same
flight as our big brown bat—vespertilio fuscus.

Pipistrellus kuhlii fuscatus. Common at Naivasha and
Nairobi. Very closely kin to our Myotis, or little
brown bat, with same habits. Fly high in the air
after dusk, and are easily shot. We never found its
day roosts.

Nyctinomus hindei (Free-tailed Bat). At Naivasha.
Very swift flight, almost like a swallow's, fairly high
in the air. Live in colonies; one such in a house at
Naivasha. On the Athi Plains they were found in
day time hanging up behind the loose bark of the big
yellow-trunked acacias.

Lavia frons (Great-eared Bat). Bluish body and yellowish wings; very long ears. Almost diurnal, flies well
by day; hangs from the thorn-tree branches, in the
sunlight, and flies as soon as it sees a man approaching. One young, which remains attached to the
mother until it is more than half her size.

Petalia thebaica (Large-eared Nycterine Bat). Caves in
the Rift Valley; also in the Sotik, spending the day
in the tops of the limestone wells or caverns which

seemingly unmoved by the close neighborhood of some wild dogs.

Once, on the Nile, while Loring and I were watching a monitor stealing crocodiles' eggs, we noticed a hippo in mid-stream. It was about ten in the morning. The hippo appeared regularly, at two or three minute intervals, always in the same place, breathed, and immediately sank. This continued for an hour. We could not make out what he was doing. It seemed unlikely that he could be feeding; and the current was too swift to allow him to rest; all other hippos at that time were for the most part lying in the shallows or were back among the papyrus beds.

APPENDIX C

THE following notes were made by Loring in East Africa:

Alpine Hyrax (*Procavia mackinderi*). On Mount Kenia at altitudes between 12,000 and 15,000 feet we found these animals common wherever protective rocks occurred. Under the shelving rocks were great heaps of their droppings, and in the places where for centuries they had sunned themselves the stone was stained and worn smooth. At all times of the day, but more frequently after the sun had risen, they could be seen singly, in pairs, and in families, perched on the peaks. At our highest camp (14,700 feet), where on the 22d of September more than half an inch of ice formed in buckets of water outside the tent, they were often heard. They emit a variety of chatters, whistles, and cat-like squalls that cannot be described in print, and we found them very noisy. Whenever they saw any one approaching they always sounded some note of alarm, and frequently continued to harangue the intruder until he had approached so close that they took fright and disappeared in the rocks or until he had passed. All along the base of cliffs and leading from one mass of rocks to another they made well-worn trails through the grass. At this time of the year many young ones about one-third grown were seen and taken.

Kenia Tree Hyrax (*Procavia crawshayi*). From the time that we reached the edge of the forest belt (altitude

7,000), on Mount Kenia, we heard these tree dassies every night, and at all camps to an altitude of 10,700 feet they were common. I once heard one on a bright afternoon about four o'clock, and on a second occasion another about two hours before sundown. Although I searched diligently on the ground for runways, and for suitable places to set traps, no such place was found. In a large yew-tree that had split and divided fifteen feet from the ground, I found a bed or bulky platform of dried leaves and moss of nature's manufacture. On the top of this some animal had placed a few dried green leaves. In this bed I set a steel trap and carefully covered it, and on the second night (October 14), captured a dassie containing a fœtus almost mature. We were informed by our "boys" that these animals inhabited hollow stumps and logs as well as the foliage of the live trees, but we found no signs that proved it, although, judging from the din at night, dassies were abundant everywhere in the forests.

At evening, about an hour after darkness had fully settled, a dassie would call and in a few seconds dassies were answering from all around, and the din continued for half an hour or an hour. The note began with a series of deep frog-like croaks that gradually gave way to a series of shrill tremulous screams, at times resembling the squealing of a pig and again the cries of a child. It was a far-reaching sound and always came from the large forest trees. Often the cries were directly over our heads and at a time when the porters were singing and dancing about a bright camp fire. Although we tried many times to shine their eyes with a powerful light, we never succeeded, nor were we able to hear any rustling of the branches or scraping on the tree trunks as one might expect an animal of such size to make. The porters were offered a rupee apiece for dassies, but none was brought in.

Rock Hyrax (*Procavia brucei maculata*). These animals inhabited the rocks and cliffs on Ulukenia Hills in fair numbers. None lived in burrows of their own make, but took advantage of the natural crevices for cover. I heard their shrill calls at night, usually when the moon was out. Several were shot and two trapped in traps set in narrow passages through which the animals travelled.

Klippspringer (*Oreotragus oreotragus*). Several pairs of these little antelopes were seen on Ulukenia Hills, but never were more than two found at a time. They lived on the rocky hill-sides and were quite tame, allowing one to approach within twenty-five yards before taking fright and dashing into the rocks, invariably their shelter when alarmed. When thoroughly frightened they made a loud sneezing sound. Two were collected; one of which was a female with horns. A young Boer who had lived in that neighborhood three years told me that all the females of proper age had horns.

Pygmy Gerbille (*Dipodillus harwoodi*). These little sand mice resemble very closely some of our American pocket mice (*Perognathus*). Heller took several on the Njoro O Solali and found them common, and I caught one specimen on the South Guaso Nyero River. On the sandy desert flats on the south-west side of Lake Naivasha they were abundant. The holes running obliquely into the ground were sometimes blocked with sand from the inside. On the opposite side of the lake there was less sand, and here the gerbilles were found only in spots. In sand alone their burrows resembled those described, but where the ground was hard they entered almost perpendicular, and were never blocked with sand. Often seed pods and tiny cockle burrs were strewn about the entrances.

Pygmy Mouse (*Mus* [*Leggada*] *gratus*). Various forms of this tiny little mouse were taken all along the route we travelled. They were caught in traps set at random in the brushy thickets in the lowland, as well as in the open grassy spots on the rocky hill-sides where they frequented the runways made by various species of *Mus*. A few were collected on Mount Kenia.

Athi Rock Mouse (*Epimys nieventris ulae*). This mouse proved to be a new species. It was common in and about the rocks on Ulukenia Hills, which is the only place where we found them. Those taken were caught in traps baited with peanut butter, dried apple, and rolled oats and set among the rocks.

Forest Mouse (*Epimys peromyscus*). At our camp at 8,500 feet altitude we first met with this mouse, and although a good line of traps well baited and set about stumps, tree trunks, and logs for three nights, but one mouse was captured, that being taken under a large log. Several others were trapped in the thick brush bordering the bamboo. At 10,000 feet several were caught in the bamboo, and at 10,700 feet a good series was collected on a well-thicketed and timbered rocky ridge.

Masked Tree Rat (*Thamnomus loringi*). None were taken until we reached the south-west end of Lake Naivasha. Here and also at Naivasha Station a number were collected in traps baited with rolled oats and dried apple and set at the base of large trees and in brushy thickets in groves. In some of these trees and in the bushes, nests of sticks, grass and leaves were found. While setting traps one afternoon I saw what might have been one of these rats dart from a deserted bird's nest, and run down a limb to the ground. The following morning I caught a masked tree rat in a trap set beneath the nest.

Four-striped Grass Rat (*Arvicanthus pumilio minutus*). At Naivasha we first came across this species, where it was found on the east side of the lake only, although the spotted rat was common on both the east and the west side. At Naivasha these two animals inhabited slightly different regions. In the brushy and grassy thickets bordering the lake spotted rats were abundant, but a few four-striped rats were captured. As soon as the traps were transferred to thorn-tree groves where there was plenty of under-bushes, and not so much grass and weeds, the spotted rats were found in great numbers, but no four-striped rats. All the way from Fort Hall to Mount Kenia and as high as 10,700 feet, where Dr. Mearns secured one specimen, this species was common. We also caught them along the route between Kampala and Butiaba.

Giant Rat (*Thrynomys gregorianus*). Along the skirtings of the rivers in the thick weeds, grass, and bushes at Fort Hall signs of these animals were common. There were no well-defined paths. Footprints the size and shape of those made by our muskrats (*Fiber*) were found in the mud at the water's edge, and here and there were clusters of grass and weed stems cut in lengths averaging six inches. In sections where the vegetation had been burned were innumerable holes where some animal had dug about the base of grass tufts. Their signs did not extend further than fifty feet from water. While passing through a thicket close to the water, I started a large rodent which darted through the grass and plunged into the water.

Mole Rat (*Tachyoryctes splendens ibeanus*). Mounds of earth that these rats had thrown from the mouth of their burrows at the time that the tunnels were made, were found as far west as Oljoro O'Nyon River, but none at N'garri Narok River. At our camp on the South Guaso Nyero River a pale mole-colored mole rat took this animal's place. Some fifteen miles west of Lake Naivasha mole rats became common, and on the sandy flats within five miles of the lake they were so abundant that our horses broke into their runways nearly every step. Their underground tunnels and the mounds of earth that were thrown out were similar to those made by the pocket gophers of western United States. Many were snared by the porters and brought to camp alive. They would crawl about slowly, not attempting to run away, but looking for a hole to enter. After the lapse of a few seconds they would begin to dig. In any slight depression they began work, and when small roots or a tussock of grass intervened, they used their teeth until the obstruction was removed, and then with the nails of their front feet only, continued digging. As the hole deepened they threw the dirt out between their hind legs and with them still further beyond. After the earth had accumulated so that it drifted back they faced about and using their chest as a scoop, pushed it entirely out of the way. They were most active in the evening, at night, and in early morning. Several were found dead near their holes, having evidently been killed by owls or small carnivorous mammals.

Alpine Mole Rat (*Tachyoryctes rex*). Mole rat mounds were common about the West Kenia Forest Station, but none were seen between 7,500 and 8,500 feet, and from this altitude they ranged to 11,000 feet. They inhabited all of the open grassy plots in the bamboo belt and in the open timber. The " boys " snared many in nooses ingeniously placed in the runs that were opened and closed after the trap was set. While digging into the burrows, several times I found bulky nests of dried grass in side pockets just off the main runway. Most of them were empty, but one was filled with the animal's droppings.

Kapiti Blesmol (*Myoscalops kapiti*). This mole rat, which proved to be new to science, was first encountered at Potha on Kapiti Plains and it was again met with at Ulukenia Hills. I was shown several skins that were taken about fifteen miles east of Nairobi. They were the most difficult of all mole rats to catch because they lived in the very sandy soil and almost invariably covered the trap with sand without themselves getting into it. I found a number of their skulls in the pellets of barn and other species of owls.

Springhaas (*Pedetes surdaster*). Very common at Naivasha station where their burrows were numerous on a sandy flat practically in the town, and many were taken within a hundred yards of the station. They are nocturnal, although one instance came under my observation where a springhaas was seen on a dark day to run from one burrow to another. By hunting them on dark nights, with the aid of an acetylene light we were able to secure a good series of skins. When the light was flashed on them, their eyes shone

like balls of fire the size of a penny, and it was
not uncommon to see from two to five and six within
the radius of the light at one time. They were usually
flashed at a distance of about a hundred yards, and
as the light drew near they would watch it, frequently
bobbing up and down. Often they hopped away to
right or to left, but very seldom did their fright carry
them into their burrows unless a shot was fired; in
fact even then we sometimes followed up one of their
companions and secured it. Some allowed us to approach within ten feet before moving, and then off
they would go in great bounds, but I was never able
in the dim light to see whether or not their tails aided
them in jumping. I once shot a fox from a cluster
of eyes that I am positive were those of springhaas;
this together with the fact that the stomachs of all of
the foxes killed contained termites and insects, leads
me to believe that these two animals are more or
less congenial. Doctor Mearns saw a springhaas sitting with its tail curled around to one side of its body,
similar to the position often assumed by a house cat.

Several small colonies of springhaas were discovered on sandy flats near Ulukenia Hills. Two females taken from the same burrow showed great vari-
ation in size, one having a tail several inches longer
and ears larger than the other. Although I never discovered a burrow that was completely blocked with
sand, in the morning one could find quantities of fresh
sand that had been thrown out of the entrance during
the night.

Great-eared Fox (*Otocyon virgartus*). This new species
of fox we discovered at Naivasha and found it very
common there. All of the seven specimens secured
were taken by "jacking" at night, although while

travelling over the Uganda Railroad we frequently saw them singly or in pairs in broad daylight. The white people knew nothing of a fox in this country and had always called them "jackals." They seemed to live in pairs and groups of three to six. On dark nights it was usually easy to shine their eyes and approach within shooting range. We would shine a fox, then suddenly the glare of its eyes would disappear and we would walk about casting the light in all directions until we again saw the two balls of fire glaring some fifty or a hundred yards away. Often the foxes would slink about for some time before we got within gunshot range. Frequently we saw two and sometimes three and four standing so close together that it was surprising that the spread of the shot did not kill more than one. One evening Dr. Mearns and I started out about nine o'clock and returned about midnight. Most of the hunting was done on an elevated brushy plateau within short distance of a native village where the occupants were singing, dancing, and playing their crude stringed instruments. We ran into a bunch of five of these foxes and got four of them, none of which was the young of the year. After shooting one, we would search about in the dark until the light picked up another pair of eyes, and in this way we kept circling about close to the village. One fox was killed within two hundred yards of the railroad station, and at dusk one evening I saw a fox emerge from a burrow close to a group of natives and scamper across the flat. The stomachs of several were examined and found to contain about a quart of termites and other insects.

Giant Shrew (*Crocidura nyansæ*). Giant shrews were common at Lake Naivasha, where most of them were caught in the thick reeds and rank grass bordering the lake. One was taken at Nyeri and another on Mount Kenia at an altitude of 10,700 feet. They seemed to be as much diurnal as nocturnal and were captured in traps baited with rolled oats, dried apple, and raw meat. They inhabited the dense parts of the thickets where the foliage had to be parted and a clearing made for the traps. These localities were the home of a large rat, and many of the rats captured were decapitated or partly eaten by animals that probably were giant shrews. A shrew captured alive was very ferocious and would seize upon anything that came within its reach. When fully excited and lifted into the air by its tail, it would emit a loud shrill chirping note.

Short-Tailed Shrew (*Surdisorex noræ*). Collected between altitudes of 10,000 and 12,100 feet on Mount Kenia. With the exception of those collected at 10,000 feet, where they were trapped in open grassy and brushy parks in the bamboo, most of them were taken in runways of *Otomys,* and all of those taken at 12,100 were caught in such runways in tall marsh grass.

Elephant Shrew (*Elephantulus pulcher*). Both diurnal and nocturnal. While riding over the country I frequently saw them darting through the runways from one thicket to another. Nearly every clump of bushes and patch of rank vegetation in the Sotik and Naivasha districts was traversed with well-worn trails used by different species of *Mus* and shrews. The elephant shrews were most common on the dry flats where clumps of fibre plants grew, and their trails usually led into some thorny thicket and finally entered the ground.

Yellow-Winged Tree Bat (*Lavia frons*). These large semi-diurnal bats lived in the thorn-tree groves and thick bush along the Athi, South Guaso Nyero, and Nile rivers where we found them more or less common, and at the latter place abundant. At the first two named places they were almost always found in pairs hanging from the thorn-trees by their feet, their wings folded before their faces. When disturbed they fly a short distance and alight, but when we returned to the spot a few minutes later they would often be found in the same tree from which they had been started. On the Nile at Rhino Camp, and in suitable places all along the trail between Kampala and Butiaba, it was not unusual to find three and four in a single thorn-tree. On dark days, and once in the bright sunlight, I saw these bats flying about and feeding. At evening they always appeared an hour or so before the sun went down. Their method of feeding was quite similar to that of our fly-catching birds. They would dart from the branches of a thorn-tree, catch an insect, then return and hang head downward in the tree while they ate the morsel. One was captured with a young one clinging to it head downward, its feet clasped about its mother's neck.

APPENDIX D

Dr. Mearns, accompanied by Loring, spent from the middle of September to after the middle of October, 1909, in a biological survey of Mount Kenia. I take the following account from his notes. In them he treats the mountain proper as beginning at an altitude of 7,500 feet.

Mount Kenia is the only snow-capped mountain lying exactly on the equator. Its altitude is about 17,200 feet. The mountain is supposed to support 15 glaciers; those that Mearns and Loring examined resembled vast snow banks rather than clear ice-glaciers. The permanent snow line begins at the edge of the glacial lakes at 15,000 feet; on October 18th there was a heavy snow-storm as low down as 11,000 feet. For some distance below the snow line the slopes were of broken rock, bare earth, and gravel, with a scanty and insignificant vegetable growth in the crannies between the rocks. These grasses and alpine plants, including giant ground-sells and lobelias, cover the soil. At 13,000 feet timber line is reached.

The Kenia forest belt, separating this treeless alpine region from the surrounding open plains, is from 6 to 9 miles wide. The forest zone is only imperfectly divided into successive belts of trees of the same species; for the species vary on different sides of the mountain. Even the bamboo zone is interrupted. On the west side the zones may be divided into:

(1) A cedar zone from 7,000 or 7,500 to 8,500 feet. The cedars are mixed with many hardwood trees.

(2) A belt composed mainly of bamboo and yellow-wood (African yew) from 8,500 to 10,700 feet. Here the true timber zone ends.

(3) A zone of giant heath, mixed with giant groundsells and shrubs, extending to 13,-000 feet. The heaths may be 30 feet high and can be used as fuel. In this zone are many boggy meadows.

Loring and Mearns occupied five collecting camps in the forest zone and one above it, at 13,700 feet. One day Mearns followed the snow line for a mile without seeing any traces of large animals, although leopards and smaller cats sometimes wander to this height. The grove-toothed rat, otomys, was numerous in the grass bordering the glacial lakes at a height of 15,000 feet; so were the big mountain hyrax; and Mearns shot one of these animals at 15,500 feet, by a snow bank; it was the highest point at which any mammal was collected. Various kinds of rats and shrews were numerous about the 13,700 foot camp. Above 12,000 feet only three small birds were seen: a long-tailed sunbird, a stone chat, and a fantail warbler.

On the entire Mount Kenia trip 1,112 birds, of 210 species, were collected; 1,320 mammals and 771 reptiles and batrachians were collected, but the species represented were much fewer. Mearns also made an excellent collection of plants and a good collection of invertebrates. Fresh-water crabs were numerous in the streams up to 10,000 feet, frogs went as high as 10,700, a chameleon was taken at 11,000, and a lizard at 12,100.

Loring ascended the mountain to the base of the pinnacle, at about 16,500 feet. He started from the highest camp, where the water froze each night. The ascent was easy and he carried his camera; but the glare of the snow gave him snow blindness.

APPENDIX E

PROTECTIVE COLORATION

Mr. Dugmore has made a wonderful series of photographs of African big game. Mr. Kearton has made a series of moving pictures of various big animals which were taken alive by Buffalo Jones and his two cow-boys, Loveless and Meany, on his recent trip to East Africa; a trip on which they were accompanied by a former member of my regiment, Guy Scull. All three men are old-time Westerners and plainsmen, skilled in handling both horse and rope. They took their big, powerful, thoroughly trained cow horses with them, and roped and captured a lioness, a rhinoceros, a giraffe, and other animals. I regard these feats of my three fellow-countrymen as surpassing any feats which can possibly be performed by men who hunt with the rifle.

For the natural history of African big game, probably the three most valuable books—certainly the most valuable modern books—are Selous's "African Nature Notes," Schilling's "Flashlight and Rifle," and Millais's "Breath from the Veldt." The photographer plays an exceedingly valuable part in nature study, but our appreciation of the great

value of this part must never lead us into forgetting
that as a rule even the best photograph renders its
highest service when treated as material for the best
picture, instead of as a substitute for the best picture; and that the picture itself, important though it
is, comes entirely secondary to the text in any book
worthy of serious consideration either from the
stand-point of science or the stand-point of literature. Of course this does not mean any failure to
appreciate the *absolute* importance of photographs
—of Mr. Dugmore's capital photographs, for instance; what I desire is merely that we keep in
mind, when books are treated seriously, the *relative*
values of the photograph, the picture, and the text.
The text again, to be of the highest worth, must be
good both in form and in substance; that is, the
writer who tells us of the habits of big game must
be a man of ample personal experience, of trained
mind, of keen powers of observation, and, in addition, a man possessing the ability to portray vividly,
clearly, and with interest what he has seen.

Experience in the field is of great value in helping to test various biological theories. One of the
theories which has had a very great vogue of recent
years is that of the protective coloration of animals.
It has been worked out with a special elaborateness
in Mr. Thayer's book on " Concealing Coloration
in the Animal Kingdom." I do not question the
fact that there are in all probability multitudes of

cases in which the coloration of an animal is of protective value in concealing it from its prey or its foes. But the theory is certainly pushed to preposterous extremes; its ultra-adherents taking up a position like that of some of the earlier champions of the glacial theory; who, having really discovered notable proofs of glacial action in parts of Europe and North America, then went slightly crazy on their favorite subject, and proceeded to find proofs of glacial action over the entire world surface, including, for instance, the Amazon Valley. As regards many of the big game animals, at any rate, which are claimed by the ultra-exponents of the protective coloration theory as offering examples thereof, there is not the least particle of justification for the claim.

I select Mr. Thayer's book because it is a really noteworthy book, written and illustrated by men of great ability, and because it contains much that is of genuine scientific value.* I have no question whatever, for instance, that concealing coloration is of real value in the struggle for existence to certain mammals and certain birds, not to mention invertebrates. The night hawk, certain partridges and grouse, and numerous other birds which seek to es-

---

* In passing I wish to bear testimony to the admirable work done by various members of the Thayer family in preserving birds and wild life—work so admirable that if those concerned in it will go on with it they are entitled to believe anything in the world they wish about protective coloration!

cape observation by squatting motionless, do un-questionably owe an immense amount to the way in which their colors harmonize with the surround-ing colors, thus enabling them to lie undetected while they keep still, and probably even protecting them somewhat if they try to skulk off. In these cases, where the theory really applies, the creature benefited by the coloration secures the benefit by act-ing in a way which enables the coloration to further. its concealment. A night hawk, or a woodcock, or a prairie chicken, will lie until nearly trodden on, the bird showing by its action that its one thought is to escape observation, and its coloration and squatting attitude enabling it thus to escape obser-vation; as Mr. Beddard puts it in his book on " Ani-mal Coloration," " absence of movement is absolute-ly essential for protectively colored animals, whether they make use of their coloration for defensive pur-poses or offensive purposes." So far as Mr. Thayer's book or similar books confine themselves to pointing out cases of this kind, and to working on hypotheses where the facts are supplied by such cases, they do a real service. But it is wholly dif-ferent when the theory is pushed to fantastic ex-tremes, as by those who seek to make the coloration of big game animals such as zebras, giraffes, harte-beests, and the like, protective. I very gravely doubt whether some of the smaller mammals and birds to which Mr. Thayer refers really bear out his

theory at all. He has, for instance, a picture of
blue jays by snow and blue shadow, which is de-
signed to show how closely the blue jay agrees with
its surroundings (I would be uncertain from the
picture whether it is really blue water or a blue
shadow). Now it is a simple physical impossibility
that the brilliant and striking coloration of the blue
jay can be protective both in the bare woods when
snow is on the ground and in the thick leafy woods
of midsummer. Countless such instances could be
given. Mr. Thayer insists, as vital to his theory,
that partridges and other protectively colored animals owe their safety, not at all to being inconspic-
uously colored, that is, to being colored like their
surroundings, but to their counter-shading, to their
being colored dark above and light below. But as
a matter of fact most small mammals and birds
which normally owe their safety to the fact that
their coloration matches their surroundings, crouch
flat whenever they seek to escape observation; and
when thus crouched flat, the counter-shading on
which Mr. Thayer lays such stress almost, or completely, disappears. The counter-shading ceases to
be of any use in concealing or protecting the animal
at the precise moment when it trusts to its coloration for concealment. Small rodents and small dull-
colored ground birds are normally in fear of foes
which must see them from above at the critical moment if they see them at all; and from above no such

shading is visible. This is true of almost all the small birds in question, and of the little mice and rats and shrews, and it completely upsets Mr. Thayer's theory as regards an immense proportion of the animals to which he applies it; most species of mice, for example, which he insists owe their safety to counter-shading, live under conditions which make this counter-shading of practically no consequence whatever in saving them from their foes. The nearly uniform colored mice and shrews are exactly as difficult to see as the others.

Again, take what Mr. Thayer says of hares and prongbucks. Mr. Thayer insists that the white tails and rumps of deer, antelope, hares, etc., help them by " obliteration " of them as they flee. He actually continues that " when these beasts flee at night before terrestrial enemies, their brightly displayd sky-lit white sterns blot out their foreshortened bodies against the sky." He illustrates what he means by pictures, and states that " in the night the illusion must often be complete, and most beneficent to the hunted beast," and that what he calls " these rear-end sky-pictures are worn by most fleet ruminants of the open land, and by many rodents with more or less corresponding habits, notably hares " and smaller things whose enemies are beasts of low stature, like weasels, minks, snakes, and foxes; " in short, that they are worn by animals that are habitually or most commonly looked up at by their enemies." Mr. Thayer gives several pictures of the prongbuck, and of the northern rabbit, to illustrate his theory, and actually treats the extraordinarily conspicuous white rump patch of the prongbuck as an " obliterative " marking. In reality, so far from hiding the animal, the white rump is at night often the only cause of the animal's being seen at all. Under one picture of the prongbuck, Mr. Thayer says that it is commonly seen with the white rump against the sky-line by all its terrestrial enemies, such as wolves and cougars. Of course, as a matter of fact, when seen against the sky-line, the rest of the prongbuck's silhouette is so distinct that the white rump mark has not the slightest obliterative value of any kind. I can testify personally as to this, for I have seen prongbuck against the sky-line hundreds of times by daylight, and at least a score of times by night. The only occasion it could ever have such obliterative value would be at the precise moment when it happened to be standing stern-on in such a position that the rump was above the sky-line and all the rest of the body below it. Ten steps further back, or ten steps further forward, would in each case make it visible instantly to the dullest-sighted wolf or cougar that ever killed game, so that Mr. Thayer's theory is of value only on the supposition that both the prongbuck and its enemy happen to be so placed that the enemy never glances in its direction save at just the one particular moment when, by a combination of circumstances which might not occur once in a million times, the prongbuck happens to be helped by the obliterative quality of the white rump mark. Now, in the first place, the chance of the benefit happening to any individual prongbuck is so inconceivably small that it can be neglected, and, in the next place, in reality the white rump mark is exceedingly conspicuous under all ordinary circumstances, and for once that it might help the animal to elude the attention, must attract attention to it a least a thousand times. At night, in the darkness, as any one who has ever spent much time hunting them knows, the white rump mark of the antelope is almost always the first thing about them that is seen, and is very often the only thing that is ever seen; and at night it does not fade into the sky, even if the animal is on the sky-line. So far as beasts of prey are guided by their sight at night, the white rump must always under all circumstances be a source of danger to the prong-buck, and never of any use as an obliterative pattern. In the daytime, so far from using this white rump as obliterative, the prongbuck almost invariably erects the white hairs with a kind of chrysanthemum effect when excited or surprised, and thereby doubles its conspicuousness. In the daytime, if the animals are seen against the sky-line, the white rump has hardly the slightest effect in making them less conspicuous; while if they are not seen against the sky-line (and of course in a great majority of cases they are not so seen), it is much the most conspicuous feature about them, and attracts attention from a very long distance.   But this is not all. Any one acquainted with the habits of the prong-buck knows that the adult prongbuck practically never seeks to protect itself from its foes by conceal-ment or by eluding their observation; its one desire is itself to observe its foes, and it is quite indifferent as to whether or not it is seen.   It lives in open ground, where it is always very conspicuous; ex-cepting during the noonday rest, when it prefers to lie down in a hollow, almost always under condi-tions which render the white rump patch much less conspicuous than at any other time.   In other words, during the time when it is comparatively off its guard and resting, it takes a position where it does not stand against the sky-line—as according to Mr. Thayer's ingenious theory it should; and, again contrary to this same theory, it usually lies down so that any foe would have to look down at it from above.   Whenever it does lie down, the white patch becomes less conspicuous; it is rarely quiet for any length of time except when lying down.   The kids of the prongbuck, on the other hand, do seek to escape observation, and they seek to do so by lying perfectly flat on the ground, with their heads outstretched and the body pressed so against the ground that the effect of the white rump is minimized, as is also the effect of the " counter-shading"; for the light-colored under parts are pressed against the earth, and the little kid lies motionless, trusting to escape observation owing to absence of movement, helped by the unbroken color surface which is exposed to view. If the adult prongbucks really ever gained any benefit by any " protective " quality in their coloration, they would certainly act like the kids, and crouch motionless. In reality the adult prongbuck never seeks to escape observation, never trusts in any way to the concealing or protective power of any part of its coloration, and is not benefited in the slightest degree by this supposed, but in reality entirely non-existent, concealing, or protective power. The white rump practically never has any obliterative or concealing function; on the contrary, in the great majority of instances, it acts as an advertisement to all outside creatures of the prongbuck's existence. Probably it is an example of what is known as directive coloration, of coloration used for purposes of advertisement or communication with the animal's followers. But however this may be, it is certain that there is not the smallest justification for Mr. Thayer's theory so far as the prongbuck is concerned.

It is practically the same as regards the rabbit or the hare. Any one who has ever been in the woods must know, or certainly ought to know, that when hares are sitting still and trying to escape observation, they crouch flat, so that the white of the tail and rump is almost concealed, as well as the white of the under parts, while the effect of the counter-shading almost or entirely vanishes. No terrestrial foe of the hare would ever see the white rump against the sky-line unless the animal was in rapid motion (and parenthetically I may observe that even then it would only see the rump against the sky-line in an infinitesimally small number of cases). Of course as soon as the animal is in motion it is conspicuous to even the most dull-sighted beast of prey; and Mr. Thayer's idea that the white rear patch may mislead a foe as it jumps upon it is mere supposition, unsustained by any proof, and contrary to all the facts that I have observed. Civilized man, who is much more dull-sighted than most wild things, can always see a rabbit when it runs because its white is then so very conspicuous. Here again I do not think there is the slightest value in Mr. Thayer's theory. The white rump is certainly not a protective or obliterative marking; it is probably a directive or advertisement marking.

The Virginia deer, utterly unlike the prongbuck, does often seek to evade observation by lying close, or skulking. When it lies close it lies flat on the ground like a hare, and its white tail is almost invisible, while of course even the most low-creeping foe would not under such circumstances get it against the sky-line. When it skulks it moves off

with head and neck outstretched and tail flattened
down with the white as much obscured as possible.
The white is never shown in conspicuous fashion
until the animal is frightened and no longer seeks
concealment. It then bounds off openly, crashing
through the brush, with its white tail flaunted, and
under such circumstances the white mark is extremely conspicuous.

Indeed I feel that there is grave ground to question the general statement of Mr. Thayer that " almost all mammals are equipped with a full obliterative shading of surface colors; that is, they are
darkest on the back and lightest on the belly, usually with connected intermediate shades." This is
undoubtedly true as a statement of the coloration,
but whether this coloration is in fact obliterative
needs further investigation. Of course if it is
obliterative, then its use is to conceal the mammals.
Mr. Thayer's whole thesis is that such is the case.
But as a matter of fact, the great majority of these
mammals, when they seek to escape observation,
crouch on the ground, and in that posture the light
belly escapes observation, and the animal's color
pattern loses very much of, and sometimes all of,
the " full obliterative shading of surface colors " of
which Mr. Thayer speaks. Moreover, when
crouched down in seeking to escape observation,
the foes of the animal are most apt to see it from
above, not from below or from one side. This is

also the case with carnivorous animals which seek
to escape the observation of their prey. The cougar crouches when lying in wait or stalking, so that
it is precisely when it is seeking to escape observation that its lighter-colored under parts are obscured,
and the supposed benefit of the " obliterative shading pattern " lost. I do not intend without qualifi-
cation to take ground one way or the other on this
general question; but it is certainly true that any
such sweeping statement as that quoted above from
Mr. Thayer is as yet entirely unproved. I have no
doubt that in most cases animals whose colors harmonize with their environment, and which also seek
to escape observation by remaining motionless when
they think there is danger, are very materially helped
by their concealing coloration; but when this concealment is said to be due to the obliterative shading as
described by Mr. Thayer, it is certainly worth while
considering the fact that the so-called obliterative
pattern is least shown, or is not shown at all, at the
only time when the animal seeks to escape observation, or succeeds in escaping observation—that is,
when it crouches motionless, or skulks slowly, with
the conscious aim of not being seen. No color
scheme whatever is of much avail to animals when
they move unless the movement is very slow and
cautious; rats, mice, gophers, rabbits, shrews, and
the enormous majority of mammals which are colored in this fashion are not helped by their special

coloration pattern at all when they are in motion. Against birds of prey they are practically never helped by the counter-shading, but merely by the general coloration and by absence of movement. Their chief destroyers among mammals—such as weasels, for instance—hunt them almost or altogether purely by scent, and though the final pounce is usually guided by sight, it is made from a distance so small that, as far as we can tell by observation, the " counter-shading " is useless as a protection. In fact, while the general shading of these small mammals' coats may very probably protect them from certain foes, it is as yet an open question as to just how far they are helped (and indeed in very many cases whether they really are helped to any appreciable extent) by what Mr. Thayer lays such especial stress upon as being " full obliterative shading (counter-shading) of surface coloring."

Certainly many of the markings of mammals, just as is the case with birds, must be wholly independent of any benefit they give to their possessors in the way of concealment. Mr. Thayer's pictures in some cases portray such entirely exceptional situations or surroundings that they are misleading—as, for instance, in his pictures of the peacock and the male wood-duck. An instant's reflection is sufficient to show that if the gaudily colored males of these two birds are really protectively colored, then the females are not, and *vice versa;* for the males and females inhabit similar places, and if the elaborate arrangement of sky or water and foliage in which Mr. Thayer has placed his peacock and wood-drake represented (which they do not) their habitual environment, a peahen and wood-duck could not be regarded as protectively colored at all; whereas of course in reality, as every one knows, they are far more difficult to see than the corresponding males. Again, he shows a chipmunk among twigs and leaves, to make it evident that the white and black markings conceal it; but a weasel which lacks these markings would be even more difficult to see. The simple truth is that in most woodland, mountain and prairie surroundings, any small mammal that remains motionless is, unless very vividly colored, exceedingly apt to escape notice. I do not think that the stripes of the chipmunk are of any protective value; that is, I believe (and the case of the weasel seems to me to prove) that its coloration would be at least as fully "protective" without them. The striped gophers and gray gophers seem equally easy to see; they live in similar habitats and the stripes seem to have no protective effect one way or the other.

It is when Mr. Thayer and the other extreme members of the protective coloration school deal with the big game of Africa that they go most completely wide of the mark. For instance, Mr. Thayer speaks of the giraffe as a sylvan mammal with a checkered sun-fleck and leaf-colored pattern of coloration accompanied by complete obliterative shading, and the whole point of his remarks is that the giraffe's coloration " always maintains its potency for obliteration." Now of course this means nothing unless Mr. Thayer intends by it to mean that the giraffe's coloration allows it to escape the observation of its foes. I doubt whether this is ever under any circumstances the case; that is, I doubt whether the giraffe's varied coloration ever " enables " it to escape observation save as the dark monochrome of the elephant, rhinoceros, or buffalo may " enable " one of these animals to escape observation under practically identical conditions. There is of course no conceivable color or scheme of color which may not under some conceivable circumstances enable the bearer to escape observation; but if such coloring, for once that it enables the bearer to escape observation, exposes the bearer to observation a thousand times, it cannot be called protective. I do not think that the giraffe's coloration exposes it to observation on the part of its foes; I think that it simply has no effect whatsoever. The giraffe never trusts to escaping observation; its sole thought is itself to observe any possible foe. At a distance of a few hundred yards the color pattern becomes indistinct to the eye, and the animal appears of a nearly uniform tint, so that any benefit given by the color pattern must be comparatively close at hand. On the very rare occasions when beasts of prey—that is, lions—do attack giraffes, it is usually at night, when the coloration is of no consequence; but even by daylight I should really doubt whether any giraffe has been saved from an attack by lions owing to its coloration allowing it to escape observation. It is so big, and so queerly shaped, that any trained eyes detect it at once, if within a reasonable distance; it only escapes observation when so far off that its coloration does not count one way or the other. There is no animal which will not at times seem invisible to the untrained eyes of the average white hunter, and any beast of any shape or any color standing or lying motionless, under exceptional circumstances, may now and then escape observation. The elephant is a much more truly sylvan beast than the giraffe, and it is a one-colored beast, its coloration pattern being precisely that which Mr. Thayer points out as being most visible. But I have spent over a minute in trying to see an elephant not fifty yards off, in thick forest, my black companion vainly trying to show it to me; I have had just the same experience with the similarly colored rhinoceros and buffalo when standing in the same scanty bush that is affected by giraffes, and with the rhinoceros also in open plains where there are ant-hills. It happens that I have never had such an experience with a giraffe. Doubtless such experiences do occur with giraffes, but no more frequently than with elephant, rhinoceros, and buffalo; and in my own experience I found that I usually made out giraffes at considerably larger distances than I made out rhinos. The buffalo does sometimes try to conceal itself, and, Mr. Thayer to the contrary notwithstanding, it is then much more difficult to make out than a giraffe, because it is much smaller and less oddly shaped. The buffalo, by the way, really might be benefited by protective coloration, if it possessed it, as it habitually lives in cover and is often preyed on by the lion; whereas the giraffe is not protected at all by its coloration, and is rarely attacked by lions.

Elephants and rhinoceroses occasionally stand motionless, waiting to see if they can place a foe, and at such times it is possible they are consciously seeking to evade observation. But the giraffe never under any circumstances tries to escape observation, and I doubt if, practically speaking, it ever succeeds so far as wild men or wild beasts that use their eyes at all are concerned. It stands motionless looking at the hunter, but it never tries to hide from him. It is one of the most conspicuous animals in Nature. Native hunters of the true hunting tribes pick it up invariably at an astonishing distance, and, nearby, it never escapes their eyes; its coloration is of not the slightest use to it from the stand-point of concealment. Of course, white

men, even though good ordinary hunters, and black
men of the non-hunting tribes, often fail to see it,
just as they often fail to see a man or a horse, at a
distance; but this is almost always at such a distance that the coloration pattern cannot be made out
at all, the animal seeming neutral tinted, like the rest
of the landscape, and escaping observation because
it is motionless, just as at the same distance a rhinoceros may escape observation. A motionless man,
if dressed in neutral-tinted clothes, will in the same
manner escape observation, even from wild beasts,
at distances so short that no giraffe could possibly
avoid being seen. I have often watched game come
to watering-places, or graze toward me on a nearly
bare plain; on such occasions I might be unable to
use cover, and then merely sat motionless on the
grass or in a game trail. My neutral-tinted clothes,
gray or yellow brown, were all of one color, *without any counter-shading;* but neither the antelope
nor the zebra saw me, and they would frequently
pass me, or come down to drink, but thirty or forty
yards off, without ever knowing of my presence.
My "concealment" or "protection" was due to
resting motionless and to wearing a neutral-tinted
suit, although there was no counter-shading, and
although the color was uniform instead of being
broken up with a pattern of various tints.

The zebra offers another marked example of the
complete break-down of the protective coloration

theory. Mr. Thayer says: " Among all the bolder
obliterative patterns worn by mammals, that of the
zebra probably bears away the palm for potency."
The zebra's coloration has proved especially attractive to many disciples of this school, even to
some who are usually good observers; but, as a
matter of fact, the zebra's coloration is the reverse
of protective, and it is really extraordinary how any
fairly good observer of accurate mind can consider
it so. One argument used by Mr. Thayer is really
funny, when taken in connection with an argument
frequently used by other disciples of the protective
coloration theory as applied to zebras. Mr. Thayer
shows by ingenious pictures that a wild ass is
much less protectively colored than a zebra; some
of his fellow disciples triumphantly point out that
at a little distance the zebra's stripes merge into one
another and that the animal then becomes protectively colored because it looks exactly like a wild ass!
Of course each author forgets that zebras and wild
asses live under substantially the same conditions,
and that this mere fact totally upsets the theory that
each is beneficially affected by its protective coloration. The two animals cannot both be protectively
colored; they cannot each owe to its coloration an
advantage in escaping from its foes. It is absolutely impossible, if one of them is so colored as to
enable it to escape the observations of its foes, that
the other can be. As a matter of fact, neither is,

and neither makes any attempt to elude observation by its foes, but trusts entirely to vigilance in discerning them and fleetness in escaping from them; although the wild ass, unlike the zebra, really is so colored that because thereof it may occasionally escape observation from dull-sighted foes.

Mr. Thayer's argument is based throughout on a complete failure to understand the conditions of zebra life. He makes an elaborate statement to show that the brilliant cross bands of the zebra have great obliterative effect, insisting that, owing to the obliterative coloration, zebras continually escape observation in the country in which they live. He continues: "Furthermore, all beasts must have water, and so the zebras of the dry plains must needs make frequent visits to the nearest living sloughs and rivers. There, by the water's edge, tall reeds and grasses almost always flourish, and there, where all beasts meet to drink, is the great place of danger for the ruminants, and all on whom the lion preys. In the open land they can often detect their enemy afar off, and depend on their fleetness for escape; but when they are down in the river bed, among the reeds, he may approach unseen and leap among them without warning. It is probably at these drinking-places that the zebra's pattern is most beneficently potent. From far or near the watching eye of the hunter (bestial or human) is likely to see nothing, or nothing but reed-stripes, where it

might otherwise detect the contour of a zebra."
In a foot-note he adds that however largely lions
and other rapacious mammals hunt by scent, it is
only sight that serves them when they are down
wind of their quarry; and that sight alone must
guide their ultimate killing dash and spring.

Now this theory of Mr. Thayer's about the benefit of the zebra's coloration at drinking-places, as a
shield against foes, lack even the slightest foundation in fact; for it is self-evident that animals when
they come down to drink necessarily move. The
moment that any animal the size of a zebra moves,
it at once becomes visible to the eye of its human
or bestial foes, unless it skulks in the most cautious
manner. The zebra never skulks, and, like most of
the plains game, it never, at least when adult, seeks
to escape observation—indeed in the case of the
zebra (unlike what is true of the antelope) I am not
sure that even the young seek to escape observation.
I have many times watched zebras and antelopes—
wildebeest, hartebeest, gazelle, waterbuck, kob—
coming down to water; their conduct was substantially similar. The zebras, for instance, made no
effort whatever to escape observation; they usually
went to some drinking-place as clear of reeds as
possible; but sometimes they were forced to come
down to drink where there was rather thick cover,
in which case they always seemed more nervous,
more on the alert, and quicker in their movements.

They came down in herds, and they would usually move forward by fits and starts; that is, travel a few hundred yards, and then stop and stand motionless for some time, looking around. They were always very conspicuous, and it was quite impossible for any watcher to fail to make them out. As they came nearer to the water, they seemed to grow more cautious. They would move forward some distance, halt, perhaps wheel and dash off for a hundred yards, and then after a little while return. As they got near the water they would again wait, and then march boldly down to drink—except in one case where, after numerous false starts, they finally seemed to suspect that there was something in the neighborhood, and went off for good without drinking. Never in any case did I see a zebra come down to drink under conditions which would have rendered it possible for the most dull-sighted beast to avoid seeing it. Of course I usually watched the pools and rivers when there was daylight; but after nightfall the zebra's stripes would be entirely invisible, so that their only effect at the drinking-place must be in the daytime; and in the daytime there was absolutely no effect, and the zebras that I saw could by no possibility have escaped observation from a lion, for they made no effort whatever thus to escape observation, but moved about continually, and, after drinking, retired to the open ground.

The zebra's coloration is certainly never of use

to him in helping him escape observation at a drinking-place. But neither is it of use to him in escaping observation anywhere else. As I have said before, there are of course circumstances under which any pattern or coloration will harmonize with the environment. Once I came upon zebras standing in partially burned grass, some of the yellow stalks still erect, and here the zebras were undoubtedly less conspicuous than the red-coated hartebeests with which they were associated; but as against the one or two occasions where I have seen the zebra's coat make it less conspicuous than most other animals, there have been scores where it has been more conspicuous. I think it would be a safe estimate to say that for one occasion on which the coloration of the zebra serves it for purposes of concealment from any enemy, there are scores, or more likely hundreds, of occasions when it reveals it to an enemy; while in the great majority of instances it has no effect one way or the other. The different effects of light and shade make different patterns of coloration more or less visible on different occasions. There have been occasions when I have seen antelopes quicker than I have seen the zebra with which they happened to be associated. More often, the light has been such that I have seen the zebra first. Where I was, in Africa, the zebra herds were on the same ground, and often associated with, eland, oryx, wildebeest, topi, harte-

beest, Grant's gazelle and Thomson's gazelle. Of
all these animals, the wildebeest, because of its dark
coloration, was the most conspicuous and most
readily seen. The topi also usually looked very
dark. Both of these animals were ordinarily made
out at longer distances than the others. The gazelles, partly from their small size and partly from
their sandy coloration, were, I should say, usually
a little harder to make out than the others. The
remaining animals were conspicuous or not, largely
as the light happened to strike them. Ordinarily,
if zebras were mixed with elands or oryx I saw the
zebras before seeing the eland and oryx, although
I ought to add that my black companions on these
occasions usually made out both sets of animals at
the same time. But in mixed herds of hartebeests
and zebras, I have sometimes seen the hartebeests
first and sometimes the zebras.*

The truth is that this plains game never seeks to
escape observation at all, and that the coloration
patterns of the various animals are not concealing
and are of practically no use whatever in protecting
the animals from their foes. The beasts above

* Mr. Thayer tries to show that the cross stripes on the legs
of zebras are of protective value; he has forgotten that in
the typical Burchell's zebra the legs are white; whether they
are striped or not is evidently of no consequence from the
protective standpoint. There is even less basis for Mr. Thayer's theory that the stripings on the legs of elands and one or
two other antelopes have any, even the slightest, protective
value.

enumerated are colored in widely different fashions. If any one of them was really obliteratively colored, it would mean that some or all of the others were not so colored. But, as a matter of fact, they are none of them instances of concealing coloration; none of the beasts seek to escape observation, or trust for safety to eluding the sight of their foes. When they lie down they almost always lie down in very open ground, where they are readily seen, and where they can hope to see their foes. When topi, roan antelope, hartebeest, and so forth, are standing head-on, the under parts look darker instead of lighter than the upper parts, so that in this common position there is no " counter-shading." The roan and oryx have nearly uniform colored coats which often do harmonize with their surroundings; but their bold face markings are conspicuous.* None of these big or medium sized plains animals, while healthy and unhurt, seeks to escape observation by hiding.

This is the direct reverse of what occurs with many bush antelopes. Undoubtedly many of the latter do seek to escape observation. I have seen waterbucks stand perfectly still, and then steal cautiously off through the brush; and I have seen

* A curious instance of the lengths to which some protective-coloration theorists go is afforded by the fact that they actually treat these bold markings as obliterative or concealing. In actual fact the reverse is true; these face markings are much more apt to advertise the animal's presence.

duiker and steinbuck lie down and stretch their heads out flat on the ground when they noticed a horseman approaching from some distance. Yet even in these cases it is very hard to say whether their coloration is really protective. The steinbuck, a very common little antelope, is of a foxy red, which is decidedly conspicuous. The duiker lives in the same localities, and seems to me to be more protectively colored—at any rate, if the coloration is protective for one it certainly is not for the other. The bushbuck is a boldly colored beast, and I do not believe for a moment that it ever owes its safety to protective coloration. The reedbuck, which in manners corresponds to our white-tailed deer, may very possibly at times be helped by its coloration, although my own belief is that all these bush creatures owe their power of concealment primarily to their caution, noiselessness, and power to remain motionless, rather than to any pattern of coloration. But all of these animals undoubtedly spend much of their time in trying to elude observation.

On the open plains, however, nothing of the kind happens. The little tommy gazelle, for instance, never strives to escape observation. It has a habit of constantly jerking its tail in a way which immediately attracts notice, even if it is not moving otherwise. When it lies down, its obliterative shading entirely disappears, because it has a very vivid black line along its side, and when recumbent—or

indeed for the matter of that when standing up—
this black line at once catches the eye. However,
when standing, it can be seen at once anyhow. The
bigger Grant's gazelle is, as far as the adult male
is concerned, a little better off than the tommy, because the bucks have not got the conspicuous black
lateral stripe; but this is possessed by both the
young and the does—who stand in much more need
of concealing coloration. But as I have already so
often said, neither concealment nor concealing coloration plays any part whatever in protecting these
animals from their foes. There is never any difficulty in seeing them; the difficulty is to prevent
their seeing the hunter.

Mr. Thayer's thesis is "that all patterns and
colors whatsoever of all animals that ever prey or
are preyed on are under certain normal circumstances obliterative." Either this sentence is entirely incorrect or else it means nothing; either no
possible scheme of coloration can be imagined
which is not protective (in which case of course
the whole theory becomes meaningless) or else the
statement so sweepingly made is entirely incorrect.
As I have already shown, there are great numbers of animals to which it cannot apply; and some
of the very animals which do escape observation
in complete fashion are colored utterly differently
when compared one with the other, although their
habitats are the same. The intricate pattern of the

leopard and the uniform, simple pattern of the cougar seem equally efficient under precisely similar conditions; and so do all the intermediate patterns when the general tint is neutral; and even the strikingly colored melanistic forms of these creatures seem as well fed and successful as the others. Mono-colored cougars and spotted jaguars, black leopards and spotted leopards, and other cats of all tints and shades, broken or unbroken, are frequently found in the same forests, dwelling under precisely similar conditions, and all equally successful in eluding observation and in catching their prey.

One of the most extreme, and most unwarrantable, of the positions taken by the ultra-advocates of the protective coloration theory is that in reference to certain boldly marked black and white animals, like skunks and Colobus monkeys, whose coloration patterns they assert to be obliterative. In skunks, the coloration is certainly not protective in any way against foes, as every human being must know if he has ever come across skunks by night or by day in the wilderness; their coloration advertises their presence to all other creatures which might prey on them. In all probability, moreover, it is not of the slightest use in helping them obtain the little beasts on which they themselves prey. Mr. Thayer's " sky-pattern " theory about skunks cannot apply, for bears, which are equally good mousers and insect grubbers, have no white on them, nor have fishers, weasels, raccoons, or foxes; and in any event the "sky-pattern" would not as often obliterate the skunk from the view of its prey as it would advertise it to its prey. It is to the last degree unlikely that any mouse or insect is ever more easily caught because of the white "sky-pattern" on the skunk; and it is absolutely certain that any of these little creatures that trust to their eyes at all must have their vision readily attracted by the skunk's bold coloration; and the skunk's method of hunting is incompatible with deriving benefit from its coloration. Besides, it usually hunts at night, and at night the white "sky-pattern" is *not* a sky-pattern at all, but is exceedingly conspicuous, serving as an advertisement.

The big black and white Colobus monkey has been adduced as an instance of the "concealing" quality of bold and conspicuous coloration patterns. Of course, as I have said before, there is no conceivable pattern which may not, under some wholly exceptional circumstances, be of use from the protective stand-point; a soldier in a black frock coat and top hat, with white duck trousers, might conceivably in the course of some city fight get into a coal cellar with a white-washed floor, and find that the "coloration pattern" of his preposterous uniform was protective; and really it would be no more misleading to speak of such a soldier's dress as protective compared to khaki, than it is to speak of the Colobus monkey's coloration as protective when compared with the colorations of the duller colored monkeys of other species that are found in the same forests. When hunting with the wild 'Ndorobo I often found it impossible to see the ordinary monkeys, which they tried to point out to me, before the latter fled; but I rarely failed to see the Colobus monkey when it was pointed out. In the tops of the giant trees, any monkey that stood motionless was to my eyes difficult to observe, but nine times out of ten it was the dull colored monkey, and not the black and white Colobus, which was most difficult to observe. I questioned the 'Ndorobos as to which they found hardest to see and, rather to my amusement, at first they could not understand my question, simply because they could not understand failing to make out either; but when they did understand, they always responded that the black and white Colobus was the monkey easiest to see and easiest to kill. These monkeys stretch nearly across Africa, from a form at one extremity of the range which is almost entirely black, to a form at the other extremity of the range which is mainly or most conspicuously white. Of course it is quite impossible that both forms can be protectively colored; and as a matter of fact neither is.

I am not speaking of the general theory of protective coloration. I am speaking of certain phases thereof as to which I have made observations at first-hand. I have studied the facts as regards big game and certain other animals, and I am convinced that as regards these animals the protective coloration theory either does not apply at all or applies so little as to render it necessary to accept with the utmost reserve the sweeping generalizations of Mr. Thayer and the protective coloration extremists. It is an exceedingly interesting subject. It certainly seems that the theory must apply as regards many animals; but it is even more certain that it does not, as its advocates claim, apply universally; and careful study and cautious generalizations are imperatively necessary in striving to apply it extensively, while fanciful and impossible efforts to apply it where it certainly does not apply can do no real good. It is necessary to remember that some totally different principle, in addition to or in substitution for protective coloration, must have been at work where totally different colorations and color patterns seem to bring the same results to the wearers. The bear and the skunk are both catchers of small rodents, and when the color patterns of the back, nose, and breast, for instance, are directly opposite in the two animals, there is at least need of very great caution in deciding that either represents obliterative coloration of a sort that benefits the creature in catching its prey. Similarly, to say that white herons and pelicans and roseate-colored flamingoes and spoon-bills are helped by their coloration, when other birds that live exactly in the same fashion and just as successfully, are black, or brown, or black and white, or gray, or green, or blue, certainly represents mere presumption, as yet unaccompanied by a vestige of proof, and probably represents error. There is probably much in the general theory of concealment coloration, but it is not possible to say how much until it is thoroughly tested by men who do not violate the advice of the French scientific professor to his pupils: " Above all things remember in the course of your investigations that if you determine to find out something you will probably do so."

I have dealt chiefly with big game. But I think it high time that sober scientific men desirous to find out facts should not leave this question of concealing coloration or protective coloration to theorists who, however able, become so interested in their theory that they lose the capacity to state facts exactly. Mr. Thayer and the various gentlemen who share his views have undoubtedly made some very interesting discoveries, and it may well be that these discoveries are of wide-spread importance. But they must be most carefully weighed, considered, and corrected by capable scientific men before it is possible to say how far the theory applies and what limitations there are to it. At present all that is absolutely certain is that it does not apply anywhere near as extensively as Mr. Thayer alleges, and that he is so completely mistaken as to some of his facts as to make it necessary carefully to reconsider most of the others. I have shown that as regards most kinds of big game which inhabit open places and do not seek to escape observation but trust to their own wariness for protection, his theories do not apply at all. They certainly do not apply at all to various other mammals. Many of his sweeping assertions are certainly not always true, and may not be true in even a very small number of cases. Thus, in his introductory, Mr. Thayer says of birds that the so-called "nuptial colors, etc., are confined to situations where the same colors are to be found in the wearer's background, either at certain periods of his life or all the time," and that apparently not one of these colors "exists anywhere in the world where there is not every reason to believe it the very best conceivable device for the concealment of its wearer, either throughout the main part of this wearer's life or under certain peculiarly important circumstances." It is really difficult to argue about a statement so flatly contradicted by ordinary experience. Taking at random two of the common birds around our own homes, it is only necessary to consider the bobolink and the scarlet tanager. The males of these two birds in the breeding season put on liveries which are not only not the " very best conceivable " but, on the contrary, are the very worst conceivable devices for the concealment of the wearers. If the breeding cock bobolink and breeding cock tanager are not colored in the most conspicuous manner to attract attention, if they are not so colored as to make it impossible for them to be more conspicuous, then it is absolutely hopeless for man or Nature or any power above or under the earth to devise any scheme of coloration whatsoever which shall not be concealing or protective; and in such case Mr. Thayer's whole argument is a mere play upon words. In sufficiently thick cover, whether of trees or grass, any small animal of any color or shape may, if motionless, escape observation; but the coloration patterns of the breeding bobolink and breeding tanager males, so far from being concealing or protective, are in the highest degree advertising; and the same is true of multitudes of birds, of the red-winged blackbird, of the yellow-headed grackle, of the wood-duck, of the spruce grouse, of birds which could be mentioned offhand by the hundred, and probably, after a little study, by the thousand. As regards many of these birds, the coloration can never be protective or concealing; as regards others, it may under certain rare combinations of conditions, like those set forth in some of Mr. Thayer's ingenious but misleading colored pictures * serve, for concealment or protection, but in an infinitely larger number of cases it serves simply to advertise and attract attention to the wearers. As regards these cases, and countless others, Mr. Thayer's theories seem to me without substantial foundation in fact, and other influences than those he mentions must be responsible for the coloration. It may be that his theories really do not apply to a very large number of animals which are colored white, or are pale in tint, beneath. For instance, in the cases of creatures like those snakes and mice—where the white or pale tint beneath can never be seen by either their foes or their prey—this "counter-shading" may be due to some cause wholly different from anything concerned with protection or concealment.

There are other problems of coloration for which Mr. Thayer professes to give an explanation where this explanation breaks down for a different reason. The cougar's coloration, for instance, is certainly in a high degree concealing and protective, or at any rate it is such that it does not interfere with the animal's protecting itself by concealment, for the cougar is one of the most elusive of creatures, one of the most difficult to see, either by the hunter who follows it or by the animal on which it preys. But

* Some of the pictures are excellent, and undoubtedly put the facts truthfully and clearly; others portray as normal conditions which are wholly abnormal and exceptional, and are therefore completely misleading.

the cougar is found in every kind of country—in northern pine woods, in thick tropical forests, on barren plains and among rocky mountains. Mr. Thayer in his introduction states that "one may read on an animal's coat the main facts of his habits and habitat, without ever seeing him in his home." It would be interesting to know how he would apply this statement to the cougar, and, if he knew nothing about the animal, tell from its coat which specimen lived in a Wisconsin pine forest, which among stunted cedars in the Rocky Mountains, which on the snow-line of the Andes, which in the forest of the Amazon, and which on the plains of Patagonia. With which habitat is the cougar's coat supposed especially to harmonize? A lioness is colored like a cougar, and in Africa we found by actual experience that the very differently colored leopard and lioness and cheetah and serval were, when in precisely similar localities, equally difficult to observe. It almost seems as if with many animals the matter of coloration is immaterial, so far as concealment is concerned, compared with the ability of the animal to profit by cover and to crouch motionless or slink stealthily along.

Again, there seems to be much truth in Mr. Thayer's statement of the concealing quality of most mottled snake skins. But Mr. Thayer does not touch on the fact that in exactly the same localities as those where these mottled snakes dwell, there are often snakes entirely black or brown or green, and yet all seem to get along equally well, to escape equally well from their foes, and prey with equal ease on smaller animals. In Africa, the two most common poisonous snakes we found were the black cobra and the mottled puff adder. If the coloration of one was that best suited for concealment, then the reverse was certainly true of the coloration of the other.

But perhaps the climax of Mr. Thayer's theory is reached when he suddenly applies it to human beings, saying: "Among the aboriginal human races, the various war-paints, tattooings, head decorations, and appendages, such as the long, erect mane of eagle feathers worn by North American Indians —all these, whatever purposes their wearers believe they serve, do tend to obliterate them, precisely as similar devices obliterate animals." Now this simply is not so, and it is exceedingly difficult to understand how any man trained to proper scientific observation can believe it to be so. The Indian, and the savage generally, have a marvellous and wild-beast like knack of concealing themselves. I have seen in Africa 'Ndorobo hunters, one clad in a white blanket and one in a red one, coming close toward elephants, and yet, thanks to their skill, less apt to be observed than I was in dull-colored garments. So I have seen an Indian in a rusty frockcoat and a battered derby hat make a successful stalk on a deer which a white hunter would have had some difficulty in approaching. But when the Ndorobos got to what they—not I—considered close quarters, they quietly dropped the red or white blankets; and an Indian would take similar pains when it came to making what he regarded as a difficult stalk. The feathered head-dress to which Mr. Thayer alludes would be almost as conspicuous as a sun umbrella, and an Indian would no more take it out on purpose to go stalking in than a white hunter would attempt the same feat with an open umbrella. The same is true of the paint and tattooing of which Mr. Thayer speaks, where they are sufficiently conspicuous to be visible from any distance. Not only do the war-bonnets and war-paint of the American Indians and other savages have no concealing or protective quality, as Mr. Thayer supposes, but, as a matter of fact, they are highly conspicuous; and this I know by actual experience, by having seen in the open, savages thus arrayed, and compared them with the aspect of the same savages when hunting.

APPENDIX F

THE original list of the "Pigskin Library" was as follows:

Bible.
Apocrypha.
Borrow . . . .   Bible in Spain.
                            Zingali.
                            Lavengro.
                            Wild Wales.
                            The Romany Rye.
Shakespeare.
Spenser . . . .   Faerie Queene.
Marlowe.
Mahan . . . .   Sea Power.
Macaulay . . . .   History.
                            Essays.
                            Poems.
Homer . . . .   Iliad.
                            Odyssey.

Chanson de Roland.
Nibelungenlied.
Carlyle . . . .   Frederick the Great.
Shelley . . . .   Poems.
Bacon . . . .   Essays.
Lowell . . . .   Literary Essays.
                            Biglow Papers.
Emerson . . . .   Poems.
Longfellow.
Tennyson.
Poe . . . .   Tales.
                            Poems.

Keats.

Milton . . . .   Paradise Lost (Books I and II).

Dante . . . .   Inferno (Carlyle's translation).

Holmes . . . .   Autocrat.
Over the Teacups.

Bret Harte . . . . . .   Poems.
Tales of the Argonauts.
Luck of Roaring Camp.

Browning . . . .   Selections.

Crothers . . . .   Gentle Reader.
Pardoner's Wallet.

Mark Twain . . . . . .   Huckleberry Finn.
Tom Sawyer.

Bunyan's "Pilgrim's Progress."

Euripides (Murray's translation) . . . .   Hippolytus.
Bacchæ.

The Federalist.

Gregorovius . . . . . .   Rome.

Scott . . . .   Legend of Montrose.
Guy Mannering.
Waverley.
Rob Roy.
Antiquary.

Cooper . . . .   Pilot.
Two Admirals.

Froissart.

Percy's Reliques.

Thackeray . . . . . .   Vanity Fair.
Pendennis.

Dickens . . . .   Mutual Friend.
Pickwick.

I received so many inquiries about the " Pigskin Library " (as the list appeared in the first chapter of my African articles in *Scribner's Magazine* [see page 28]), and so many comments were made upon it, often in connection with the list of books recently made public by ex-President Eliot, of Harvard, that I may as well myself add a word on the subject.

In addition to the books originally belonging to the " library," various others were from time to time added; among them, " Alice in Wonderland " and " Through the Looking-Glass," Dumas's " Louves de Machekoule," " Tartarin de Tarascon " (not until after I had shot my lions!), Maurice Egan's " Wiles of Sexton Maginnis," James Lane Allen's " Summer in Arcady," William Allen White's " A Certain Rich Man," George Meredith's " Farina," and d'Aurevilly's " Chevalier des Touches." I also had sent out to me Darwin's " Origin of Species " and " Voyage of the Beagle," Huxley's Essays, Frazer's " Passages from the Bible," Braithwaite's " Book of Elizabethan Verse," FitzGerald's " Omar Khayyám," Gobineau's " Inégalité des Races Humaines " (a well-written book, containing some good guesses; but for a student to approach it for serious information would be much as if an albatross should apply to a dodo for an essay on flight), " Don Quixote," Montaigne, Molière, Goethe's " Faust," Green's " Short History of the English People," Pascal, Voltaire's " Siècle de Louis XIV " the " Mémoires de M. Simon " (to read on the way home), and " The Soul's Inheritance," by George Cabot Lodge. Where possible I had them bound in pigskin. They were for use, not ornament. I almost always had some volume with me, either in my saddle-pocket or in the cartridge-bag which one of my gun-bearers carried to hold odds and ends. Often my reading would be done while resting under a tree at noon, perhaps beside the carcass of a beast I had killed, or else while waiting for camp to be pitched; and in either case it might be impossible to get water for washing. In consequence the books were stained with blood, sweat, gun oil, dust, and ashes; ordinary bindings either vanished or became loathsome, whereas pigskin merely grew to look as a well-used saddle looks.

Now, it ought to be evident, on a mere glance at the complete list, both that the books themselves are of unequal value and also that they were chosen for various reasons, and for this particular trip. Some few of them I would take with me on any trip of like length; but the majority I should of course change for others—as good and no better—were I to start on another such trip. On trips of various length in recent years I have taken, among many other books, the " Memoirs of Marbot," Æschylus, Sophocles, Aristotle, Joinville's " History of St. Louis," the Odyssey (Palmer's translation), volumes of Gibbon and Parkman, Lounsbury's Chaucer, Theocritus, Lea's " History of the Inquisition,"

Lord Acton's Essays, and Ridgeway's " Prehistoric Greece." Once I took Ferrero's " History of Rome," and liked it so much that I got the author to come to America and stay at the White House; once De La Gorce's " History of the Second Republic and Second Empire "—an invaluable book. I did not regard these books as better or worse than those I left behind; I took them because at the moment I wished to read them. The choice would largely depend upon what I had just been reading. This time I took Euripides, because I had just been reading Murray's " History of the Greek Epic." * Having become interested in Mahaffy's essays on Hellenistic Greece, I took Polybius on my next trip; having just read Benjamin Ide Wheeler's " History of Alexander," I took Arrian on my next hunt; something having started me reading German poetry, I once took Schiller, Koerner, and Heine to my ranch; another time I started with a collection of essays on and translations from early Irish poetry; yet another time I took Morris's translations of various Norse Sagas, including the Heimskringla, and liked them so much that I then incautiously took his translation of Beowulf, only to find that while it had undoubtedly been translated out of Anglo-Saxon, it had not been translated into

* I am writing on the White Nile from memory; the titles I give may sometimes be inaccurate, and I cannot, of course, begin to remember all the books I have at different times taken out with me.

English, but merely into a language bearing a specious resemblance thereto. Once I took Sutherland's " History of the Growth of the Moral Instinct "; but I did not often take scientific books, simply because as yet scientific books rarely have literary value. Of course a really good scientific book should be as interesting to read as any other good book; and the volume in question was taken because it fulfilled this requirement, its eminent Australian author being not only a learned but a brilliant man.

I as emphatically object to nothing but heavy reading as I do to nothing but light reading—all that is indispensable being that the heavy and the light reading alike shall be both interesting and wholesome. So I have always carried novels with me, including, as a rule, some by living authors, but (unless I had every confidence in the author) only if I had already read the book. Among many, I remember offhand a few such as " The Virginian," " Lin McLean," " Puck of Pook's Hill," " Uncle Remus," " Aaron of the Wild Woods," " Letters of a Self-made Merchant to His Son," " Many Cargoes," " The Gentleman from Indiana," " David Harum," " The Crisis," " The Silent Places," " Marse Chan," " Soapy Sponge's Sporting Tour," " All on the Irish Shore," " The Blazed Trail," " Stratagems and Spoils," " Knights in Fustian," " Selma," " The Taskmasters," Edith

Wyatt's " Every Man to His Humor," the novels and stories of Octave Thanet—I wish I could remember more of them, for personally I have certainly profited as much by reading really good and interesting novels and stories as by reading anything else, and from the contemporary ones I have often reached, as in no other way I could have reached, an understanding of how real people feel in certain country districts, and in certain regions of great cities like Chicago and New York.

Of course I also generally take out some of the novels of those great writers of the past whom one can read over and over again; and occasionally one by some writer who was not great—like " The Semi-attached Couple," a charming little early-Victorian or pre-Victorian tale which I suppose other people cannot like as I do, or else it would be reprinted.

Above all, let me insist that the books which I have taken were and could only be a tiny fraction of those for which I cared and which I continually read, and that I care for them neither more nor less than for those I left at home. I took " The Deluge " and " Pan Michael " and " Flight of a Tartar Tribe," because I had just finished " Fire and Sword "; " Moby Dick," because I had been rereading " Omoo " and " Typee "; Gogol's " Taras Bulba," because I wished to get the Cossack view of what was described by Sienkiewicz from the Polish side; some of Maurice Jokai, and " St. Peter's Umbrella " (I am not at all sure about the titles), because my attention at the moment was on Hungary; and the novels of Topelius when I happened to be thinking of Finland. I took Dumas's cycle of romances dealing with the French Revolution, because I had just finished Carlyle's work thereon —and I felt that of the two the novelist was decidedly the better historian. I took " Salammbo " and " The Nabob " rather than scores of other French novels simply because at the moment I happened to see them and think that I would like to read them. I doubt if I ever took anything of Hawthorne's, but this was certainly not because I failed to recognize his genius.

Now, all this means that I take with me on any trip, or on all trips put together, but a very small proportion of the books that I like; and that I like very many and very different kinds of books, and do not for a moment attempt anything so preposterous as a continual comparison between books which may appeal to totally different sets of emotions. For instance, one correspondent pointed out to me that Tennyson was " trivial " compared to Browning, and another complained that I had omitted Walt Whitman; another asked why I put Longfellow " on a level " with Tennyson. I believe I did take Walt Whitman on one hunt, and I like Browning, Tennyson, and Longfellow, all of them, without thinking it necessary to compare them. It is largely a matter of personal taste. In a recent English review I glanced at an article on English verse of to-day in which, after enumerating various writers of the first and second classes, the writer stated that Kipling was at the head of the third class of " ballad-mongers "; it happened that I had never even heard of most of the men he mentioned in the first two classes, whereas I should be surprised to find that there was any one of Kipling's poems which I did not already know. I do not quarrel with the taste of the critic in question, but I see no reason why any one should be guided by it. So with Longfellow. A man who dislikes or looks down upon simple poetry, ballad poetry, will not care for Longfellow; but if he really cares for " Chevy Chase," " Sir Patrick Spens," " Twa Corbies," Michael Drayton's " Agincourt," Scott's " Harlaw," " Eve of St. John " and the Flodden fight in " Marmion," he will be apt to like such poems as the " Saga of King Olaf," " Othere," " The Driving Cloud," " Belisarius," " Helen of Tyre," " Enceladus," " The Warden of the Cinque Ports," " Paul Revere," and " Simon Danz." I am exceedingly fond of these, and of many, many other poems of Longfellow. This does not interfere in the least with my admiration for " Ulysses," " The Revenge," " The Palace of Art," the little poems in " The Princess," and in fact most of

Tennyson. Nor does my liking for Tennyson prevent my caring greatly for "Childe Roland," "Love Among the Ruins," "Proteus," and nearly all the poems that I can understand, and some that I can merely guess at, in Browning. I do not feel the slightest need of trying to apply a common measuring-rule to these three poets, any more than I find it necessary to compare Keats with Shelley, or Shelley with Poe. I enjoy them all.

As regards Mr. Eliot's list, I think it slightly absurd to compare any list of good books with any other list of good books in the sense of saying that one list is "better" or "worse" than another. Of course a list may be made up of worthless or noxious books; but there are so many thousands of good books that no list of small size is worth considering if it purports to give the "best" books. There is no such thing as *the* hundred best books, or *the* best five-foot library; but there can be drawn up a very large number of lists, each of which shall contain *a* hundred good books or fill *a* good five-foot library. This is, I am sure, all that Mr. Eliot has tried to do. His is in most respects an excellent list, but it is of course in no sense a list of the best books for all people, or for all places and times. The question is largely one of the personal equation. Some of the books which Mr. Eliot includes I would not put in a five-foot library, nor yet in a fifty-foot library; and he includes various good books which are at least no better than many thousands (I speak literally) which he leaves out. This is of no consequence so long as it is frankly conceded that any such list must represent only the individual's personal preferences, that it is merely a list of *good* books, and that there can be no such thing as a list of the *best* books. It would be useless even to attempt to make a list with such pretensions unless the library were to extend to many thousand volumes, for there are many voluminous writers, most of whose writings no educated man ought to be willing to spare. For instance, Mr. Eliot evidently does not care for history; at least he includes no historians as such. Now, personally, I would not include, as Mr. Eliot does, third or fourth rate plays, such as those of Dryden, Shelley, Browning, and Byron (whose greatness as poets does not rest on such an exceedingly slender foundation as these dramas supply), and at the same time completely omit Gibbon and Thucydides, or even Xenophon and Napier. Macaulay and Scott are practically omitted from Mr. Eliot's list; they are the two nineteenth-century authors that I should most regret to lose. Mr. Eliot includes the Æneid and leaves out the Iliad; to my mind this is like including Pope and leaving out Shakespeare. In the same way, Emerson's " English Traits " is included and Holmes's " Autocrat " excluded—an incomprehensible choice from my stand-point. So with the poets and novelists. It is a mere matter of personal taste whether one prefers giving a separate volume to Burns or to Wordsworth or to Browning; it certainly represents no principle of selection. "I Promessi Sposi" is a good novel; to exclude in its favor "Vanity Fair," "Anna Karénina," "Les Misérables," "The Scarlet Letter," or hundreds of other novels, is entirely excusable as a mere matter of personal taste, but not otherwise. Mr. Eliot's volumes of miscellaneous essays, "Famous Prefaces" and the like, are undoubtedly just what certain people care for, and therefore what they ought to have, as there is no harm in such collections; though personally I doubt whether there is much good, either, in this "tidbit" style of literature.

Let me repeat that Mr. Eliot's list is a good list, and that my protest is merely against the belief that it is possible to make any list of the kind which shall be more than a list as good as many scores or many hundreds of others. Aside from personal taste, we must take into account national tastes and the general change in taste from century to century. There are four books so pre-eminent—the Bible, Shakespeare, Homer, and Dante—that I suppose there would be a general consensus of opinion among the cultivated men of all nationalities in putting them foremost;* but as soon as this narrow

* Even this may represent too much optimism on my part. In Ingres's picture on the crowning of Homer, the foreground

limit was passed there would be the widest diver-
gence of choice, according to the individuality of
the man making the choice, to the country in which
he dwelt, and the century in which he lived. An
Englishman, a Frenchman, a German, an Italian,
would draw up totally different lists, simply because
each must necessarily be the child of his own
nation.*

We are apt to speak of the judgment of " posterity " as final; but " posterity " is no single entity,
and the " posterity " of one age has no necessary
sympathy with the judgments of the " posterity "
that preceded it by a few centuries. Montaigne,

is occupied by the figures of those whom the French artist
conscientiously believed to be the greatest modern men of
letters. They include half a dozen Frenchmen—only one of
whom would probably have been included by a painter of
some other nation—and Shakespeare, although reluctantly
admitted, is put modestly behind another figure, and only
a part of his face is permitted to peek through.

* The same would be true, although of course to a less
extent, of an American, an Englishman, a Scotchman, and
an Irishman, in spite of the fact that all speak substantially
the same language. I am entirely aware that if I made an
anthology of poems, I should include a great many American poems—like Whittier's " Snow-Bound," " Ichabod," and
" Laus Deo "; like Lowell's " Commemoration Ode " and
" Biglow Papers "—which could not mean to an Englishman
what they mean to me. In the same way, such an English
anthology as the " Oxford Book of English Verse " is a good
anthology—as good as many other anthologies—as long as it
confines itself to the verse of British authors. But it would
have been far better to exclude American authors entirely;
for the choice of the American verse included in the volume,
compared in quantity and quality with the corresponding
British verse of the same period which is selected, makes it
impossible to treat the book seriously, if it is regarded as a
compendium of the authors of both countries.

in a very amusing and, on the whole, sound essay
on training children, mentions with pride that when
young he read Ovid instead of wasting his time on
" ' King Arthur,' ' Lancelot du Lake,' . . . and such
idle time-consuming and wit-besotting trash of
books, wherein youth doth commonly amuse itself."
Of course the trashy books which he had specially
in mind were the romances which Cervantes not
long afterward destroyed at a stroke. But Malory's
book and others were then extant; and yet Montaigne, in full accord with the educated taste of his
day, saw in them nothing that was not ridiculous.
His choice of Ovid as representing a culture and
wisdom immeasurably greater and more serious
shows how much the judgment of the " posterity "
of the sixteenth century differed from that of the
nineteenth, in which the highest literary thought
was deeply influenced by the legends of Arthur's
knights and hardly at all by anything Ovid wrote.
Dante offers an even more striking instance. If
" posterity's " judgment could ever be accepted as
final, it would seem to be when delivered by a man
like Dante in speaking of the men of his own calling
who had been dead from one to two thousand years.
Well, Dante gives a list of the six greatest poets.
One of them, he modestly mentions, is himself, and
he was quite right. Then come Virgil and Homer,
and then Horace, Ovid and *Lucan!* Nowadays we
simply could not understand such a choice, which

omits the mighty Greek dramatists (with whom in the same canto Dante shows his acquaintance), and includes one poet whose works come about in the class of the " Columbiad."

With such an example before us, let us be modest about dogmatizing overmuch. The ingenuity exercised in choosing the " Hundred Best Books " is all right if accepted as a mere amusement, giving something of the pleasure derived from a missing-word puzzle. But it does not mean much more. There are very many thousands of good books; some of them meet one man's needs, some another's; and any list of such books should simply be accepted as meeting a given individual's needs under given conditions of time and surroundings.

KHARTOUM, *March* 15, 1910.

INDEX

INDEX

665

Index

Hornbills, 332.

Horne, Mr., 311, 346, 351.

Horses, the, 341, 439.

Humphery, Mr., District Commissioner, 52, 82.

Hunt, Leigh, 541, appendix A.

Hurlburt, Mr., 179.

Hutchinson, Captain, R.N.R., 479, 480.

Hyena, 73, 74, 76, 77, 201, 202, 227; difficulty in determining sex of, 407, 411, 427, 440.

Hyraxes, 388, 444.

Ibis stork, 274.

Impalla, 54, 135, 136, 137, 138, 393.

Indian trader, letter from an, 330.

Ingowa, an, a war-dance of the natives, 330.

Ivory, 295, 296, 322; poachers of, 483.

Jackal, 348.

Jackson, Lieutenant-Governor, 8, 78, 178, 329.

Jordaan, Mr., 431, 432.

Judd, H., 48, 133, 276.

Juja Farm, 125, 130, 151.

Juma Yohari, Kermit's gun-bearer, 411, 449, 535.

Jungle, the, 311, 312.

Jusserand, M., French ambassador, 199.

Kafu River, 477.

Kamiti Ranch, 154.

Kamiti River, 156, 157.

Kampalla, 454.

Kangani, 363.

Kapiti Plains, 20, 53.

Kassitura, Kermit's gun-bearer, 411, 491, 535, 551.

Kavirondo crane, 162, 280, 343, 358.

Kearton, Mr., 329.

Kenia, Mount, 287, 333; biological survey of, 395, 396; appendix D.

Khartoum, parting from comrades at, 566.

Kijabe, 179, 181, 280, 451.

Kikuyu savages, 130, 131, 264, 279; dance of, 286, 288, 310, 330, 337.

Kilimakiu, 47, 108.

Kilimanjaro, 38.

Kilindini, 448.

King's African Rifles, the, encamped at Neri, 329.

Kirke, Mr., 430, 432, 436.

Kisumu, 451.

Kitanga, hills of, 37, 38.

Klipspringers, 70, 229.

Klopper, Mr., 47, 50.

Knowles, Mr., District Commissioner, 454; struck by lightning, 463.

Kob, Uganda, 416, 417, 511, 559; lechwe, 554, 555, 556, 558, 562; Vaughn's, 559; white-eared, 554, 562, 563.

Koba, 483.

THE END